AF540769

SOCIAL INEQUALITY

Amit Kumar

CENTRUM PRESS
NEW DELHI-110002 (INDIA)

CENTRUM PRESS
H.O.: 4360/4, Ansari Road, Daryaganj,
New Delhi-110002 (India)
Tel: 23278000, 23261597, 23255577, 23286875
B.O.: No. 1015, Ist Main Road, BSK IIIrd Stage,
IIIrd Phase, IIIrd Block, Bangalore-560085 (INDIA)
Tel: 080-41723429
Email: centrumpress@gmail.com
Visit us at: www.centrumpress.com

Social Inequality

First Edition, 2011

ISBN 978-93-80921-73-0

PRINTED IN INDIA

Printed at Tarun Offset Printers, Delhi-110053

Contents

Preface

Social inequality refers to a position in which individuals in a society do not have the same social status. Vicinity of potential social inequality include: voting rights, freedom of speech and assembly, the extent of property rights and access to education, health care, quality housing and other social goods. Social inequality is dissimilar from economic inequality, although the two are connected.

Economic inequality refers to disparities in the sharing of economic resources and income. Though economic inequality is caused by the unequal distribution of wealth, social inequality survives because the not have of wealth in convinced areas prohibits these people from obtaining the similar housing, health care, etc., as the wealthy, in societies where access to these social goods depends on wealth. Social inequality is linked to racial inequality and wealth inequality. The way people behave socially, through racism and other forms of discrimination, tends to trickle down and affect the opportunities and wealth individuals can generate for themselves.

This book examines a number of dimensions of social inequality, including inequality in family, education and work, health, and political participation and the formation of public policy. It pays special attention to recent trends that may threaten to sustain inequality into the future.

Author

1

Understanding the Inequality in India

INTRODUCTION

Officially, Indian policymakers have always been concerned with the reduction of poverty and inequality. However, between the first five year plan after independence in 1947 and the turn of the century, Indian economic policy making went through a sea of change. After independence and for a period of about forty years, India followed a development strategy based on central planning.

As Chakravarty pointed out, one of the reasons for adopting an interventionist economic policy was the apprehension that total reliance on the market mechanism would result in excessive consumption by upper-income groups, along with relative under-investment in sectors essential to the development of the economy. Chakravarty, policymakers in India adopted a middle path, in which "there was a tolerance towards income inequality, provided it was not excessive and could be seen to result in a higher rate of growth than would be possible otherwise."

In this context however, the macroeconomic sensitivity to inflation as fallout from growth reflected government concerns regarding the redistributive effects of inflation, which typically affected workers, peasants and unorganized sectors more. From the mid-1980s, the Indian government gradually adopted market-oriented economic reform policies. In the early phase, these were associated with an expansionist fiscal strategy that involved additional fiscal allocations to the rural areas, and thus counterbalanced the redistributive effects of the early liberalization. The pace of policy change accelerated during the early 1990s, when the explicit adoption of neo-liberal reform programmes marked the beginning of a period of intensive economic liberalization and changed attitudes towards state intervention in the economy.

The focus of economic policies during this period shifted away from state intervention for more equitable distribution towards liberalization, privatization and globalization. This study focuses on the period when these neo-liberal and market-oriented economic policies were being implemented in India. However, it should be noted that the Indian experience with such policies over this period was more limited, gradual and nuanced than in many other developing countries, with correspondingly different economic effects. This document gives an overview of the nature and causes of inequality trends since the mid-1990s and tries to explain the observed trends.

TRENDS IN INCOME AND CONSUMPTION INEQUALITY IN INDIA

The debate on economic policy and reform began in India in the 1980s, and continues today. Prior to the extensive introduction in 1991 of the new economic policy, as it came to be known, there was widespread apprehension that liberalization and excessive reliance on market forces would lead to increases in regional, rural-urban and vertical inequalities in India. Nearly fifteen years later, the issue is still under debate, with various studies unable to give an unequivocal verdict.

Economists continue to disagree on whether income and consumption inequality increased in India during the reform period. A number of studies based on the National Sample Survey estimates of household consumption expenditure reveal mixed evidence on aggregate and regional trends. For example, Bhalla reported that both urban and rural Gini coefficients declined between 1993-1994 and 1999-2000. Rural inequality decreased in 15 out of 16 major states of India, and urban inequality declined in 8 of the 17 states over this period. He therefore concluded that inequality had not worsened in India during the period of reform. Another study by Singh and others could not find strong evidence of increases in household inequality for the period 1993-1994 to 1999-2000.

"There are some indications of increases in regional inequality, but they are neither uniform nor overly dramatic". Singh and others also studied convergence of economic performance at a sub-state level. Using a set of five variables, their study found that during the post reform period, some states experienced increasing within-state inequality.

The Government of India National Human Development Report published the state-wide Gini coefficients for the years 1983, 1993-1994 and 1999-2000. These coefficients were estimated using the 38th, 50th and 55th rounds of Household Consumer Expenditure survey conducted by the National Sample Survey of India. Comparing the level of inequality between 1993-1994 and 1999-2000, among the 32 states and union territories reported showed that seven states experienced an increase in rural inequality and fifteen states experienced an increase in urban inequality.

There were five states where both urban and rural inequalities increased. It is interesting to note that all these five states were located in the North-Eastern part of India. It is also notable that during the reform period, urban inequality in India was much higher than rural inequality for most of the states. In fact, in 31 of the 32 states and union territories, urban inequality was higher than rural inequality.

This was also reflected in the all India figures, which showed that urban inequality remained higher than rural inequality in all the reference years. Moreover, it could also be seen that from 1983 to 1999-2000, the rural Gini declined consistently, but there was a gradual rise in urban inequality during the same period. Using data from different rounds of the National Sample Surveys, Jha calculated rural and urban inequality in India. The period 1993-1994 to 1999-2000. It shows that both rural and urban Gini coefficients increased in the period between 1993-1994 and 1997, and declined between

1997 and 1999-2000. However, as Jha pointed out, changes in the methodology used in the 55th round National Sample Survey meant that the results for 1999-2000 were not comparable to earlier rounds. Therefore, care should be taken not to interpret the lower Gini coefficients of 1999- 2000 as a sign of declining inequality in India.

Most studies have used various rounds of NSS consumption expenditure survey statistics for calculating per capita incomes and Gini coefficients. But there is a well known problem of lack of comparability of NSS statistics between the latest round and the earlier ones. As Sen pointed out, the reference periods in the Consumer Expenditure Survey of the 55th round of NSS survey were changed from the uniform 30 day recall, used till then, to both seven and 30 day questions for items of food and intoxicants and to 365 day questions for items of clothing, footwear, education, institutional medical expense and durable goods.

As Deaton and Dreze explained, the change from 30 to 365 days in the reporting period for these low frequency items possibly led to lower poverty and inequality estimates. The longer reporting period reduced the mean expenditures on these items, but because a much larger fraction of people reported something over the longer reporting period, the bottom tail of the consumption distribution was pulled up, and as a result, both inequality and poverty were reduced.

The new methodology lowered the measured rural poverty in India by almost 50 million. As a consequence, rural inequality measures were also affected. Revised estimates of rural inequality had been calculated by Deaton and Dreze, Sundaram and Tendulkar and Sen and Himanshu. In general, these studies revealed that although the unadjusted data showed decreasing inequality between rounds 50 and 55, the adjusted data suggested that rural inequality had, in fact, gone up in India between 1993-1994 and 1999-2000.

Sen and Himanshu argued that the adjusted figures indicated that the more accurate change in rural inequality between the 50th and 55th rounds was an almost three Gini point increase, rather than a two Gini point decline. Deaton and Dreze and Sundaram and Tendulkar also came to the conclusion that rural inequality increased in the period between 1993-1994 and 1999-2000. Sen and Himanshu provided striking evidence about increased inequality in India in the post-reform period.

Based on indices of real Mean Per Capita Expenditure by fractile groups, Sen and Himanshu showed that whereas the consumption level of the upper tail of the population, including the top 20 per cent of the rural population, went up remarkably during the 1990s, the bottom 80 per cent of the rural population suffered during this period. This graph clearly shows that the consumption disparities between the rich and the poor and between urban and rural India increased during the 1990s.

These findings are based on the NSS 'thin sample' surveys, conducted annually since 1986. These surveys are not as comprehensive as the NSS comprehensive rounds or the 'thick sample' surveys, but provide sufficiently good estimates at the national level. Also, these thin sample results are comparable because they use a common type of questionnaire. Similarly, using adjusted NSS data, Deaton and Dreze found three distinct trends of changing patterns of inequality during the 1990s.

They showed that there is strong evidence of divergence in per capita consumption across states. Secondly, their estimates of state-wise per capita expenditure revealed that rural-urban inequality in per capita expenditure significantly increased at an all-India level. They also found strong evidence of increased rural-urban inequalities within states between 1993-1994 and 1999-2000. Jha also concluded that in both rural and urban sectors, all-India level inequality was higher during the post reform period than it was during the crisis period of the early 1990s.

Banerjee and Piketty also highlighted disproportionately large income/consumption gains by the upper tail of the population. Based on income tax reports, they found that in the 1990s, the real incomes of the top one per cent of income earners in India increased by about 50 per cent. Furthermore, among this top one per cent, the richest one per cent increased their real incomes by more than three times during the 1990s. The real income of the top one per cent of income earners in India as a share of total income. Banerjee and Piketty argued that the U-shaped pattern depicted was broadly consistent with the evolution of economic policy in India. While the 'socialist policies' of the early part of the planning period shrank the income share of the top earners very substantially until the mid-1980s, more open and pro-market policies have since allowed the ultra-rich to increase their share substantially.

Sen and Himanshu also provided state wide rural and urban Gini coefficients for the 50th round and the 55th round NSS surveys. These Gini coefficients were comparable because they were based on adjusted data for the 50th and 55th rounds. It can be seen that for the rural sector, eight of the fifteen states experienced a decline in inequality, while in seven others, inequality increased. On the other hand, it was noteworthy that for all the 15 major states, urban inequality increased by 1999-2000 as compared to 1993-1994.

REGIONAL INEQUALITY

There was a sharp increase in regional inequality in India during the 1990s. In 2002-2003, the per capita Net State Domestic Product of the richest state, Punjab, was about 4.7 times that of Bihar, the poorest state. This ratio had increased from 4.2 in 1993-1994. A time-series graph of this ratio shows that the disparity between the richest and poorest state shot up remarkably during the 1990s.

This has been highlighted by Ghosh and Chandrasekhar, who showed that interstate inequality increased sharply in India during the reform period. As the authors pointed out, based on per capita SDP, the basic hierarchy of the Indian states remained the same during the reform period, with Punjab, Haryana and Maharashtra at the top, and Bihar and Orissa at the bottom. They also noted that the gap between the richest and poorest states opened up considerably after 1990-1991. To show this, the authors benchmarked the average per capita net SDP of the three richest states. Ahluwalia also highlighted the trend of increasing inequality among states by using per capita gross state domestic product data for the period 1980-1981 to 1998-1999.

The trend of the Gini coefficient indicating interstate inequality which confirms that interstate inequality grew steadily in India with liberalization. More evidence on increasing interstate inequality came from Singh and others, who used regressions to check convergence in per capita consumption expenditures across states.

The study found absolute divergence of interstate per capita consumption expenditures for the periods 1983 to 1999-2000 and 1993-1994 to 1999-2000. A convergence exercise by Jha indicated that the ranking of states with respect to inequality had not changed in the reform period. Interstate convergence of the level of inequality was weak.

POVERTY TRENDS IN THE 1990S

In addition to the discussion on inequality in India during the 1990s, there is a similar debate on the extent of poverty reduction during this same period. This debate essentially centres on two controversial and interlinked issues. During the early 1990s, it was observed that average consumption estimates, measured using National Accounts Statistics data, tended to be consistently higher than NSS consumption data. Consequently, NSS data showed higher poverty in India than NAS data.

It must be emphasized here that NAS data are not the most appropriate to use because poverty estimates crucially depend on the distribution of incomes, and reliable poverty estimates cannot be directly obtained from NAS data in the absence of income distribution data. However, in spite of this NAS data limitation, the discrepancy between NAS and NSS poverty estimates fuelled a debate about the relative merit of sample surveys and national accounts statistics in India. Some proponents of the reform measures suggested that in the absence of any real evidence that consumption inequality has widened among the poor, NAS data essentially indicated that the National Sample Survey Organization survey results were not giving the right picture. They argued that surveys were unreliable and error prone, and urged a revision of the NSSO survey methodology to bridge the discrepancy between NSS and NAS data. Among the pro-reformers, the opposition to the NSS methodology drew strength from the fact that for the NSS rounds 46 to 54, poverty was higher than for the 45th round.

These trends further fuelled the criticism that NSS surveys tended to underestimate consumption and eventually led to the changes in the NSS methodology for the 55th round. Following criticism of the NSS poverty estimates, the methodology used to carry out a large scale consumer expenditure survey by the NSSO was modified in 1999-2000. This led to serious compatibility issues between the 55th round and the previous rounds of NSS surveys. This debate has revolved around the changes introduced in the questionnaire for the 55th round of the sample survey and the resultant changes in the data.

These changes exaggerate the consumption data of the surveyed households, and thereby reduce measured poverty very sharply. It is not surprising that the 55th round NSS survey showed a sharp decline in poverty in India. Unadjusted 55th round estimates showed that the headcount ratio of poverty declined from 37.3 per cent in 1993-1994 to 27 per cent in 1999-2000. Surprisingly, in spite of the well-established shortcomings of the 55th round, the Indian Government accepted these figures as the official poverty estimates.

However, experts readily recognized that these figures could be misleading and spurious. Most economists tried to make a more meaningful estimate of the decline in poverty in India by attempting a reconciliation of the methodologies used in the 50th and 55th rounds of NSSO surveys. They attempted different techniques to attain this goal, and not surprisingly, even the comparable results showed considerable variation. At one end of the spectrum is Bhalla, who used NAS data for the computation of poverty, and claimed that there was a very sharp decline of poverty in India. The official poverty figure of 27 per cent for 1999-2000 was a gross overestimate. His calculations indicated that for the year 1999, poverty in India was less than 12 per cent. However, Bhalla's optimism was not shared by those who use the NSS data. Deaton, for example, attempted to reconcile the differences between the 50th round and the 55th round of NSS survey, using a methodology suggested by Tarozzi.

This approach took into account the items in the questionnaire which were kept unchanged between the 50th and 55th rounds. Deaton found that expenditure on these items highly correlated with total household expenditure. Using the expenditure pattern on these items, Deaton constructed adjusted and comparable estimates of poverty for the 50th and 55th rounds.

Calculations by Deaton showed that poverty declined from 37.3 per cent in 1993-1994 to 30.2 per cent in 1999-2000. These results suggested a slightly lower decline of poverty than the official estimates. In a series of documents, Sundaram and Tendulkar also tried to reconcile the results obtained from the 50th and the 55th rounds. These authors argued that for 'high' and 'intermediate' frequency goods, the difference between the 50th and the 55th rounds was insignificant.

Corrections were only required for low frequency items and for items like clothing, durables, education expenses and institutional medical expenses. Using a set of assumptions, Sundaram and Tendulkar found significant poverty reduction during the second half of the 1990s. Poverty declined from 32.15 per cent in 1993-1994 to 27.32 per cent in 1999-2000, which indicated a smaller decline in poverty than suggested either by the official figures or by Deaton.

However, there remain some reservations about Sundaram and Tendulkar's measures because some of their assumptions underlying their calculations are considered moot. Secondly, and probably more importantly, they used a different poverty line than the standard one suggested and used by the Planning Commission. Sen and Himanshu differed from both Deaton as well as Sundaram and Tendulkar in their approach to the problem.

Sen and Himanshu relied mainly on recalculation of unit-level NSS data from rounds 43, 50 and 55, and made fewer assumptions than the others. Their estimates showed that both Deaton as well as Sundaram and Tendulkar had overestimated the decline in poverty. The head-count poverty ratio in India declined by three percentage points at most between the 50th and the 55th rounds, but the number of poor in the country actually increased during this period.

These authors also argued that the change in methodology for the 55th round of the survey was ill-advised because there was hardly any validity in the criticisms of the 1990-1997 NSS data and their alleged mismatch with NAS figures. The growth rate of the NSS nominal consumption expenditure was almost identical to that from the then current National Accounts series with its 1980-1981 base. Some indication of the varying results that can be obtained by using different methods but the essential conclusion of a slowdown in the rate of poverty reduction after 1993 remains.

EMPLOYMENT GROWTH AND THE DISTRIBUTION OF INCOME GENERATING OPPORTUNITIES

The most significant link between growth and poverty reduction is employment generation, which is why patterns of employment growth are usually critical in determining both changes in income distribution and the incidence of poverty. During the 1990s, the employment growth rate in India plummeted. A very significant deceleration of employment generation in both rural and urban areas, with the annual growth rate of rural employment falling to only 0.67 per cent over the period 1993-1994 to 1999-2000.

This is not only less than one-third the rate of the previous period 1987-1988 to 1993-1994, but it is also less than half the projected growth rate of the labour force in the same period. In fact, it turns out that this is the lowest growth rate of rural employment in post-independence history. The decline in rural employment can be directly attributed to the stagnation of agricultural employment during the 1990s. NSSO data indicated that total employment in the agriculture sector increased from 190.72 million in 1993- 1994 to 190.94 million in 1999-2000, registering an annual growth rate of only 0.02 per cent during this period. This was much lower than the population growth rate over the same period, and also lower than the corresponding figures for earlier periods. In fact, the agricultural employment growth rate plummeted to its lowest ever mark since the NSS began recording employment data in the 1950s.

One of the major reasons behind the poor employment generation during the second half of the 1990s could have been attributable to the sharp decline in the employment elasticity of output growth during this period. Among the sectors, employment elasticities fell in agriculture, mining and quarrying, manufacturing, electricity, gas and water, transport, storage and communication, finance and insurance and services sectors.

In general, the employment elasticity of output growth was highest in the tertiary sector, followed by the secondary sector. In the reform period, the employment elasticity of agriculture was the lowest, and among the lowest observed in Indian agriculture since 1961. Along with the stagnation of employment generation in the agricultural sector, the real wage growth rate of agricultural labourers also stagnated during the 1990s.

As Deaton and Dreze showed, if one compared the growth rate of real wages for agricultural labourers with that of public sector salaries, real agricultural wages grew at about 2.5 per cent per year during the 1990s, whereas public sector salaries grew at about 5 per cent per year during the same period. This partly explained the increased rural-urban inequality of the 1990s in India.

Sen and Himanshu pointed out that though real wage growth of agricultural labourers was positive, its impact on rural per capita income was less significant because the number of agricultural labourers grew faster than the available days for wage employment. The authors showed that just as to NSS estimates, the percentage of the rural population in agricultural labour households increased from 27.6 per cent to 31.1 per cent between rounds 50 and 55, implying an average of 3.7 per cent annual growth of this population. Against this, it reported less than 1.5 per cent average annual growth of wage paid days of employment in agriculture. As a result, agricultural unemployment was on the rise, and the increase in real wages had not resulted in an increase in the per capita income for rural agricultural workers. Another observable employment trend was a steady increase in the casualization of the labour force in India.

The proportion of casual workers increased steadily in rural India. This was matched by a steady decrease in the self-employment of workers, both male and female, in rural India. Regular employment for rural workers was also abysmally low in India, accounting for less than 7 per cent of all workers. However, for urban areas, the share of casual employment for female workers came down over the years and regular employment rose. But for male workers, the shares of casual workers and self-employed workers steadily increased, and there was a marginal decline in the share of regular employment.

The decline in self-employment in agriculture, which was especially sharp for women, may have been related to changes in production conditions, which forced some peasants out of direct cultivation. There was strong evidence of the declining viability of cultivation in India over the 1990s. A recent study of farm business incomes found that average farm business income at current prices deflated by the CPIAL grew at only 1.02 per cent per annum over the 1990s, compared to 3.21 per cent in the 1980s.

Rising input costs and fluctuating output prices were found to be the dominant cause of this trend. These numbers were averages for farmers of all size holdings; clearly, the situation had been much worse for small and marginal farmers with inferior access to both input and product markets. This, in turn, led to a loss of assets, including land, by the small peasantry. It is now clear that this period witnessed a significant degree of concentration of operated holdings, reflecting changes in both ownership and tenancy patterns.

Many small and very marginal peasants lost their land over this period, and therefore were forced to search for work as landless labourers. Meanwhile, micro-level surveys reported increased leasing—in by large farmers from small landowners.

There was a very large increase in landless households as a percentage of total rural households, from around 35 per cent in 1987-1988 to as much as 41 per cent in 1999-2000. This would definitely have affected the degree of labour intensity on farms. The sector-wise distributions of the workforce showed some interesting patterns. Sundaram showed that if one took a broad definition of the agricultural sector, the work force participation rate in agriculture declined steadily between 1961 and 1999- 2000.

There was a 16 percentage point decline in the share of the agricultural sector in the total workforce. Moreover, between 1993-1994 and 1999-2000, the share of the agricultural sector in the total workforce declined twice as fast as the rate of decline over the 33-year period between 1961 and 1994. As a result, as noted earlier, there was hardly any change in the absolute number of workers in the agricultural sector.

Sundaram also showed that of the 16 percentage point decline in the share of the agriculture sector, the manufacturing sector and the construction sector gained about 3 per cent each of total employment. But the services sector, as a group, recorded a 10 percentage point gain in its share of the workforce. About 50 per cent of this increase was caused by the relatively high employment growth rate in the trade, hotels and restaurants sector.

The transport, storage and communications, as well as the community, social and personal services sectors each gained 2 percentage points in their shares of the workforce. Agriculture still employs about 75 per cent of the total female workforce in India. For rural female workers, dependence on agriculture is much higher at around 84 per cent. Data from earlier NSS rounds also showed that in 8 of the 17 major states, the share of agriculture in total female rural employment exceeded 90 per cent; in 15 states, their share was no less than 75 per cent in 1999-2000.

Only in West Bengal and Kerala, did rural females account for a somewhat higher proportion of non-agricultural employment. This trend was contrary to the trend observed for male workers. As the NSS data showed, there was a steady decline in the proportion of male workers dependent upon the primary sector. Increasingly higher proportions of male workers were getting employed in secondary, tertiary and other non-farm activities, increasing from 22 per cent in 1983 to 29 per cent in 1999-2000.

In this context, the difference between the occupational structures of rural and urban female workers is worth noting. Whereas 37.8 per cent of urban female workers are employed in the services sector, the corresponding figure for rural female workers is 4.3 per cent. In spite of the fact that the tertiary sector is the fastest growing sector in the Indian economy, the share of rural female workers in this sector has not improved in the post-liberalization era.

This difference between rural and urban female workers is a consequence of the fact that in poor developing countries like India, the ability of rural female workers to make inter-sectoral shifts in occupation is severely limited by various social and economic factors including their education and skill level. It is notable here that in most Indian states, the differences in the education and literacy standards between males and females are quite significant.

The lopsided nature of employment growth in India is evident which shows that employment in all sub-sectors of the services sector increased much faster than in the rest of the economy. However, in spite of the high rate of employment generation in the services sector, poor performance in agriculture and in some industrial sectors has brought down the overall rate of employment generation.

In India, only about eight to ten per cent of the population is involved in the organized sector. But employment generation in this sector suffered during the 1990s, mainly because of a decline in employment generated by the public sector. However, due to the better performance of the private sector, total employment generated by the organized sector grew marginally in the period 1995-2001. The deceleration in organized sector employment was one of the more disconcerting features of the 1990s, especially since industrial output increased manifold and the service sector, in which much organized employment was based, was the most dynamic element in national income growth. So, along with the deceleration of employment generation in the rural areas, urban employment generation also suffered during the 1990s.

However, there was some increase in employment opportunities in certain service sub-sectors such as information technology, communications and entertainment related services. But the numbers involved remained very small relative to the size of the labour force and these jobs remain concentrated in the larger cities.

So this really created some islands of prosperity in an otherwise desperate employment scenario. There was also a strong gender dimension in the growth rate of organized sector employment. For male workers, employment in the organized sector has steadily declined since 1997. Both in private and public sector companies, employment of male workers fell. Female workers, on the other hand, have done better, and there has been an increase in aggregate organized sector employment for them. State wise employment generation data also revealed higher levels of inequalities in 1999-2000 than in 1993-1994.

The coefficient of variation across states increased from 53.7 in 1993-1994 to 63.7 in 1999- 2000. Out of the fifteen major states and union territories, only three experienced a decline in the unemployment rate during this period.

HEALTH INEQUALITIES, NUTRITION AND EDUCATION

India's performance in health is one area which has been extremely disappointing over the years. Though there have been improvements in some health related indicators like birth and death rates, India's performance in a number of health-related development indicators has been worse than Sub-Saharan Africa's. Also, the improvements have not been uniform throughout the country.

Health services are much better in urban areas, and there are differences in the population's health across different regions. Dreze and Sen pointed out that India has fared much worse than Sub-Saharan Africa in nutrition-related indicators such as the proportions of undernourished children, low birth weight babies and pregnant women with anaemia. The proportion of females to males in the population is also lower in India than in Sub-Saharan Africa.

World Bank data suggest that about 53 per cent of children are undernourished, and the proportion of pregnant women with anemia is as high as 88 per cent. In fact, as far as these indicators are concerned, for all the countries for which data are available, none-except Bangladesh-has fared worse than India. Also, if one looks at basic gender inequality data, India is again right at the bottom of the world table, along with Pakistan.

On certain other indicators like infant mortality and life expectancy, India's performance is relatively much better, but these figures hide considerable interstate variations as well as persistent vulnerabilities of some segments of the population. For example, life expectancy at birth is about 55 in Madhya Pradesh, but in Kerala, it is more than 73. Similarly, the number of women per 1000 males varies from 861 in Punjab to about 1058 in Kerala.

South Indian states have done much better on development-related indicators, including health indicators. For example, Kerala's health indicators are in many ways comparable to those of mid-income and high income countries. Kerala's fertility rate is about 1.8 per cent, which is lower than that of the USA and is comparable to West European rates.

On the other hand, Dreze and Gazdar show that the performance of Uttar Pradesh and Bihar, two of the most populous states of India, has been worse than many Sub-Saharan African countries on a large number of health indicators. The Human Development Index of India also shows considerable variations across the states. However, the dispersion of HDI was lower in 2001 than in 1991. It is also interesting to note that the interstate variations in health related indicators do not always correlate with poverty levels. Poverty, as measured by the head-count ratio, is higher in the eastern states of Bihar and Orissa, but child death rates are much higher in the central and northern states of Uttar Pradesh, Madhya Pradesh and Rajasthan. Despite poverty being lower in Uttar Pradesh, child mortality is more than twice as high in the state as compared to Tamil Nadu.

Also, gender discrimination is most pronounced in the states of Punjab and Haryana, two of the most prosperous states of India. In fact, one of the most disturbing developments in the 1990s was the decline in the female-male ratios in the relatively prosperous states of India. The female-male ratio among children declined from 945 girls per 1,000 boys in 1991, to 927 girls per 1,000 boys in 2001.

This decline was mainly driven by a combination of social discrimination against female children and the spread of prenatal sex-determination technology and sex-selective abortion. Since the largest declines in the female-male ratios have occurred in the more prosperous states of Gujarat, Haryana, Himachal Pradesh, Punjab and Delhi, it appears that economic growth may have facilitated the spread of sex-selective abortion by making sex-determination technology and sex-selective abortion more affordable.

Though prenatal sex determination has subsequently been banned by the government, given the social stigma, corruption and availability of technology, it is difficult to say how effective the ban will be. One of the main reasons behind the poor state of health care facilities in India and the high health related inequalities across the states is the very low level of public health expenditure, which happens to be among the lowest in the world, at 5.1 per cent of Gross Domestic Product. Further, nutrition conditions are acknowledged to have a close relationship with overall health, and here, the conditions may even have worsened in recent years.

There have been disturbing changes in consumption patterns, as revealed by the NSSO and other sources. Per capita food-grain consumption declined from 476 grams per day in 1990 to only 418 grams per day in 2001, while aggregate calorific consumption per capita declined from just over 2,200 calories per day in 1987-1988 to around 2,150 in 1999-2000. This decline was marked, even among the bottom 40 per cent of the population, where it was unlikely to reflect Engel's curve type shifts in consumer choice, but rather relative prices and the inability to consume enough food due to income constraints. In India, the literacy rate has been increasing steadily, but still too slowly over the last few decades. The Census of India has calculated the country's overall literacy rate at 65 per cent in 2001, up from about 43 per cent in 1981 and 52 per cent in 1991.

The male-female gap in literacy improved from 26.6 per cent in 1981 to 21.6 per cent in 2001, but remains large. There are significant interstate inequalities in literacy rates. Even in 2001, Bihar, the state with lowest literacy rate below 50 per cent, was about 18 percentage points below the national average. For female literacy, the gap was even wider at about 21 per cent. By contrast, Kerala, the state with the highest literacy in India, had an average literacy rate of 90.92 per cent, with more than 86 per cent female literacy.

Though the difference in literacy rates between the top and the bottom states has narrowed in recent years, it remains significant. Along with interstate differences, there exist large disparities between the rural and urban sectors of the country. In particular, the literacy rate is still shockingly low among rural women, with less than half classed as literate, even with a restricted definition of literacy.

Primary school enrolment in India may have increased steadily over the years, but is low even by South Asian standards. Countries like Sri Lanka and Bangladesh have higher primary school enrolment rates than India. Estimates suggest that more than 70 million children in the 6 to 14 years age group are either school dropouts or have never been enrolled in school at all.

Many more children may be formally registered, but barely attend. This is not surprising because the bulk of primary schools in the country lack the most basic resources such as, teachers, buildings, blackboards, toilets, and textbooks. Dropout rates from schools are very high in India, with girls more prone to withdrawing. However, the dropout rate did decline marginally over the 1990s. Another factor contributing to increased inequality in education in India has been the rapid growth of private schools. Over the years, the shares of private un-aided schools have gone up significantly at primary, mid-primary and secondary school levels. There has also been a commensurate decline in the share of government schools in these categories.

The growth of private un-aided schools has been much higher at the secondary and higher secondary levels. These private un-aided schools are mostly located in urban areas, and charge much higher fees than the government or local body schools. Since these private schools mainly cater to the richer parts of the population, their rapid growth is indicative of increasing education inequality in India.

FACTORS BEHIND GROWING INEQUALITY AND PERSISTENT POVERTY

The earlier discussion shows a perceptible increase in inter- and intra-regional inequality in India during the reform period. This inequality is evident, not only in income terms, but also in terms of health and access to education. This part discusses some factors which might be responsible for the increase in inequality in India during the reform period.

FISCAL POLICY

An important element of the economic reform process adopted in India was the belief that a high fiscal deficit level was responsible for the 1991 crisis, and the deficit should therefore be brought down to a certain pre-determined target. It was argued that a high fiscal deficit is bad for an economy because it can be inflationary, can give rise to external deficits, can lead to high interest rates and therefore crowd-out private investment, and can put an unsustainable interest rate burden on an economy through accumulation of public debt. The IMF programme required the government to bring down the fiscal deficit to a level of five to six per cent of GDP from the average of seven per cent of GDP for the period 1985-1990. However, it was also part of the macro-policy paradigm that taxes should be rationalized and direct tax rates should be cut so as to improve "efficiency" and provide incentives to private investors. In addition, indirect tax rates were cut because of import liberalization and associated domestic duty reductions.

This meant that fiscal balance could not be achieved through increased tax revenues, but would have to depend upon expenditure cuts. Therefore, to achieve this targeted fiscal deficit, the government undertook major expenditure cuts during the 1990s. Not surprisingly, the government found it difficult to cut current expenditure, so massive reductions were made in capital expenditure.

As a result, central government capital expenditure, as a share of GDP, declined steadily from 7.02 per cent for the period 1986-1987 to 1989-1990 to 2.74 per cent for the period 1999-2000 to 2002-2003. Public investments in crucial areas like agriculture, rural development, infrastructure development and industry were scaled down. This adversely affected the already fragile state of infrastructure in the economy and led to a virtual collapse of public services in areas like education, public health and sanitation.

As discussed by Chandrasekhar and Ghosh, not only were the plan targets for expenditure scaled down, but there were also huge shortfalls in public investment, even relative to these reduced targets, during most years of the decade. In addition, there was a decline in the central government's current expenditure on rural development accompanied by an overall decline in per capita government expenditure in rural areas. The decline of government investment in rural areas marked a sharp turnaround from the trend observed during the early 1980s, when there was a large increase in expenditure on the rural sector.

Political developments of the 1980s induced various governments to increase the flow of resources to this sector. This led to higher demand generation in the rural sector, and consequently resulted in lower poverty, economic diversification and increased rural employment generation.

However, over the 1990s, many policies which had contributed to this rural development were reversed. Central government expenditure on rural development schemes like agricultural programmes , rural employment programmes and anti-poverty schemes were cut. This had a negative effect on rural poverty and employment generation during the 1990s. Along with the cutback of central government expenditure on the rural sector, there was a gradual reorganization of the tax system, which led to reduced financial transfers to state governments.

The central government reduced the Central Sales Tax, introduced non-shareable levies in direct taxes, and adopted a value-added tax, all of which reduced the ability of states to generate resources. Since state governments were the dominant provider of basic services and rural infrastructure, the reduced ability of the state to finance these activities resulted in even lower levels of investment in rural sectors. This again, adversely affected demand and employment generation in the rural sector.

As part of the cost cutting exercise, subsidies given for food, fertilizer and exports were also reduced significantly. The reduction of the food subsidy crippled the public distribution system for food, which provided fair-priced food items to a very large number of low-income households. To reduce the food subsidy, the government introduced the targeted public distribution system.

In this system, only the households which belonged to the BPL category were eligible for subsidized food through the public distribution system. To reduce the budgetary expenditure on food, in 1999-2000, the government tried to increase food prices to equal the economic cost of the Food Corporation of India. This led to a doubling of food prices for the above poverty line household. Food prices for BPL households were also raised by about 80 per cent during this period.

At the same time, over the 1990s, the government increased the procurement prices of some major food-grains to placate the politically powerful farmer lobby. The increase in food prices led to a decline in food purchases by the public from the PDS, so stocks held by the FCI increased to three times the desired food-grain stock level, leading to very high stock holding costs. So, the attempt to reduce food subsidies by increasing prices paid by consumers had the paradoxical effect of increasing the public costs of holding food-grain stocks, and thus increased the food subsidy!

Over this period, per capita food-grain availability in the country actually declined from 510 grams in 1991 to 458 grams in 2000. Downsizing of employment in a number of key public sector industries was also undertaken in line with the expenditure-cutting exercise. This severely affected employment generation in the public sector but, as most studies pointed out, generated only notional fiscal benefits. Widespread disinvestment and sale of the equity of profitable public sector units were also undertaken during the 1990s. It was argued by the policymakers that disinvestment of public sector units would ensure fiscal discipline and would lead to higher levels of efficiency.

However, as many economists suspected, the real motivation behind the sale of PSUs was the accumulation of resources to meet the IMF fiscal deficit target. The disinvestment process pursued all through the 1990s turned out to be a disaster, as the controversial disinvestment of PSUs involved a number of profit making PSUs being sold at low and discounted prices to their global and domestic competitors.

Not only did this result in a loss to the government exchequer, putting a recurring burden on the exchequer, but it also distorted the markets for several commodities and services. There were also persistent allegations about corruption and malpractice in the sale of PSUs. As part of fiscal consolidation, a number of loss-making PSUs were closed down. Since some of these actually provided important services to farmers, small enterprises and people in general, their closure also had unfortunate productive and distributive implications. Many of these PSUs were not established solely as profit making companies, but were supposed to achieve various socio-economic targets. So, as a result of this process of disinvestment, the fiscal situation of the government did not improve, while many were deprived of the socio-economic benefits provided by many of these PSUs. This is one reason why the new government of the United Progressive Alliance, led by the Congress Party, declared that it would halt this process of mindless privatization, especially of profit-making public companies. Privatization of basic services like electricity and transport also raised the prices of these services in many places across India. This definitely contributed to the increased inequality observed during the 1990s.

The relatively backward regions, where private participation in industry is low, were the worst hit. The attempt by the government to undergo fiscal adjustment was essentially a one-track approach. In line with the expenditure cutting exercise, very little emphasis was put on improving revenue generation in the economy. The dictates of market-friendly neo-liberal economic policies did not allow for increases in direct tax rates or import tariffs.

As a result, the central government's tax to GDP ratio declined from about 11.8 per cent for the period 1987-1988 to 1989-1990 to about 9.6 per cent from 1999- 2000 to 2002-2003. A number of factors contributed to this decline. First, India initiated trade liberalization from the early 1990s, and levels of customs duties were reduced on a large number of goods. During the mid-1990s, tariff rates were reduced further, sometimes even going beyond the level required by WTO obligations.

As a result, customs duties declined steadily from about 3.6 per cent of GDP in 1990-1991 to about 1.8 per cent in 2001-2002. Secondly, a range of excise duty concessions were introduced to boost private sector demand and to encourage the growth of private industry. Also, to attract foreign direct investment and foreign portfolio investment, a number of fiscal concessions were given to foreign investors. Huge amounts of tax revenue were foregone on these accounts. Consequently, excise taxes declined from 4.3 per cent of GDP in 1990-1991 to 3.2 per cent in 2001-2002. During the mid-1990s, a number of direct tax concessions were also given as incentives to boost domestic savings and investment. It was argued that lowering direct tax rates would lead to higher tax revenue following the Laffer curve argument and would increase the buoyancy of tax receipts. However, Reserve Bank of India data show that over the Eighth and Ninth Plan periods, the buoyancy of central government taxes deteriorated from 0.9 to 0.8.

Though this decline happened mainly on account of indirect taxes, the buoyancy in direct tax collection stagnated at 1.3, and did not compensate adequately for the fall in buoyancy of indirect taxes. The restructuring of both direct and indirect taxes effected since the early 1990s, coupled with the structural shift in the composition of GDP towards the less-taxed services sector, appears to have affected the growth in tax revenue.

Thus, it can be concluded that the fiscal policy measures initiated in the reform period did not allow the government to build up productive capacity in the economy. Lack of public investment dampened aggregate demand, negatively affected private investments, created infrastructure bottlenecks to future growth, and adversely affected the provision of important public services.

Moreover, in a developing country, where capital expenditure on infrastructure and social services tends to crowd in private investment, reduced expenditure on these sectors led to the crowding out of private investment. As a result of reduced public and private investment, there was inadequate productive employment generation, both in rural and urban areas. This was a key factor behind the increased inequality and slow down of poverty reduction in the country.

FINANCIAL SECTOR REFORM

The crisis of 1991 hastened the process of financial liberalization pursued by the Indian government since the mid-1980s. Financial liberalization was designed to accomplish the following objectives: a) make the central bank more independent; b) relieve financial repression by freeing interest rates, and introduce various new financial instruments and innovations in the Indian financial system; c) reduce directed and subsidized credit; and d) allow greater openness and freedom for various forms of external capital flows. It should be noted that these objectives were not realized in full, and indeed, the lack of completeness of such financial liberalization has been one important reason for the relative financial stability of the country, unlike several other 'emerging markets.' The most adverse effect of financial liberalization on inequality came from policies which eased 'priority sector' lending norms for nationalized banks.

Until the 1980s, nationalized banks had obligations to fulfill priority sector lending targets. But post-liberalization, the priority sector definition was widened to include many more activities, and the emphasis in banking shifted instead towards maintaining the capital adequacy level prescribed by the Basle accord. As a result, most banks now avoid lending to small farmers and small scale industries, as they are perceived to be less creditworthy customers. This has had dramatic effects on the viability and cultivation of small enterprises, which are the largest employers in the country, and has therefore indirectly impacted income distribution and poverty reduction.

A report by a Reserve Bank of India working group concluded that the recent slowdown in priority sector lending principally owes to risk aversion due to a high proportion of non-performing loans. However, the composition of the non-performing assets of Indian public and private sector banks shows a somewhat different picture. As of 31 March 2002, 77.91 per cent of total NPAs in private sector banks were in non-priority sectors, while priority sectors accounted for only 21.8 per cent of total NPAs. For public sector banks, 53.5 per cent of NPAs were accounted for by non-priority sectors, 44.5 per cent of total NPAs were in priority sectors.

Anecdotal evidence suggests that a number of big Indian business houses are responsible for a substantial share of the non-priority sector NPAs. Collusion of big business houses with the political elite has prevented strong legal measures against defaulters. The decline in priority sector lending has led to a significant reduction in rural credit from formal channels, which has had major effects in terms of costs and the feasibility of cultivation. The irony is that the rural sector continues to contribute savings in the form of deposits into the banking system, leading to low and falling ratios of credits to deposits in rural banks. The reduced access to and higher cost of agricultural credit obviously means not just increased costs of cultivation, which has not been given adequate policy attention, but also adversely affected private investment in agriculture. Another consequence of financial liberalization has been the high inflow of foreign private capital into India.

A look at the RBI balance sheet shows that since 1993-1994, there has been a sharp increase in the Net Foreign Exchange Assets of the RBI. To moderate the growth of Reserve Money, which is defined as the sum of Net Foreign Exchange Assets and Net Domestic Assets of the RBI, the RBI had to constrain the growth of NDA. This was partly done by selling domestic currency bonds in the market, and partly by restricting RBI credit to the domestic sector.

As a result, the share of NFEA increased from 20.44 per cent in 1992-1993 to 65.01 per cent in 2000-2001. The figures show that in recent years, net foreign exchange asset accretion by the banking system became the most important source of money supply expansion in India. External compulsion of this kind can have serious implications for macroeconomic and monetary management of the country.

If the central bank has to accommodate large increases in foreign capital inflow, base money supply can only be controlled by sterilization involving a reduction in central bank credit to the domestic sector. While there are obvious analytical problems with the view that such sterilization has an effect on broader measures of money supply, the point is that sterilization affects the government's own perception of the possibilities of domestic monetary expansion, and therefore constrains its fiscal behaviour.

The principal area for such reductions is with regard to central bank credit to the government. This substantially increases the fiscal vulnerability of the state, reducing its ability to stimulate growth, sustain welfare measures like subsidies, and increase outlays on social sectors like health, education and meeting the basic needs of the population. This further constrained fiscal policy.

LIBERALIZATION OF FOREIGN AND DOMESTIC INVESTMENT

Extremely skewed interstate distribution of domestic and foreign direct investment has also contributed to increased inter-regional disparities in India. State-wise data on FDI approvals between 1991 and 2002 show that only a handful of states have managed to attract a very high share of FDI. It can be seen that the top 10 Indian states attracted more than 63 per cent of total foreign direct investment in India.

In contrast, the bottom 10 states together received less than 1 per cent of total FDI. There is also a strong regional disparity in the pattern of FDI flows, with the southern and western states faring much better than the other parts of the country. Three southern states received more than 20 per cent of total FDI, while Maharashtra and Gujarat received 17.35 per cent and 7.7 per cent of FDI respectively. In contrast, the seven North-Eastern states together received only 0.03 per cent of total FDI during the same period.

This unequal distribution of FDI across states in India is not unexpected, as FDI inflows tend towards states with better infrastructure and development. The concentration of FDI in a few pockets in India therefore did not help to reduce inequality during the reform period. Apart from its very skewed regional distribution, FDI flows in India also exhibit a strong sect oral bias. In India, a very high proportion of FDI has gone into high-end consumer goods and financial services like banks, insurance companies and consultancy services. It has also flowed into information technology related areas where India's human resources and research and development base have pockets of international competitiveness.

A large part of the inflow also went into the non-tradable infrastructural sector, attracted by special concessions, including guaranteed returns, offered by the government for such investments. However, benefits accruing from FDI in terms of fixed investments, exports and technological upgrading have been less than expected. This happened because since the 1990s, a significant part of FDI came in the form of mergers and acquisitions. As opposed to green-field FDI investment, M&As do not create productive capacity and hence do not benefit the host country as much. In fact, there are some negative consequences if M&As lead to the formation of monopoly powers in an industry. Also, typically with such mergers, employment stagnates or falls.

This often counterbalances or even negates the increase in employment of multi-national corporation affiliates, so that employment increases tend to be the least buoyant of all the major variables associated with MNC production. Secondly, though FDI worth around $30 billion has come into India since 1991, it has not contributed to an increase in exports.

Most analysts suggest that a high proportion of FDI came into India during the early 1990s to jump the 'tariff wall' and service the Indian market, rather than to use the country as an export hub. There were also apprehensions that the initial inflow of direct investment would be followed by large and persistent outflows on account of imports, royalties, technical fees and dividends, with adverse balance of payments consequences.

There have also been a few instances of anticompetitive practices by some large foreign companies in India. The most famous cases include the tussle between the government of Maharashtra and the energy giant Enron, and the buyout of a rival Indian cold drink company Parle Exports by Coca Cola. However, despite the liberalization of rules regarding FDI, India's performance in attracting FDI was not particularly impressive in this period.

Whereas China has managed to increase its FDI stock from $24 billion in 1990 to $448 billion in 2002, India's FDI stock increased from $1.6 billion in 1990 to $25.7 billion during 2002. FDI also financed only about 2-3 per cent of India's gross domestic capital formation, whereas the corresponding figure for China was around 10-11 per cent. Patterns of FDI inflow in India suggest that the inflows are highly concentrated in a few states and in some sectors where India can offer either a big domestic market or cheap and skilled labour. The concentration of FDI in relatively small areas has created some illusion of prosperity, but has hardly done anything to reduce overall levels of poverty or inequality in India. On the other hand, in a bid to attract FDI to their states, many state governments have completely overlooked the rural sector and concentrated their development expenditures in the urban areas. This has resulted in increased rural-urban inequality, and has given rise to political tension in these states.

In the 2004 elections, mainly due to rural discontent, the chief minister of Andhra Pradesh was voted out of office even though Hyderabad, the capital of the state, is one of the main hubs of the software industry in India and one of the most favoured FDI destinations in the country. Along with FDI, domestic private investment has also been regionally skewed. In the reform period, decontrol of investment licensing eliminated the central government's ability to direct investment to particular areas, especially to backward or undeveloped regions.

As a result, private corporate investment increasingly located in areas that could provide them with better support at lower cost. Ahluwalia argued "Private corporate investment is potentially highly mobile across states and is therefore likely to flow to states which have a skilled labour force with a good 'work culture', good infrastructure especially power, transport and communications, and good governance generally." As a result of the increased mobility of private capital and the reduced power of the state to direct investment to certain areas, the poorer performing states, which suffer from infrastructure deficiencies, remain at a serious disadvantage in attracting private investment.

This has led to the concentration of domestic investment in a few enclaves, and resulted in higher levels of interstate inequality in India. To address this disparity, it is essential that public investment be used to build economic and social infrastructure in these states to help them attract a larger flow of private investment.

TRADE LIBERALIZATION

Trade liberalization is essentially inequitable in nature since it distributes income in favour of the export sector and against the import competing sector. Unless the gains from trade are redistributed, trade liberalization will always change income distribution, which may imply higher inequality. In India, a similar phenomenon can be observed, but not necessarily along the lines predicted by traditional Hecksher-Ohlin trade theory.

The more employment-intensive sectors have been adversely affected, rather than encouraged, by trade liberalization. Opening up trade has helped certain sub-sectors, both in manufacturing and services, where India is internationally competitive, but mainly in activities using relatively skilled labour in the Indian context. By expanding the markets for these sectors, trade liberalization has definitely created some pockets of prosperity in India, but on the other hand, it has negatively affected most other manufacturing sectors and agriculture.

The situation in agriculture is most disturbing because about 70 per cent of the population depends upon this sector. Continued subsidization of agriculture by developed countries and the resultant distortion of global agricultural trade is one of the important factors behind the poor performance of agriculture. Yet, other macroeconomic policies, such as patterns of public spending and financial policies have also played a role. Small and medium enterprises in the manufacturing sector have also been hit by trade liberalization.

Typically, employment intensive domestic production has been displaced by imports of similar goods using more capital intensive production methods abroad. There is also a possibility that increased globalization and reforms may increase the cost of labour, and this would encourage capital intensive industrialization. This can happen because: an increase in relative food prices would increase the cost of labour in the form of higher wages; reduction of tariff s in capital goods sector may lead to cost advantages in favour of capital; foreign competition and greater export drive may also encourage more capital intensity. Therefore, a freer trade regime may not necessarily lead to higher employment generation in a country; this is supported by India's experience thus far. In this context, it is notable that in a liberalized trade regime, it is important that most workers possess some ability to shift jobs between sectors because trade liberalization is likely to induce the relocation of labour. Opening up trade leads to job losses in import competing industries and increases employment opportunities in export sectors.

If socio-economic conditions prevent workers from making this transition smoothly, or if the rate of new job creation is not fast enough, then it may result in even higher levels of inequality than those already prevailing in the economy. It is the duty of the government to equip and train workers to build up the requisite skills to make such inter-sectoral shifts.

However, the increased withdrawal of the state in India from most welfare-related issues suggests that the adjustment to trade liberalization is going to be a painful process, and the gap between the beneficiaries of trade liberalization and those who have not managed to benefit from it, will increase in the immediate future unless alternative policies are introduced.

CONCLUSION

In India, although there are claims that inequality has decreased in the post-liberalization period, careful analysis of data shows that these views are mostly unsubstantiated. Comparable estimates of the 50th and 55th rounds of National Sample Survey data reveal that inequality increased both in rural and urban India. Several authors have also pointed out that though the richer parts of the population benefited in the post-liberalization period, there has been a stagnation of incomes for the majority, with the bottom rung of the population severely negatively affected by this process.

There is also evidence that, both at the national and the state levels, income disparities between the rural and urban sectors increased during this period. State-level data also showed that not only had the income gap between the poorest and the richest states increased during the 1990s, but urban inequality increased for all the 15 major states in India. Inequality also alarmingly increased in the North-Eastern part of the country, where all the states experienced increased rural and urban poverty during this same period.

One of the reasons behind the increased income inequality observed in India in the post-reform period has been the stagnation of employment generation in both rural and urban areas across the states. Open unemployment increased in most parts of the country, and the rate of growth of rural employment hit an all time low. Declining employment elasticity in several sectors, including agriculture, was one of the main reasons behind this decline.

Low employment generation in the agriculture sector has also been associated with a steady, but significant increase in casualization of the labour force in India. Due to large scale downsizing and privatization of public sector units, employment generation in the organized sector also suffered. However, the services sector performed relatively better during this period.

The employment growth rate in this sector was higher than in other sectors of the economy. Particularly in some sub-sectors like information technology, communication and entertainment, employment generation and wages increased substantially in this period. However, these sectors employed only a very small part of the labour force, and their impact on the overall employment scenario has been minimal.

One countervailing force to the lower employment generation has been increased economic migration, typically to other countries in Asia and the Middle East. This has been especially important in certain regions and provided an important alternative source of transfer income to local residents through remittances.

However, these flows have had little to do with domestic policies and more to do with international economic processes. The discussion of health and education related indicators shows that though there has been some progress by India in these areas, this progress has been unsatisfactory, even when compared to other developing countries. Huge interstate disparities in health and education related indicators remain across the country. State involvement and investment in these sectors has historically remained very low and declined even further during the 1990s.

Gradual withdrawal of the state from these sectors and increased reliance on the private sector are likely to further exacerbate the already inequitable distribution of health and education services in India. A number of policies adopted during the reform period essentially increased the level of inequality in India. Liberalization of trade helped some sectors where India was internationally competitive, but it also negatively affected the other sectors.

The agriculture sector, as well as small and medium enterprises, which account for the bulk of employment, were the worst hit by the trade liberalization undertaken by policymakers since the mid-1990s. The inflow of FDI into India has only marginally improved gross domestic capital formation, but its incidence has been confined to some very small pockets, both geographically and sectorally.

This has increased interstate and inter-sectoral inequalities in the country. Emphasis on reduction of the fiscal deficit also increased inequality in India during the reform period. Due to pressures from powerful lobbies, direct and indirect tax rates declined in India. The government's failure to reduce current expenditure implied that most of the adjustment to reduce the fiscal deficit was carried out by reducing capital expenditure and rural expenditure generally, as well as by selling PSUs to generate one-time revenue.

Reduction of capital expenditure reduced public investment in key infrastructural areas and social welfare schemes. In a country like India, where the level of infrastructure development is poor, public investment in infrastructure is critical, not only for its direct developmental effects, but also because it brings in private investment through its crowding in effects. Attempts to reduce government expenditure on food subsidies and social welfare schemes have also had serious negative effects on inequality in the country.

In their zeal to adopt market-oriented reform measures, Indian policymakers have tended to overlook the fact that not only the so-called 'market economies' of Europe and America, but also the industrialization success stories of East Asia, all spend a very high percentage of their GDP on health, education and social security.

Notwithstanding the free market rhetoric, these countries have steadily increased their public expenditure on social services since the 1980s. Other market-oriented reform measures, like closure of non-profit making PSUs, have seriously undermined the social objectives of the PSUs and negatively affected employment and economic development in some parts of the country.

The closure of non-profit-making PSUs hurt the backward regions of the country more severely because the profit-maximizing private sector often does not find these areas economically attractive. Opening up the economy and financial sector liberalization also had major negative consequences for weaker parts of the population.

The introduction of prudential norms for private and public sector banks and the Basle NPA benchmark made wary banks avoid lending to borrowers in agriculture and to small enterprises. As a result, credit flows to agriculture and to small and medium enterprises went down drastically in recent years. This reinforced the problems faced by these sectors due to trade liberalization and the complete removal of quantitative restrictions on imports.

All of this points to conclusions with implications for government policy. The first is the crucial importance of continued and increased public expenditure for productive investments in infrastructure as well as for social expenditures and ensuring food access.

Both aggregate expenditure and the pattern of public expenditure are important. In addition, fiscal federalism-relations between the central and provincial governments-are very significant in large countries like India. Methods of raising resources for government expenditure, such as the pattern of taxation, also impact this connection. The relationships between growth patterns and the extent and type of employment generated have been extremely important as well. Trade liberalization has had disequalizing effects; while it provided more opportunities for some export activities, there were adverse effects for those employed in import-competing sectors, especially in small-scale activities. FDI patterns have tended to reinforce existing inequalities, possibly even more than domestic investment.

2

Water, Hindu Mythology and Unequal Social Order

INTRODUCTION

Vedic philosophy, the structural basis of currently practised Hinduism identifies that water and the human body in the Hindu social system are not merely physical entities. Water has, since the Vedic periods, been recognised as a primordial spiritual symbol. Similarly, Vedic philosophy describes the symbolic division of Purusa, or the Eternal Man, into four varnas or classes, Brahmans, Rajanyas, Vaisyas and Sudras.

The social hierarchy of the caste system in Hindu society is said to have originated from this four-fold class system. The caste system, a product of post-Vedic philosophy, ascribes states of ritual purity and pollution to the human body on account of caste or rather caste-based occupation and gender. Water has since then been recognised as an instrument to determine the rigours of socio-ritual purity and pollution of the human body.

Field research on water use in a rural Hindu society in the Kumaon region of the Central Himalayas in Uttaranchal state in India reveals that caste based socially hierarchy is determined locally through notions of purity and pollution. These notions are used in local culture in determining and reinforcing an inequitable access to, control over and distribution of water and water use rights. It is argued that popular policy visions of restoring the community's supremacy in water management can be counter-productive and reinforce existing inequality if the basis and reality of social inequality is ignored and the existence of a 'unitary, egalitarian and altruistic' community is assumed.

WATER, SOCIAL STRATIFICATION AND HINDUISM

'This knife has been with our family for generations. We did change the handle several times and the blade, sometimes, yet it is still the same knife.' Analysing social relations in contemporary India, Dube declares that, 'Caste is not dead and its boundaries and hierarchies are articulated by gender'. Jaiswal similarly propounds that the institution of caste continues to pose serious problems in the restructuring of Indian society, as traditional practices of discrimination on account of birth and gender tenaciously persist.

Others, however, claim that social inequality persists, but is no longer determined by the traditional social hierarchy of the caste system. Traditionally dominant castes are no longer the most powerful, as parametres determining social dominance have changed and continue to change with history. Despite the contradiction, it is agreed generally that the basis of the caste system is determined by notions of purity and pollution, themes which are identified as central to Hindu culture.

Impurity is symbolised by the peripheral extremities of the human body. 'All margins...and matter issuing from them are considered polluting... hair, nails...spittle, blood, semen, urine, faeces or even tears'. Human bodies in the act and process of producing bodily secretions or associating with these matters are recognised as polluting. Impurity is also incurred during birth and death; however, while birth signifies 'auspicious impurity' death is considered as 'inauspicious impurity'.

In the socially graded system, Brahmans are considered to be the purest, as a result of their occupational involvement in ritual and religious activities. These tasks are considered to be the most superior and purest of all social activities. At the other end of the social continuum, the Sudras are identified as defiled as a result of the defiling activities that they have socially been obliged to engage in. Sudras have historically been assigned the tasks of cremating the human dead, handling dead animals, handling human faeces, cutting hair, nails and washing and cleaning processes associated with bodily excrements.

As a result of their occupational association with polluted social events and polluted human matter, they are considered as eternally polluted and polluting. It is believed that in the Vedic period, individuals with a certain aptitude for these activities chose to perform such tasks.

In later periods, as the classes became transformed into a rigid social system of castes, tasks were determined not by aptitude or preference but were inherited at birth. Thus Sudras remained bound to performing these tasks through generations. Similarly, all women, regardless of their social caste, cyclically incur pollution through the bodily processes of menstruation and childbirth.

The core concern of Hindu ritualism is concerned with the manipulation and maintenance of purity and impurity. Purity is increased by associating or coming into contact with things and actors assigned pure status and by reducing association with things and actors of impure status.

There are essentially two ways to bring about a condition of purity, one is to distance oneself from objects signifying impurity and the other is to purify oneself by things recognised to have the ability to absorb and thus remove pollution directly. Water is the most common medium of purification. It is considered to have an intrinsic purity and the capacity to absorb pollution and carry it away.

To unfold the context of social stratification in Indian Hindu society and to determine the role of water in the regulation of social order it is essential to go back into history to trace the origin of the institution of these belief systems and forward into existing social and cultural contexts to identify whether the institution of the caste system still exists and if it does then in what shape, context and pattern in relation to water use practices.

THE VEDIC PERIOD—SANCTIFICATION OF WATER

In Vedic texts, water is referred to as Apah, or literally the Waters. The Waters are considered to be purifying in a spiritual context. 'Hail to you, divine, unfathomable, all purifying Waters...' The Rig Veda identifies the Waters as the first residence or ayana of Nara, the Eternal Being and therefore water is said to be pratishtha, the underlying principle, or the very foundation of this universe.

'Water may pour from the heaven or run along the channels dug out by men; or flow clear and pure having the Ocean as their goal... In the midst of the Waters is moving the Lord, surveying men's truth and men's lies. How sweet are the Waters, crystal clear and cleansing... From whom... all the Deities drink exhilarating strength, into whom the Universal Lord has entered...'.

Early Vedic texts also identify water as a manifestation of the feminine principle, known commonly as Sakti. 'I call the Waters, Goddesses, wherein our cattle quench their thirst; Oblations to the streams be given...'. It is said that the primordial cosmic man or Purusa was born of the Waters. Similarly later Vedic texts identify that, 'Water is female...' Vedic philosophy thus bestows a sacred character on water, which is then identified as a medium to attain spiritual enlightenment.

The concept of purification in early Vedic texts was essentially spiritual, rather than moral and/or physical. Understanding the primary meaning and force of water was considered to supersede all ritual and rite. The Vedas identify water as the very essence of spiritual sacrifice or 'the first door to attain the divine order'. The use of water in daily life as well as in ritualistic ceremony was referred to as spiritual sacrifice, a process of attaining eternity cleansing bath was believed to liberate one from sin and impurity:

'...Whatever sin is found in me, whatever wrong I may have done, if We have lied or falsely sworn, Waters remove it far from me...' The act of bathing was considered intensely spiritual and it was believed that physical acts of imperfection were removed and spiritual oneness with the Eternal Self was attained during the process. It was not the act of taking a bath itself, but the coming into contact with the sacredness of water, and the attainment of such knowledge and proximity that made one sinless and guided the individual to the Eternal Self. Water was considered sacred but it was clarified that man does not pray to water, the physical entity, but to the source of life and spirituality within water. 'Water is the purified as well as the purifier, the real and spiritually conceived source of life'.

SOCIAL ORDER IN VEDIC PHILOSOPHY

In the early Vedic period, social stratification in human society existed on the basis of colour, class, individual capacity, occupational aptitude and moral and intellectual worth, rather than on the later determined caste system, which is based on inheritance-based rights and privileges. The first instance of social distinction is made on the colour and culture differences between the fair skinned Aryas and the dark skinned Dasas. Then, the division of mankind into four varnas from the Purusa or the Eternal Man is described in the hymn, Purusa Sukta of the Rg Veda:

'When they divided Man, how many did they make Him. The Brahman was his mouth; his arms were made the Rajanya; his thighs were the Vaisya; from his feet the Sudra was born.'

Social hierarchy in the early Vedic society is believed to have been divinely-ordained. Historians argue that the varna system was an 'open class system' of flexible membership and the construction of castes and the rigid caste system did not begin in the early Vedic period. 'The Vedic quadripartition of classes or colours is not to be confused with the notion of caste or jati as this was merely a social model based on a cosmic paradigm of hierarchy'.

However the system of social stratification was established in the early Vedic period, even if it was flexible and not inherently binding. The Rg Veda defines varnas and designated occupations, 'One to high sway, one to exalted glory one to pursue his gain and one to his labour.' 'Brahmans were to be the teachers of mankind, Kshatriyas were to carry weapons and protect people, Vaisyas were to provide food for the people and the Sudras were to be the footmen or servants of the other varnas, even if they had all originated from the same Eternal Man'. Despite the obvious social stratification in the early Vedic period, historians identify that there was no concept of untouchability, of physical purity and pollution, of prevention of social relations between individuals of different varnas in early Vedic literature.

However it is agreed that by the later Vedic periods, social hierarchy had been established and the Brahmans, men devoted to learning and priesthood had come to be regarded as superior by mere birth. Similarly the inferiority of certain jatis or social groups within the Sudra varna, such as the Candalas or those undertaking cremation tasks, had been established.

POST VEDIC PERIODS AND INSTITUTIONALISATION OF WATER-RELATED SOCIAL INEQUALITY

In contrast to the notion of spirituality in early Vedic texts, Smrtis or post Vedic literature constructed the notion of ritualism. Water governed the ritualistic or bodily purification of human existence. Ritualism was related to the construct of Dharma or moral law and the most authoritative text on the subject of Dharma is the 'Laws of Manu', or Manusmrti. Manu is blamed for creating the caste system, however some authors argue that he may have simply recorded the system of social order that existed then.

What matters though, is that Manu and other lawmakers of this period codified the social order as morally appropriate social behaviour, social duties and obligations. Social obligations and duties were classified as contributing to religious ritualism, which explains why the religiously inclined Hindus tenaciously practise Dharma as their culture. 'Dharma persists steadfastly in Hindu society, despite the fact that there is no watchdog, like the Western Church, to enforce moral regulations'.

Murray lists the structural features of the caste system, as expounded by Manu, which are said to have changed little in contemporary social practice. These include, 'the Brahmans' continuous cultural prominence in religious ritualism; a rigid caste status assigned solely on the basis of inheritance; the centrality of a person's caste in his/her social life; prohibition of mobility across caste boundaries maintained by the regulation of marriage and eating arrangements; enormous social energies devoted to maintaining caste boundaries and extensive norms and elaborate rituals prescribed for regulating social stratification based on the centrality of the concept of Dharma.'

The lawbooks or Dharmasastras defined in very clear terms how Sudras were, on the basis of their inherited status to undertake defiling and/or polluting tasks. In order to maintain purity, the Sudras who were essentially bound to undertake polluting tasks were excluded physically, socially and morally from the larger village commune.

Sudras, identified in the Dharmasastras as the very essence of pollution, were required to live outside the village confines. Fa Hein, the Chinese traveller to India, writes about how in a public place the Candalas had to give notice of their approach by striking a piece of wood, to warn others to avoid contact with them. Any physical association of a Sudra, especially a Sudra male with women of other castes, was a severely punishable act for the Sudra, which could lead to castration or even death, even if the association was mutually desired. Purification of touch by a Sudra involved taking a cleansing bath; talking to a Sudra was purified by talking to a Brahman; and the sight of a Sudra was purified by looking at the sun, moon or stars and rinsing the mouth with water.

In the Dharmasastras, water was identified as a medium to purify the pollution obtained through the Sudras. The Manusmriti also elaborates how water and food cooked in water, offered or touched by the Sudras, was polluting. It was stated that when Sudras touch a well or any other stagnant water source, the source and the water is polluted. Manu went to the extent of elaborating rituals to be performed to purify such polluted water. The Sudras had no God and therefore were to be excluded from all religious knowledge and ritualism, which was the very basis of Hindu existence. It is fair to say that in the post-Vedic period the Sudras were isolated from the other social, now caste groups and thus contextually removed from the class of humans and assigned the status similar to that ascribed to animals. There are numerous parallels drawn in the Dharmasastras between socially belittled animals, like dogs and pigs, and the Sudras.

Apart from the eternally polluted Sudras, all persons became polluted and therefore 'untouchable' during birth and death in the house. Those touching members mourning during death, touching the corpse and/or carrying the corpse to the cemetery were identified as polluted. Drawing parallel with the notion of pollution accorded to death, Sudras were likened by him to 'a living cemetery'.

Women, on account of their bodily secretions during their menstrual cycle and immediately after childbirth, were identified as polluting regardless of their caste. During this period, all of the restrictions detailed for the Sudras were exercised on them. Those touching menstruating women or touching women during the first ten days after childbirth were also considered as polluting. Water was ascribed as a medium to purify all these forms of pollution.

RITUALLY-DETERMINED SOCIAL STRATIFICATION IN CONTEMPORARY HINDU SOCIETY

Theoretical texts endlessly debate the validity of history in interpreting local culture. Sax, argues that, '...the hackneyed dualities of Hindu history, of sacred and profane, of body and ...spirit, are trojan horses, as the notions were historically determined and culturally specific.' However, his statement appears relevant only in particular political contexts. Srinivas identifies that Brahmans are not the dominant caste in rural India today. 'Economic, political and 'western' axes of power determine dominance.

The agriculturally landed and the numerically strong are the dominant social groups today.' Srinivas' claim that the traditionally determined patterns of caste-specific familial occupation, or Jajman are changing, is challenged by those who argue that despite reform, legislation and wider potential for choosing occupation types, 'A Brahman still performs the function of the priest and the Sudra remains responsible for ritually polluting occupations. In every region, women and men of specific "untouchable" castes remain responsible for the essential task of removing pollution of upper and clean castes'. This implies that social positions may have changed for the more and less dominant social groups, but culturally and ritually little has changed for the 'untouchables' or Sudras as the social order of Dharma persists as both social belief and culture.

The 'untouchables' remain ritually polluted, therefore polluting and therefore untouchable. Further, Srinivas' claim of western influences on the dilution of social hierarchy, though visible, may actually be peripheral. Assayag reports recent claims in this way, 'At the office I remove my caste, which I again put on at home'. In the rural context, where offices are rare, such influences may be even less significant.

SPIRITUALITY, RITUALISM AND SOCIAL EXCLUSION THROUGH WATER IN CHUNI VILLAGE

To observe cultural interpretations of social stratification and the role of water in determining this structure in local contexts, the water behaviour and order in a remote, rural mountain village, Chuni, in the Kumaon hills was studied and compared with observations made in villages in other parts of North India.

Chuni is known locally as a water-abundant village. The ancient Jal Devi temple located in the village is said to keep the waters in the traditional irrigation channels, or guls, flowing, as well as to bestow other blessings on Chuni residents. The traditional water springs or Naulas used by the 'upper castes' are also said to be the abode of the Jal Devi, therefore revered and worshipped.

The Naula is built by constructing a stone-wall across a groundwater spring. Throughout mountain villages, 'Naulas are traditionally held in deep reverence and rituals are made while constructing these systems'. Water from the spring is used daily in ritual worship at home and the springs are ritualistically important during marriage, and in local customary and traditional Hindu festivals. In keeping with Vedic philosophy, water as well as the water source itself, is spiritually sacred to the local people and this belief is manifested in the rituals governing social life.

Water is also purifying. The concept of purity exists as a theme, which is central to local life, almost in the same way as defined by Manu. This concept is used to exclude the polluted from water sources, which are considered sacred. In death and birth for the family, and menstruation and childbirth for women, water from the Naulas is mixed with water from the holy river Ganga, if available, and is sprinkled on the polluted to purify them before they are re-integrated into the social system and also before they can actually access the Naulas themselves.

Dalits, here as elsewhere, are considered polluted and capable of polluting. When the 'upper castes' come in close contact with Dalits they are purified by the sprinkling of Naula water, a practice known locally as Chod. After Dalits leave an 'upper caste' household, the place where they sat in the courtyard is washed or sprinkled with water, or sometimes with a mixture of cow-dung, also identified as pure, and water.

Officially The Kumaon and Garhwal Water Act, 1975, terminated the customary rights of individuals and village communes and just as to the Act, the 'State took over the power... for collection, conservation and distribution of water and control of water sources'. However, in the village, specific hamlets and/or families exercise control over these formally 'state owned' Naulas as well as other water sources and determine social inclusion and exclusion in access to water and water sources.

Ritually determined local culture excludes the Dalits in Chuni from accessing or using any Naula in the village except the one that is assigned as theirs. Ganga Devi, a Tamta woman, tells of an ancient folktale, 'A Dalit man in the forest ate some gooseberries from a tree. He then came to a Naula belonging to the "upper castes". Very thirsty and seeing no one around, he stole and drank some water and found it very sweet. He said to himself, No wonder we are not allowed to access such sweet water.' Ganga Devi confirms that this practice continues. Her small nephew was recently beaten for stealing cool water on a hot summer day from the Naula belonging to the Goswamis. To purify the Naula, defiled by the touch of this small Dalit boy, the water was thrown out. The Goswami family performed a ritualistic prayer to the Jal Devi and warned the boy's parents that if the act was repeated the family would no longer be given land for sharecropping.

Even the spaces around the Naulas are considered sacred and therefore to be protected from the polluted. The concept of Dharma is exercised as a self-regulatory mechanism to ensure exclusion. Good Dalits and good women are those who do not violate this social doctrine. This is a social belief locally, even amongst women and the Dalits.

When the water in the Naulas reduces, women are blamed for accessing the spring in an impure condition. Both women and men say, 'Big white snakes appear in the Naulas as the first sign of the Goddess' wrath and then the water slowly dries up. The remedy is a purifying Devi Path and also presentation of a calf to the Brahman performing the ritual.' Dalits are not blamed so readily; blaming them would mean legitimising that they can and do access the Naulas secretly; which would be politically more damaging.

However, when Dalits access Naulas forbidden to them, the consequences are graver. In a nearby village, a Dalit schoolteacher, who was not a local, was socially ostracised and finally forced to leave the village. His defiance in fetching drinking water from the Naula used by the 'upper castes' was not tolerated, especially as there was an officially provided tap, which villagers identified he could safely use.

Taps, in contrast to Naulas are not sacred. However, water from taps like these, which are provided through officially implemented projects, carry water mostly from storm water drains, a source that is inferior to the Naula. Also, water from the tap is hot in summer and cold in winter, having flowed through exposed metal pipes and not like the Naula water, which is cool in summer and warm in winter, as well as sweet and refreshing. Locally, this defiance was said to be a display of an uncouth attitude, an example of what happens when the Dalits, not having the innate constitution for education, become educated. 'It makes them more perverse.' Despite legislation that makes such treatment a criminal offence, even educated Dalits like this schoolteacher do not pursue legal prosecution. In the mountain villages, Dalits living as a minority are well aware of what suits their specific interests better.

Factors of social exclusion for 'impure' women vary in intensity between villages. In most mountain villages, women when impure live in small huts outside the domains of the main house. In severely orthodox communities, women are made to live in small settlements outside the village boundary. Exclusion from the Naulas is however seen in all villages for 'impure' women.

This means that women are not able to access water from the Naulas especially during periods when they are most in need of water for personal hygiene. During such periods, women do not fetch drinking water or cook food and remain dependent on other members of their family for performing this work, which is essentially theirs at other times.

However, they still perform tasks like washing clothes, and fetch water for uses at home, which are not considered polluting. For this they have to get water from other water sources, like the storm water drains and rivers. Drains are not considered sacred, and rivers though considered sacred are believed to be capable of absorbing and absolving all pollution because they flow continuously.

If such alternative sources are not available, women depend on others for water needed to perform these tasks as well as for water for personal use. For the Dalits, Naulas except their own are permanently inaccessible and for the Dalit women, when doubly impure, their own springs are also inaccessible.

Can Dalits not be satisfied using the Naulas assigned to them? Why this complaint of inequality? The social geography of the mountain villages shows that historically dominant landowning groups have occupied water abundant sites in the village setting. Closely parallel the relative access to preferred sources of water and water adequacy in Chuni. Dalits and the other service providers were settled in the least attractive peripheries of the village.

The 8 Dalit families in this hamlet have access to one Naula, in comparison to one Khanka family's sole legitimate access to one Naula. Even when numerically equal, inequality persists on the basis of untouchability.

In remote mountain villages, traditional sources like the Naula remain widely used. Officially provided water supply systems have either not reached remote rural villages or, where provided are unreliable, poorly maintained, not the preferred source of drinking water and also identified as inappropriate for the multiple household needs of water.

The officially provided system of tap-stands in Chuni village built as a 'nine lakh rupees project' provided water for only 4 days. A big monsoon landslide washed away the pipes. This project design had anyway excluded the Dalit hamlets. It was commonly said, 'Those hamlets are uphill, the technology of gravity flow cannot make water flow uphill.' This happened even though official policy recognising caste-based inequities defines, 'Priority coverage to Scheduled Caste/ Scheduled Tribe inhabitants and Scheduled Caste/Scheduled Tribe inhabited villages'.

This policy was drawn up after identifying that, 'One of the most obnoxious disabilities suffered by the rural Dalits is the lack of access to drinking water. Loopholes in the law are exploited by higher caste villagers, with the connivance of local officials of identical castes, to classify village wells as private property. The Harijans either have to travel far to get their water or must turn to polluted sources that the higher castes do not use'.

Despite the legislation of this policy the practice of connivance continues. When discussing the problems faced by the Dalits in Chuni with the Junior Engineer of the official organisation, he said, 'But the elected head has never raised this complaint.' The elected village head is not a Dalit and the

Junior Engineer himself, also not a Dalit, has not travelled to the village. In a similar incident in a rural village in coastal Orissa, it was seen that the Dalits continue to use water from a polluted pond, as the official norm of one hand-pump for 250 persons means that hand-pumps, though provided, are not conveniently located. In this mixed-caste village, the Dalits could not access the handpumps used by their Brahman neighbours. In some places, handpumps are shared between castes, but the access is still unequal.

In water scarce Banda district of Uttar Pradesh, both Dalits and the Kurmis used the same handpump. To purify the source and water, 'Kurmi women clean the handpump with several buckets of water before filling their own bucket if the earlier user was a Dalit. ...If the other castes are filling water or using the handpump, the Dalits need to wait for hours. They cannot fill water together and the Dalits must always wait for their turn.' In the Kumaon hills, the Dalits are a numerical minority. This fact, coupled with their occupational need to spread out as service providers across villages, means that they have historically remained numerically vulnerable and thus unable to achieve any authority locally, despite supporting legislation. Other principles of lower social status also influence the fact that the Dalits remain excluded from authorities that make decisions about water at the village level.

Similarly, women, barred by social norms of exclusion from public domains, have historically remained excluded from any decision-making authorities. This explains why the design of water systems has historically not met the specific needs of Dalits specifically and women generally.

COMMUNITY MANAGEMENT IN WATER PROJECTS

What happens when the concept of community ownership is transferred to such local settings? The World Bank supported SWAJAL project specifies the need for handing over management responsibility to the local community, through the Village Water and Sanitation Committee. There is a specified criterion that thirty per cent of VWSC memberships should be reserved for women and twenty per cent for Dalits.

The World Bank project also came to Roulikhet village and brought with it benefits of non-formal education, income generation programmes and hygiene education together with improved access to drinking water and sanitation. In terms of women's increased access to water, the upper caste women in Roulikhet village do not use the tap-stands provided by the project when they are bodily impure. They continue to go to the river or ask others for water. The belief here is that, although the taps are not sacred, using the water flowing rapidly from the taps would result in the water flowing out to the village lowlands, where the temple of the powerful village Goddess is located.

Water polluted by the touch of such women would pollute the sacred spot and this would result in the Goddess's wrath, which few women in the village dare incite. During these periods, women use water sparingly so that it is absorbed in the soil and does not flow down to the temple.

CONCLUSION

The age-old Hindu philosophy of water and the human body being social constructs persists. The notions of this belief have changed with history but there is no evidence that these changes have resulted in positive outcomes for the socially deprived. Social inequality, instituted in the later Vedic periods on the basis of caste ascribed by birth and gender, persists and thrives in contemporary Hindu society and the losers in this unequal social order are the Dalits and women.

In the rural mountain villages, the social order remains unequal and behaviour in relation to water remains instrumental in determining inequality. Consequently the Dalits remain permanently excluded and women are cyclically excluded from traditional, but currently preferred and used systems of water delivery. This observation may vary in specific villages, however given the constancy of ritual purity and pollution and the role of water in defining these, one can safely assume that the situation is largely universal, especially in those areas where the Dalits remain a minority. Official policy aimed to improve access to water for the Dalits, who were identified as those who had historically been excluded from traditional water sources. However, inequity in social order at local levels, coupled with the inadequacy of official interventions, has determined that Dalits continue to lack access to reliable, appropriate and adequate water sources. New policies identify the failure of official interventions and aim to improve access to water by restoring authority to village communities. In order to socially empower women and the Dalits and to improve their access to water, such policies aim to include the formerly excluded in decision-making forums at the village level. However, policy does not identify the root causes of the principles of social exclusion operating at local levels.

When authority is handed over to local communities, local power positions determine that power remains concentrated in the hands of the socially dominant. It is in this context that Murray's argument of the need to distinguish political, economic and status mobility becomes relevant. He identifies that political and economic mobility of the Dalits has occurred in India, more in the urban context than in rural areas, but little change can be seen in the ritual status of the Dalits.

'To raise the status of some is to lower the status of others; to decrease the impurity of untouchables has the long-term consequence of eroding the Brahman's extraordinary purity'. Addressing structural social inequities and the resulting unequal access to basic resources challenges the very notions central to the Hindu way of life. Increasing political mobility for the Dalits and women will not always readily translate to mobility in status.

Such deep-rooted caste and gender inequities cannot be erased simply. To equitably improve access to water for the Dalits and women, the root causes of the determinants of social inequity need to be identified, exposed and addressed locally. Blueprint approaches construed in ignorance of deep-rooted cultural values of caste and gender hierarchies will at best result in cosmetic, but not real changes to the social fabric of Hindu society and the power-based distribution and access to basic resources in such societies.

3

Vulnerable Groups in India

VULNERABLE GROUPS; THEIR HEALTH AND HUMAN RIGHTS

Human right applies universally to all. The process of identifying vulnerable groups within the health and human right generated from the pressing reality on the ground that stemed from the fact that there are certain groups who are vulnerable and marginalized lacking full enjoyment of a wide range of human rights, including rights to political participation, health and education. Vulnerability within the right to health framework means deprivation of certain individuals and groups whose rights have been violated from the exercising agency.

Certain groups in the society often encounter discriminatory treatment and need special attention to avoid potential exploitation. This population constitutes what is referred to as Vulnerable Groups. Vulnerable groups are disadvantaged as compared to others mainly on account of their reduced access to medical services and the underlying determinants of health such as safe and potable drinking water, nutrition, housing, sanitation etc.

For example, persons with disabilities often don't get employment or adequate treatment or people living with HIV/AIDS, face various forms of discrimination that affects their health and reduces their access to health services. The issue of participation and prevention of violation is important for understanding the vulnerable groups; their health and human rights. The United Nations Economic, Social and Cultural

Rights Committee mentions that an important aspect of implementing the right to health "is the improvement and furtherance of participation of the population in the provisions of preventive and curative health services, such as the organization of the health sector, the insurance system and, in particular in political decisions relating to the right to health taken at both the community and national levels".

The General Comment 14 of the Article 12 also proscribes any discrimination in access to health care and underlying determinants of health, as well as to means and entitlements for their procurement, on the grounds of race, colour, sex, language, religion, political or other opinion, national or social origin, property, birth, physical or mental disability, health status, sexual orientation and civil, political, social or other status, which has the intention or effect of nullifying or impairing the equal enjoyment or exercise of the right to health.

The Committee stresses that measures, such as the strategies and programmes designed to eliminate health-related discrimination, can be pursued with minimum resource implications through the adoption, modification or abrogation of legislation or the dissemination of information. The Committee recalls General Comment No.3, Paragraph 12, which states that even in times of severe resource constraints, the vulnerable members of society must be protected.

Protecting and fulfilling the rights of the vulnerable groups constitutes the immediate state obligations under the Covenant for Economic Cultural and Social Rights. There are many and complex linkages between health and human rights of the vulnerable groups. Violations or lack of attention to human rights can have serious health consequences for certain groups. The manner in which health policies and programmes are designed can either protect or violate human rights of certain groups.

The chances of enjoying good health must not be unfairly disadvantaged because of sex, class, religion, age, sexual orientation, ethnic identity, perhaps their recognition of the vital role of societal environment to both health and realization of human rights. Both the approaches recognize the fact that there is a complex relation between the individual and the society that impacts their health. For example, the health of an individual or groups may depend on the conditions such as sufficient income, living conditions, access to safe drinking water, etc., and all the factors are heavily influenced by whether or not an individual belongs to a group that suffers discrimination. Public health is assumed to seek the greatest good for the greatest number of people.

Application of human rights principles to public health strategies has expanded the scope of the latter by going beyond averages and focusing attention also on those population groups in society which are considered most vulnerable. The focused attention on vulnerable and disadvantaged groups in the international human rights instruments reinforces the principle of equity. An ideal public health strategy would be the one which addresses the concerns for equity and justice in every society but in practical terms there are limitations of every health system.

This necessitates the need to focus on the immediate service delivery by prioritizing the needs. Human rights norms and standards form a strong basis for health systems to prioritize the health needs of vulnerable and marginalized population groups. Focus on the vulnerable group is very useful for human rights documentation. It allows review of context specific violations, identify the challenges faced by the specific groups and their access to healthcare, gather information on group-specific risk factors, cultural and social differences among groups and its impact on health and health-seeking behaviour, document the negative attitude of the health system resulting in denial, draws attention to how national legislation and development policies impact upon the status of such groups. This facilitates advocacy for Right to Health and empowers the disadvantaged groups by raising awareness about their rights and potential violations. Different societies have different conditions/situations that generate and perpetrate vulnerability among certain individuals and groups. Hence identifying vulnerable groups within the right to health framework is an ongoing process.

VULNERABLE GROUPS IN INDIA

In India there are multiple socio-economic disadvantages that members of particular groups experience which limits their access to health and healthcare. The task of identifying the vulnerable groups is not an easy one. Besides there are multiple and complex factors of vulnerability with different layers and more often than once it cannot be analysed in isolation.

The present document is based on some of the prominent factors on the basis of which individuals or members of groups are discriminated in India, *i.e.*, structural factors, age, disability, mobility, stigma and discrimination that act as barriers to health and healthcare.

The vulnerable groups that face discrimination include Women, Scheduled Castes, Scheduled Tribes, Children, Aged, Disabled, Poor migrants, People living with HIV/AIDS and Sexual Minorities. Sometimes each group faces multiple barriers due to their multiple identities. For example, in a patriarchal society, disabled women face double discrimination of being a women and being disabled.

VULNERABLE GROUPS FACING STRUCTURAL DISCRIMINATION

Structural norms are attached to the different relationships between the subordinate and the dominant group in every society. A group's status may for example, be determined on the basis of gender, ethnic origin, skin colour, etc. The norms act as structural barriers giving rise to various forms of inequality. Access to health and healthcare for the subordinate groups is reduced due to the structural barriers. The structural discrimination faced by the groups and their human right violations.

In India, members of gender, caste, class, and ethnic identity experience structural discrimination that impact their health and access to healthcare. Women face double discrimination being members of specific caste, class or ethnic group apart from experiencing gendered vulnerabilities. Women have low status as compared to men in Indian society.

They have little control on the resources and on important decisions related to their lives. In India, early marriage and childbearing affects women's health adversely. About 28 per cent of girls in India, get married below the legal age and experience pregnancy. These have serious repercussions on the health of women. Maternal mortality is very high in India. The average maternal mortality ratio at the national level is 540 deaths per 100,000 live births. It varies between states and regions, *i.e.*, rural-urban.

The rural Maternal Mortality Rate is 617 deaths of women age between 15-49 years per one lakh live births as compared to 267 maternal deaths per one lakh live births among the urban population. In most cases the deaths occur from preventable causes. A large proportion of women is reported to have received no antenatal care. In India, institutional delivery is lowest among women from the lower economic class as against those from the higher class.

Women face violence and it has an impact on their health. During infancy and growing years a girl child faces different forms of violence like infanticide, neglect of nutrition needs, education and healthcare. As adults they face violence due to unwanted pregnancies, domestic violence, sexual abuse at the workplace and sexual violence including marital rape and honour killings.

The experience of violence and its impact on health varies just as to the women's caste, class and ethnic identity. Caste also perpetrates inequality. Caste in Indian society is a particular form of social inequality that involves a hierarchy of groups ranked in terms of ritual purity where members who belong to a particular group or stratum share some awareness of common interest and a common identity.

The caste system is linked to the possession of natural resources, livelihood resources and in the Indian context also to land economy and land based power relations. Traditionally, caste relations were based on the hierarchy of occupations where work related to leather, cleaning dead cattle from village grounds, work related to funeral ceremonies, etc were placed at the bottom. People or castes who were performing the task of eliminating the polluted elements from society were considered 'untouchables' vis-à-vis the Brahmins who were highest in the order based on the purity-impurity principle. Structurally the lower castes were economically dependent on the higher castes for existence. The Scheduled Caste remained economically dependent, politically powerless and culturally subjugated to the upper caste.

This impacted their overall lifestyle and access to food, education and health. A major proportion of the lower castes and Dalits are still dependent on others for their livelihood. Dalits does not refer to a caste but suggests a group who are in a state of oppression, social disability and who are helpless and poor. They were earlier referred as 'untouchables' mainly due to their low occupations *i.e.,* cobbler, scavenger, sweeper. In a caste-dominated country like India, Dalits who comprises more than one-sixth of the Indian population, stand as a community whose human rights have been severely violated. Literacy rates among Dalits are only about 24 per cent. They have meager purchasing power; have poor housing conditions; lack or have low access to resources and entitlements.

In rural India they are landless poor agricultural labourers attached to rich landowners from generations or poor casual labourers doing all kinds of available work. In the city they are the urban poor employed as wage labourers at several work sites, beggars, vendors, small service providers, domestic help, etc., living in slums and other temporary shelters without any kind of social security.

The members of these groups face systemic violence in the form of denial of access to land, good housing, education and employment. Structural discrimination against these groups takes place in the form of physical, psychological, emotional and cultural abuse which receives legitimacy from the social structure and the social system. Physical segregation of their settlements is common in the villages forcing them to live in the most unhygienic and inhabitable conditions. All these factors affect their health status, access to healthcare, and quality of health service received. There are high rates of malnutrition reported among the marginalized groups resulting in mortality, morbidity and anaemia. Access to and utilization of healthcare among the marginalized groups is influenced by their socio-economic status within the society. Structural discrimination directly impedes equal access to health services by way of exclusion.

The negative attitude of the health professionals towards these groups also acts as a barrier to receiving quality healthcare from the health system. In the case of women, discrimination increases by the complex mix of two factors-being a women and being a member of the marginalized community. A large proportion of Dalit girls drop out of primary school inspite of reservations and academic aptitude, because of poverty, humiliation, isolation or bullying by teachers and classmates and punishment for scoring good grades.

The scavenger community among the Dalits is vulnerable to stress and diseases with reduced access to healthcare. The Scheduled Tribes like the Scheduled Castes face structural discrimination within the Indian society. Unlike the Scheduled Castes, the Scheduled Tribes are a product of marginalization based on ethnicity. In India, the Scheduled Tribes population is around 84.3 million and is considered to be socially and economically disadvantaged.

Their percentages in the population and numbers however vary from State to State. They are mainly landless with little control over resources such as land, forest and water. They constitute a large proportion of agricultural labourers, casual labourers, plantation labourers, industrial labourers etc. This has resulted in poverty among them, low levels of education, poor health and reduced access to healthcare services. They belong to the poorest strata of the society and have severe health problems.

They are less likely to afford and get access to healthcare services when required. The health outcomes among the Scheduled Tribes are very poor even as compared to the Scheduled Castes. The Infant Mortality Rate among Scheduled Castes is 83 per 1000 live births while it is 84.2 per 1000 per live births among the Scheduled Tribes. Among the Scheduled

Castes and the Scheduled Tribes the most vulnerable are women, children, aged, those living with HIV/AIDS, mental illness and disability. These groups face severe forms of discrimination that denies them access to treatment and prevents them from achieving a better health status. Gender based violence and domestic violence is high among women in general in India.

Girl child and women from the marginalized groups are more vulnerable to violence. The dropout and illiteracy rates among them are high. Early marriage, trafficking, forced prostitution and other forms of exploitation are also reportedly high among them. In situations of caste conflict, women from marginalized groups face sexual violence from men of upper caste *i.e*, rape and other forms of mental torture and humiliation.

VULNERABILITY OF CHILDREN AND AGED

Children and the elderly population face different kind of vulnerability. Mortality and morbidity among children are caused and compounded by poverty, their sex and caste position in society. All these have consequences on their nutrition intake, access to healthcare, environment and education. These factors directly impacts food security, education of parents and their access to correct health information and access to health care facilities. Malnutrition and chronic hunger are the important causes of death among children from poor families.

Diarrhoea, acute respiratory diseases, malaria and measles are some of the main causes of death among children, most of which are either preventable or treatable with low-cost interventions. Tetanus in newborns remain a problem in at least five states: Uttar Pradesh, Madhya Pradesh, Rajasthan, West Bengal, and Assam. Poverty has a direct impact on the mortality and morbidity among children.

Neo-natal mortality is about two times higher among people with low standard of living while Under-5 mortality among children from lower economic class is five times than that of households with high standard of living. 73.4 per cent of children have some form of anemia. In India, a girl child faces discrimination and differential access to nutritious food and gender based violence is evident from the falling sex ratio and the use of technologies to eliminate the girl child.

Among children the health indicators vary between the different social groups. High mortality and morbidity is reported among children from Scheduled Castes, Scheduled Tribes and Other Backward Classes as compared to the general population. Infant morality is higher among the rural population.

The vaccination coverage is very poor among children who live in rural India. Vaccination coverage among children between 12-23 months who have received the recommended vaccines is only 39 per cent in rural India as compared to 58 per cent in urban India. In India, children's vulnerabilities and exposure to violations of their protection rights remain spread and multiple in nature.

The manifestations of these violations are various, ranging from child labour, child trafficking, to commercial sexual exploitation and many other forms of violence and abuse. With an estimated 12.6 million children engaged in hazardous occupations, for instance, India has the largest number of child labourers under the age of 14 in the world. Child labour in the agriculture sector accounts for 80 per cent of child labour in India and 70 per cent of working children globally.

In, Sivakasi, an estimated 1, 25,000 children make the child labour force, comprising 30 per cent of the entire labour force. Those children working in the brick kilns, stone quarries, mines, carpet and zari industry suffer from occupation related diseases. In India, however there is a huge gap in the industry-specific and exposure-specific epidemiological evidence. Most of the studies are small-scale and community-based studies. There is a large proportion of children in India who are living with HIV/AIDS.

The most common sources of infection among children is the Mother-to-Child Transmission, sexual abuse, blood transfusion, unsterilised syringes, including injectable drug use. Among children, there are some groups like street children and children of sex workers who face additional forms of discrimination. A large number of children are reportedly trafficked to the neighbouring countries. Trafficking of children also continues to be a serious problem in India.

The nature and scope of trafficking range from industrial and domestic labour, to forced early marriages and commercial sexual exploitation. Moreover, for children who have been trafficked and rescued, opportunities for rehabilitation remains scarce and reintegration process arduous. While systematic data and information on child protection issues are still not always available, evidence suggests that children in need of special protection belong to communities suffering disadvantage and social exclusion such as scheduled casts and tribes, and the poor.

In India, the population of the elderly is growing rapidly and is emerging as a serious area of concern for the government and the policy planners. The age of India's population, in Census 2001, there are a little over 76.6 million people above 60 years, constituting 7.2 per cent of the population. The number of people over 60 years in 1991 was 6.8 per cent of the country's population.

The vulnerability among the elderly is not only due to an increased incidence of illness and disability, but also due to their economic dependency upon their spouses, children and other younger family members. The 2001 census, 33.1 per cent of the elderly in India live without their spouses. The widowers among older men form 14.9 per cent as against 50.1 per cent widows among elderly women.

Among the elderly, 71.1 per cent of women were widows while widowers formed only 28.9 per cent of men. Vulnerability among the elderly also depends on their living arrangement since the elderly are less capable of taking care of themselves compared to younger persons and need the care and support of others in several aspects. About 2.9 per cent of elderly in India live alone. More elderly women live alone compared to elderly men. The significance of the living arrangement among the elderly becomes evident when seen in the context of their level of economic dependence. Lack of economic dependence has an impact on their access to food, clothing and healthcare. Among the basic needs of the elderly, medicine features as the highest unmet need. Healthcare of the elderly is a major concern for the society as ageing is often accompanied by multiple illnesses and physical ailments. Pain in the joints, followed by cough and blood pressure, piles, heart diseases, urinary problems, diabetics and cancer are the common ailments reported among elderly.. One out of two elderly in India suffers from at least one chronic disease which requires life-long medications.

Providing healthcare to elderly is a burden for especially poor households. About 29 per cent of the elderly populations in India are reported to have received no medical attention before death. Among the elderly, the widows, poor and disabled constitute those who are more disadvantaged. Widows face structural disadvantages associated with gender and marital status. There is striking gender differential that exists in the ownership of property and assets and in the participation of their management.

At all India level, aged women like those in other age groups suffer from lack of ownership of property and financial assets and participation in their management compared to aged men in both urban and rural India. Lack of property ownership affects their access to resources like food, housing, health etc. Visual impairment, hearing problem, locomotor problem and problems in speech are common forms of disability among elderly. Senility and neurosis are common mental illness reported among elderly.

VULNERABILITY DUE TO DISABILITY

Disability poses greater challenges in obtaining the needed range of services. Persons with disabilities face several forms of discrimination and has reduced access to education, employment and other socioeconomic opportunities. In India, there is an increase of proportion of disabled population. The proportion of disabled population in India is about 21.9 million. The percentage of disabled population to the total population is about 2.13 per cent. There are two broad categories of disability, one is acquired which means disability acquired because of accidents and medical reasons the other is disability since the onset of birth. The National Sample Survey Organisation Report, about one-third of the disabled population have disability since their birth. There are interstate and interregional differences in the disabled population.

The disabled face various types of barriers while seeking access to health and health services. There are different types of disability and the needs of the disabled differ accordingly. Among those who are disabled women, children and aged are more vulnerable and need attention. Mental illness is a prominent form of disability. Five out of ten leading causes of disability and premature death worldwide are due to psychiatric conditions.

Depression and anxiety are the most common mental disorders. Psychotic disorders such as schizophrenia and bipolar disorder, although less common are profoundly disabling. The other area of concern is the mental health of women and the elderly. Neurotic and stress related cases are reportedly higher among women than men though among men there is reporting of higher number of cases of serious illness.

Dementia and major depression are two of the leading contributors to mental diseases in older people. But inspite of such proportion of mental illness, the health care provisions for persons with mental illness are very poor in India. People with mental illness face severe forms of human rights violations. In Special Homes, Hospitals and Asylums, they are kept in chains, denied basic needs like food, clothing and face different forms of abuse.

There is social stigma attached to mental illness. Women with mental illness are subjected to physical and sexual abuse both within families and the institutions. There are 42 mental hospitals in the country with bed availability of 20,893 in the government sector and another 5096 in the private sector hospital settings to take care of an estimated 1,02,70,165 people with severe mental illness and 5,12,51,625 people with common mental disorders. Psychiatric medicines are supplied only in a few primary health centres, community centres and district hospitals. Services like child guidance and rehabilitative services are also available only in mental hospitals and in big cities. Several states do not have mental hospitals. The Persons with Disabilities Act 1995, commonly referred as the PWD Act came into force on Feb. 7, 1996. Mental illness has been considered in the Act, but there is no reference to any provision within the Act to be given or set aside for people with mental illness. The Act also does not assure the right to treatment.

VULNERABILITY DUE TO MIGRATION

Migrants and their denial of rights have to be understood from the existing contradictions within and across countries-from skilled and voluntary migrants at one end of the spectrum to the poor and unskilled migrant population on the other end destined to be excluded from the fabric of the host nation/areas. For the latter, the intersection of human rights and migration is a negative one, with bad experiences throughout the migratory 'life cycle', in areas of origin, journey or transit and destination.

The intersection of health and human rights becomes even more complex when irregular or illegal migration clashes with the interest of the area of destination. Cases of exploitation of migrants by employers, smugglers or traffickers in such cases never meet justice. All these directly impact the rights of individual migrants.

India has a large number of international migrants. About 5.1 million persons are migrants by last residence from across the international border in India. Neighbouring countries are the main sources of origin of the international migrants to India with the bulk of these migrants coming from Bangladesh, followed by Pakistan and Nepal.

But these are migrants who have entered the country legally. There are many who enter the country illegally. Those are the one who are most vulnerable to abuse and exploitation by employers, migration agents, corrupt bureaucrats and criminal gangs. In many situations, migrants do not know what rights they are entitled to and still less how to claim them, hence the cases of abuse go unrecorded. Another area where exploitation is rampant is forced labour which takes place in the illicit underground economy and hence tends to escape national statistics. Illegal migrants often live on the margins of society, trying to avoid contact with authorities and have little or no legal access to prevention and healthcare services. They face higher risks of exposure to unsafe working conditions.

Many often they do not approach the health system of the host countries for fear of their status being discovered. Internal migration of poor labourers has also been on the rise in India. The poor migrants usually end up as casual labourers within the informal sector. This population is at high risk for diseases and faces reduced access to health services.

In India, 14.4 million people migrated within the country for work purposes either to cities or areas with higher expected economic gains during the 2001 census period. Large number of migrants are employed in cultivation and plantations, brick-kilns, quarries, construction sites and fish processing. Large numbers of migrants also work in the urban informal manufacturing construction, services or transport sectors and are employed as casual labourers, head loaders, rickshaw pullers and hawkers.

The rapid change of residence due to the casual nature of work excludes them from the preventive care and their working conditions in the informal work arrangements in the city debars them from access to adequate curative care. Among the migrants who are vulnerable, the Internally Displaced People deserve mention.

In India, the Internally Displaced People are estimated to be around 6 lakhs. Internal displacement arises out of ethnic conflicts, religious conflicts, political reasons, development projects, natural disaster etc. The Internally Displaced People are vulnerable to health risks and access to treatment. The emotional stress of displacement and the toll that this takes does have a great impact on physical as well as mental health. Large number of mental health problems are reported among Internally Displaced People. Stress disorder leads to cardiovascular stress, psycho-trauma, endocrine stress, musculo-skeletal stress, stress-belly and cranial stress. Hypertension, reactive depression and nervous breakdown are common even among the youth who are Internally Displaced People. There are reports of lack of basic facilities like food, medical supplies and sanitation in the State government organized relief camps for the internally displaced people in case of a political conflict. Women and child migrants are the most vulnerable.

In the case of internal migration in India, women and children mostly migrate as associated migrants with the main decision to migrate being taken by the male of the household. As associated migrants, they suffer greater vulnerability due to reduced economic choices and lack of social support in the new area of destination. In the case of semi-skilled, low-skilled or unskilled women migrants, this can translate into their entry into the low paying, unorganized sector with high exposure to exploitation and abuse.

International migration of women for employment has also increased. In India, there are a large number of international women migrants. Female migration to India constitutes 48 per cent of the total inmigration from other countries. Migration among women has been high from Bangladesh and Nepal as compared to other neighbouring countries. Low/skilled or semi-skilled migration has an impact on their choice of occupation and the conditions of work.

Many of the low/semi-skilled female migrants work in the unorganized sector, in hazardous conditions, live in shanty arrangements and are denied access to health and healthcare. Trafficking also contributes to the cross-border movement of a large proportion of women and children into other countries. There are established routes of trafficking in India, used to facilitate the movement of women and children from across the borders in order to sustain the underground economy. Women and children in an irregular situation are doubly vulnerable owing to their lack of proper legal status and high risk of sexual exploitation and suffer from poor antenatal care coverage, prevalence of anemia, prevalence of reproductive tract infections experience high incidences of violence.

Children of poor migrant parents suffer from malnutrition and low immunization due to their parents' perpetual low-income uncertain jobs that necessitate frequent shifts based on concentration and are more susceptible to HIV/AIDS infection.

VULNERABILITY DUE TO STIGMA AND DISCRIMINATION

There are certain attitudes and perceptions towards certain kinds of illnesses and sexual orientation which results in discrimination against individuals/groups. This part deals with the stigma and discrimination faced by the People living with HIV/AIDS and Sexual Minorities. These groups face various kinds of discrimination and have reduced access to healthcare. Stigma is the greatest barrier of health and healthcare in their context.

Negative responses and attitude of the society towards these groups are strongly linked to people's perception of the causes of HIV/AIDS and sexual orientation. The rights of People living with HIV/AIDS are violated when they are denied access to health, education, and services. They suffer when their close or extended families and friends fail to provide them the support that they need.

India's National AIDS Control Organization estimated in 2005 that there were 5.206 million HIV infections in India, of which 38.4 per cent occurred in women and 57 per cent occurred in rural areas. Many experts argue that the current figures are gross underestimations and that a significant number of AIDS cases go unreported or untracked. Prevalence estimates are based primarily on sentinel surveillance conducted at public sites.

The national information system for collecting HIV testing information from the private sector is very weak. Vulnerability to HIV is also increased by the lack of power of individuals and communities to minimize or modulate their risk of exposure to HIV infection and once infected, to receive adequate care and support. Some individuals are more vulnerable to the infection than others. Low status of woman may force a monogamous woman to engage in unprotected sex with her spouse even if he is engaging in sex with others. Similarly adolescent girls and boys may be vulnerable to HIV by being denied access to preventive information, education, and services. Sex workers may have greater vulnerability to HIV if they cannot access services to prevent, diagnose, and treat sexually transmitted infections, particularly if they are afraid to come forward because of the stigma associated with their occupation.

There are strong perceptions of the causes of AIDS, routes of transmission, and their level of knowledge about the illness. These are compounded by the marginalization and stigmatization on the basis of such attributes as gender, migrant status or behaviours that may be perceived as risk factors for HIV infection. For example, women whose husbands have died of AIDS are rejected by their own and their husband's families and they are denied property inheritance of their husbands.

The available provisions of care are inadequate. Since April 1, 2004, anti-retroviral treatment is provided free of cost in India, at government hospitals in the six high prevalence states of Tamil Nadu, Andhra Pradesh, Maharashtra, Karnakata, Manipur, and Nagaland. However, of the estimated 5.1 million people living with HIV/AIDS in 2005, 600,000 people needed antiretroviral therapy, but only 7,000 adults were receiving such treatment through the government programme.

Besides anti-retroviral drugs there is shortage of several other drugs in the public facilities which are needed by persons living with HIV/AIDS. People living with HIV/AIDS face discrimination even from the health providers who deny them quality of care. Negative attitudes from health professionals generate anxiety and fear among people living with HIV/AIDS, and as a result many do not reveal or seek treatment for their HIV status.

Another group that faces stigma and discrimination are the sexual minorities. Those identified as gay, lesbian, transgender, bisexual, kothi and hijra, experience various forms of discrimination within the society and the health system. Due to the dominance of heteronomous sexual relations as the only form of normal acceptable relations within the society, individuals who are identified as having same-sex sexual preferences are ridiculed and ostracized by their own family and are left with very limited support structures and networks of community that provide them conditions of care and support.

Their needs and concerns are excluded from the various health policies and programmes. Only the National AIDS Prevention and Control Policy recognize sexual minority and homosex in the context of identifying 'high risk behaviour'. But pervasive discrimination from the health providers delays or deters their health seeking.

Hence they remain excluded from the process of government surveillance carried among the high risk population in the context of HIV/AIDS. The surveillance amongst 'MSM' or men who have sex with men, is usually carried out by NGOs and through 'support groups', *i.e.* amongst males who are accessible to NGOs and who are willing to identify with categories, such as kothi, around which support groups are structured. They also undergo considerable amount of psychological stress.

CONSTITUTES VIOLATION OF RIGHT FOR VULNERABLE GROUPS

The violation of the right to health of vulnerable groups may result from direct government action, from failure of the government to fulfill its minimum core obligations and from the patterns of systematic discrimination.

The specific examples of violations of right to health of vulnerable groups would be:

- Deliberate withholding or misrepresentation of information on the health status of disadvantaged groups that may have been essential for the prevention and treatment of illness or disability.
- Imposing discriminatory practices affecting the group's health status and needs.
- Adopting laws and policies that interfere with the

rights of the groups, for example, women's reproductive rights.

- Failure to protect women against violence; violence against women is often systematic and serious enough to require women to seek hospital treatment for injuries and involve other health complication related to violence. When governments fail to take preemptive steps to prevent and treat victims of violence it is tantamount to violation of right.
- Failure of government to provide adequate public health measures against infectious diseases that affect the disadvantaged groups.
- Failure to cover the eligible population with child immunization packages.
- Failure to provide adequate obstetric and family planning services
- Failure to provide adequate primary healthcare, basic healthcare service to disadvantaged group.
- Inappropriate health resource allocation including disproportionate investment of public resources in ways that benefit the health of only a narrow part of the population, *i.e.*, when government spends in expensive diagnostic and curative health services and equipment that limited number of privileged people can afford and on the other hand primary and preventive health services which large part of people use, suffer due to lack of adequate funds. Such a pattern of financing is a form of indirect discrimination affecting the health and healthcare of vulnerable groups.
- Government policies and practices creating imbalances in providing health services, *i.e.*, poor infrastructure in rural areas or predominantly tribal areas.
- Systematic discrimination in access to medicines and essential drugs for particular groups, *i.e.*, HIV/AIDS drugs, reproductive health services for particular groups like women living in poverty, in rural areas, belonging to marginalized communities.

ADVOCACY ON HEALTH AND HUMAN RIGHTS OF VULNERABLE GROUPS IN INDIA

- Identify disadvantaged/marginalized groups; their health status and needs in different situations
- Review the health information and services that are available to protect the health of the poor, vulnerable, or otherwise disadvantaged groups, including their quality, accessibility, affordability and acceptability.
- Collect disaggregated information on the health disparities among the marginalized groups. Identify the unmet need, particularly those resulting from adverse discrimination
- Assess the relevance of public health messages and determine whether they are accessible and meaningful.
- Assess whether the vulnerable group's dignity is preserved by the health services made available to them; whether they have the necessary health information and services that they require; whether they are allowed freedom for the choice of treatment; whether their full, free and informed consent was obtained during specific interventions; and whether confidentiality has been a part of the treatment where it was necessary.
- Identify barriers to the implementation of relevant laws, obligations and commitments; this could mean lack of political will; weak infrastructure or mechanisms for effective administration of policies and programmes; harmful traditional practices; cultural norms or policies imposed by and as a result of adverse reforms of the health sector to funding health services
- Promote capacity-building among health professionals to ensure conformity with the right to health in service delivery.
- Examine the curricula of medical and other health professional training schools and advocate for the inclusion of health and human rights of vulnerable groups in Medical Education.

- Increase public awareness on the right to health of the vulnerable groups and engage in community education and mobilization.
- Assess government compliance with specific obligations; whether government is meeting minimum essential level of health rights; whether there is systematic discrimination associated with the treatment of poor, vulnerable and otherwise disadvantaged groups.
- Undertake advocacy to facilitate change by identifying violations to right to health; familiarize yourself with the nature of the state obligations arising from the right to health and the common ways in which government violates them; document any identified violations and use it as a basis for monitoring and advocacy.
- Work on national enforcement procedures to ensure state accountability.
- Prepare parallel reports.

ADVOCACY FOR RIGHT TO HEALTH INTERNATIONALLY

Advocacy for right to health of vulnerable groups involves identifying the barriers to health and healthcare of the vulnerable and disadvantaged groups and lobbying for their rights with the government nationally and internationally. The rights of the vulnerable groups are recognized in numerous international instruments.

The International Covenant on Economic, Social and Cultural Rights which provides the most comprehensive object on the right to health in the international human rights law recognizes the health needs of the vulnerable groups and explains by illustrations a number of steps to be taken by the State parties to achieve the full realization of the right to health of general population and vulnerable groups in particular. The signatories of the Treaty of International Covenant on Economic, Social and Cultural Rights representing nearly 155 governments of the world made an international commitment to protect and respect, Right to Health of the population of the respective nations as Parties while another 66 governments are Signatory Parties of the Covenant. The Treaty came into force on the 3rd January 1976. By ratifying international human rights treaties that affirm the right to health, a state agrees to be accountable to the international community, as well as to the people living within its jurisdiction, for the fulfillment of its obligations.

State parties to an international human rights treaty are required to adopt legislative measures and to employ all appropriate means to ensure that the population can enjoy the rights conferred by the treaty. This means that international treaty provisions must be incorporated into the domestic legislation. Individuals and communities can access effective judicial or other appropriate remedies in the face of violations of their rights.

A central advocacy principle for NGOs using a human rights approach to health hence should be that governments are accountable for their obligations under international law, regional law, and within the framework of national constitutions and legislation. Monitoring and state compliance with universal norms of human rights related to health is an essential component of the Treaty of Economic Social and Cultural Rights.

There are three forms of monitoring rights: investigative reports prepared by the special rapporteurs or working groups; individual complaint procedures by which nationals and other residents of a state can complain to international bodies for alleged violations of their human rights; and reports prepared by states which have ratified international human rights conventions and which therefore are parties to the convention.

Such reports are submitted periodically to the international expert bodies set in conformity with the convention. The periodic reports are examined in the presence of representatives from the state concerned. Reporting obligations are built into the convention as a mechanism for monitoring the human right. NGOs involved in monitoring the right to health must ensure that the governments send periodic reports to the Committee on Economic Social and Cultural Rights. They can also send parallel reports to the committee.

SCOPE AND LIMITATIONS OF THE INDIAN STATE VIS-A VIS RIGHT TO HEALTH

The Constitution of India and the laws do not accord health and healthcare as rights to the population in general. While civil and political rights are enshrined as fundamental rights that are justiciable, social and economic rights like health, education, livelihoods etc. exist as Directive Principles for the State and are hence not justiciable.

There are however instances in which cases have been filed in the various High Courts of states and Supreme Court of India on the right to life, Article 21 of the Indian Constitution, or on the various directive principles to demand access to healthcare, especially in emergency situations. International protection of human rights is only effective when they are made viable by national protection.

National-level legislation, policies and enforcement mechanisms are the key factors in rights being operationalized for individuals and groups within a nation. National laws offer variable degrees of protection against human rights violation and enables national bodies to hear cases of denial and enforce the norms.

At present there is a problem of justiciability of the Right to health in Indian Constitution since the same is not protected by national legislation. Though India has ratified the Treaty on the Economic Social and Cultural Right which covers Right to Health, that cannot be effectively used to advocate for right to health in India.

The Courts or petitioners can merely derive inspiration from the treaties on the cases on denial/violation on right to health but may not be able to use it effectively to deliver justice. The international treaties have only an evocative significance unless protected by national legislation. Absence of national legislation on right to health in India is the main reason why it cannot be realized. Health and human rights advocacy in India needs to intensify the attempts towards transforming the critical principles of the Directive principles on health and work into independent rights through rigorous judicial activism, *i.e.*, filing Public Interest Litigations, gathering testimonials for denial on right to health, etc. There needs to be a concerted move towards making a national legislation on right to health.

4

Social Group Disparities

INTRODUCTION

'Economic growth with social justice' or 'growth with equity' has been the basic objective of public policy in India since Independence and refers to a broad based strategy of development, with an emphasis on reduction of poverty. But, whether and the extent to which the poor have actually benefited from the growth process has always been an issue of heated academic debate.

In recent years, this debate has focused on the effect of economic liberalization policies on poverty in India. Such debates have not been confined to India, but have been the subject of much empirical enquiry in a global context leading to a vast body of literature on poverty, inequality and growth and their interrelations.

However, the focus of much of this literature has been on vertical inequalities *i.e.* inequalities across income or expenditure classes. In a plural society like India, with people of different castes and religions, it is equally important to focus on 'horizontal inequalities' *i.e.* disparities between certain identifiable groups in the economy. In India, there are historically marginalized 'social groups' such as the scheduled castes and scheduled tribes, who comprise a quarter of India's total population.

There are separate provisions for their welfare in the 'Constitution of India', which form the basis of targeted development policies by the State to raise the socioeconomic status of these groups in absolute terms as well as relative to the rest of society. This document seeks to provide a profile of social group disparities and poverty in India by outlining the trends in growth, poverty and inequality for these sub-groups in the economy. It then seeks to examine the factors underlying differences in levels of living between these groups and for each group separately.

HISTORICAL OVERVIEW

Scheduled castes are a constitutionally declared collection of castes, which suffered from the practice of untouchability. Scheduled tribes are identified on the basis of certain criteria such as primitive traits, distinct culture, geographical isolation and general backwardness.

However, the terms 'scheduled caste' and 'scheduled tribe' are nowhere defined in the Constitution of India. They comprise within them more than four hundred castes and tribes respectively, with large cultural heterogeneity. The former 'untouchables' were considered to be at the bottom of the Hindu social hierarchy and were not a part of the four-fold 'Varna system' comprising Brahmin, Kshatriya, Vaishya and Shudra.

They have been variously referred to as 'Avarna' and 'Ati-Shudra'. The tribal people also referred to as 'Adivasis' meaning original inhabitants of the land were not considered part of the Hindu social hierarchy.

It is important to note that scheduled castes have historically suffered from social stigma due to untouchability and thus been socially excluded, though physically they have always been a part of mainstream society. Scheduled tribes on the other hand have historically been physically or geographically excluded, but did not face any social stigma and are not socially excluded.

So, while scheduled castes even today can be found in almost all villages and urban centres in India, except perhaps the exclusive tribal regions, scheduled tribes are generally concentrated in a few geographical regions, which are relatively physically inaccessible, such as hilly regions and forests. These historically rooted different forms of exclusion have very important implications for the present-day nature and causes of poverty among these groups.

DATA SOURCE

The consumer expenditure surveys from the National Sample Survey represent the main source of data for the issues addressed in this study. The National Sample Survey Organization was started by the Government of India in 1950 to collect socio-economic data employing scientific sampling methods. Different subjects are taken up for survey in different rounds of the NSS and the surveys cover the whole of the Indian Union. The household consumer expenditure survey collects data separately for the rural and urban sectors by way of two-stage stratified random sampling.

We use data on monthly per capita expenditure, which is available for social groups from the 38th round onwards. The state-wise results in all parts of this document refer to fourteen major states of India *viz.* Andhra Pradesh, Assam, Bihar, Gujarat, Karnataka, Kerala, Maharashtra, Madhya Pradesh, Orissa, Punjab, Rajasthan, Tamil Nadu, Uttar Pradesh and West Bengal. In the first part of the document, we use data mainly from three quinquennial rounds *viz.* the 38th round, 50th round and 55th round, which are large sample rounds. The 55th round categorizes social groups as ST, SC, OBC and Others.

The earlier rounds did not specify a separate OBC category and therefore to maintain comparability, OBC has been combined with Others, for the purpose of our computations. Data on monthly per capita expenditure for the 55th round is available using two reference periods *viz.* the seven-day and thirty day reference period. The analysis in this document uses data from the thirty-day reference period.

SOCIAL GROUP DISPARITIES AND POVERTY: A PROFILE

The preamble of the Indian constitution resolves to secure to all its citizens, "Justice, social, economic and political". The Constitution directs the State to promote with special care the educational and economic interests of the scheduled castes and scheduled tribes, and protect them from social injustice and all forms of exploitation. In the spirit of the Constitution of India, there have been a multitude of affirmative action policies for the scheduled castes and scheduled tribes, which include a separate special component plan and tribal sub-plan respectively.

In economic parlance, these may be referred to as 'between-group redistributive policies', which in the context of historically marginalized sub-groups in the economy have close connections with the notion of 'equity' and 'social justice'. The trends in social group disparities and poverty in India should be evaluated keeping in view these special policies. So, along with absolute poverty, a discussion of relative deprivation also assumes significance. While recognizing the multi-dimensionality of poverty, we confine ourselves to growth, inequality and poverty defined in the consumption sphere and seek to examine the following issues:

- What are the trends in absolute poverty and composition of the poor by social group?
- What are the trends in between-group disparities and within-group inequalities and changes in the social group hierarchy in India?
- What is the nature and direction of the change in poverty for each social group, with regard to the relative role of growth and changes in distribution?
- What is the 'growth elasticity of poverty' for social groups in India?

INCIDENCE OF POVERTY AND COMPOSITION OF THE POOR

The head-count ratio of poverty measures the proportion of the population living below the poverty line. India and state-wise estimates of the head-count ratio by social group and indicates that in 1999-00, 45.83% of the ST in rural India were living below the poverty line as compared to 35.89% of the SC and 21.47% of the Others. Scheduled castes have the highest incidence of poverty in urban India. To analyse the trends in absolute poverty of different social groups, we compute the rate of change in the head count ratio for each period under consideration. The results for all-India indicate that for the overall time period under consideration and the period of the 1990s poverty has declined faster among the Others as compared to the SC and ST. From 1993-94 to 99-00, the ST showed the lowest rate of decline in the extent of poverty in both rural and urban India.

This is seen to be a common feature across rural areas of almost all states in India. The composition of the poor is slowly changing in rural India. In 1983, the SC and ST together comprised about 37% of the poor in rural all-India. In 1999-00, this share has gone up to 45%, which is much higher than their 31% share in the rural population even after accounting for changes in the composition of rural population. This may imply a trend towards a concentration of rural poverty among the SC and ST.

BETWEEN-GROUP DISPARITIES AND WITHIN-GROUP INEQUALITIES

The average monthly per capita expenditure of a social group can be taken as a proxy for the average level of living of that group. We compute compound annual growth rates in average MPCE at constant 1960-61 prices for each time period under consideration, separately for the rural and urban sectors for each social group. The period as a whole *i.e.* from 1983 to 1999-00, the growth rate in average MPCE of the SC and ST was marginally higher than the Others in rural areas, while in urban areas, the SC consistently have the lowest growth rate.

The ST in rural India had the lowest growth rate in average MPCE in the period of the nineties. These growth rates also suggest that rural-urban disparities are widening for all social groups *i.e.* the growth rate in average MPCE for the urban sector is greater than that of the rural sector for each social group, and in the aggregate between each time period under consideration. These growth rates get reflected in the social disparity ratios computed separately for rural and urban areas. So, from 1983 to 1999-00, social disparities between SC and Others in rural areas have declined, but in urban areas have increased. Social disparities between ST and Others have however widened at an all-India level between 1993-94 and 1999-00. The disparities between SC and Others in urban areas are wider as compared to rural areas, and the reverse is true for ST.

The state specific variations in social disparities also need to be noted. For example, in 1999-00 the average MPCE of the rural SC in Punjab was 68.66% that of Others, but for Assam and West Bengal, it was more than 90% that of Others. Similarly, the ST in rural Orissa had an average MPCE, which was 66.45% that of Others, but the average MPCE of ST in Assam was actually higher than that of Others. Similar variations can be observed for urban areas.

A comparison of the average consumption level of different groups provides some measure of the magnitude and direction of between-group disparities. However, disparities between groups and their change over time can also be examined by changes in the social group hierarchy, indicated by the population composition of consumption quintiles by social group.

This is obtained by first dividing the population into quintiles on the basis of their MPCE, and then computing the population composition of each quintile by social group. It can be observed that the proportion of ST and SC decreases as we move to higher quintiles, while the proportion of Others increases. In 1999-00, 83.63% and 92.53% of the top quintile comprise of the Others in rural and urban areas respectively. The population composition of quintiles by social group indicates that the Others comprise more than 50% of the population in all quintiles, which would be a reflection of their higher overall population.

An alternative profile of the social group hierarchy in India is provided by examining the percentage distribution of social group by quintiles *i.e.* distribution of the population of each social group across quintiles. For the year 1999-00, this shows that 37% of ST and 27% of SC are in the bottom quintile of the rural sector as against 15% of Others. On the whole, more than 50% of ST and SC are in the bottom two quintiles. The proportion of ST in the bottom quintile shows an increase from 34% in 1983 to 37% in 1999-00, while that of SC and Others shows a marginal decline. In urban India, the proportion of both SC and ST has increased in the bottom quintile. Within group inequalities have been measured using the Gini coefficient, which is the most commonly used measure of inequality in the empirical literature. A priori, the Others may be expected to be a much more heterogeneous group in terms of average consumption levels, as they include the 'Other Backward Classes' as well as high caste groups in Indian society.

It can be observed that though inequality within the Others is higher than within the SC and ST, the magnitude of difference is not as large as may be expected. Within-group inequalities in the rural sector have decreased for all social groups, but in the urban sector have increased for the ST and Others. The within-group disparity ratios indicate the ratio of average MPCE of the top quintile to the bottom quintile.

The average MPCE of SC and ST in the top quintile of the rural sector is 3.36 and 3.86 times respectively that in the bottom quintile. This ratio is higher in the urban sector and clearly indicates that the SC and ST are not a homogenous group in terms of levels of living. Total inequality can be decomposed into a within-group and between-group component.

The Gini coefficient is not additively decomposable into a within-group and betweengroup component and this has been done using the Theil 's entropy measure. The between-group component can be defined as the value of the inequality index for the hypothetical consumption distribution, which assigns to each person within a group, the mean consumption of the group.

The within-group component can be defined as the value of the inequality index, when the mean consumption levels for each group are equalized to the overall mean, through an equiproportional change in the consumption of every person within a group. The results indicate that between-group disparities comprise less than 5% of total inequality in both rural and urban areas. The between-group component in rural areas is larger than in urban areas and has increased in both these sectors from 1983 to 1999-00.

Thus, it would appear that it is within group inequalities that are quantitatively more important than between-group disparities within the rural and urban sectors. Kanbur points out that, the empirical literature on such decompositions for race, gender, spatial units etc in an international context indicates that the betweengroup component has not exceeded 15%, but the policy interpretation needs to be done with caution, since the social weight on these differences might be far greater than their contribution to overall interpersonal inequality.

In the context of social group disparities and poverty in India, we may say that it is the existence of differences in average socioeconomic status on the basis of caste, across time and across regions, that makes it normatively unacceptable and a cause of policy concern. Whether the unit of action for public policy should be a group or parts within a group could be a matter of debate in which a distinction needs to be made between the social and economic impacts of any such policy.

DECOMPOSITION OF CHANGE IN POVERTY

The proportion of people living below the poverty line as measured by the head count ratio is a function of the mean consumption level as given by the monthly per capita expenditure and the inequality in the distribution of monthly per capita expenditure. Therefore, poverty can be reduced with an increase in mean consumption, with inequality remaining constant; a reduction in inequality with mean consumption remaining constant or an increase in mean consumption simultaneously accompanied by a reduction in inequality of its distribution.

While the first strategy focuses on growth alone and the second on reduction of inequality or redistribution, the third strategy brings about a faster reduction in poverty and is referred to as 'redistribution with growth' or 'growth with equity'. A change in poverty between two periods can be decomposed into a growth component and a redistribution component. We do this decomposition for the SC and ST in each state and all-India for the rural sector between the time periods under consideration. The results of this decomposition would enable a better understanding of the nature and direction of poverty change for these groups. Alternative methodologies exist for doing this decomposition. We use the Datt and Ravallion methodology, which decomposes a change in poverty over time periods t and t+n as follows:

$$P_{t+n} - P_t = G(t, t+n) + D(t, t+n) + R(t, t+n)$$

Here, the three terms on the right-hand side of the equation refer to the growth component, redistribution component and residual component respectively.

The growth component of a change in the poverty measure is defined as the change in poverty due to a change in the mean consumption, with inequality in the distribution of consumption remaining constant. The redistribution component is the change in poverty due to a change in inequality while keeping the mean consumption constant. The residual will vanish only if the mean consumption level or the inequality in the distribution of consumption remains unchanged over the decomposition period. The results of the decomposition for all-India. The rural sector, both growth and redistribution have contributed to a decrease in poverty, but the growth component dominates the redistribution component.

If we include the state-wise decompositions, in general, the following five cases can be distinguished:

(1) Both growth and redistribution components have contributed to a reduction in poverty, but growth component dominates redistribution component.
(2) Both growth and redistribution components have contributed to a reduction in poverty, but redistribution component dominates growth component.
(3) Growth component has contributed to an increase in poverty, but redistribution component has contributed to a decrease.

(4) Redistribution component has contributed to an increase in poverty, but growth component has contributed to a decrease.

(5) Both growth and redistribution components have contributed to an increase in poverty.

In case of (3) and (4), the net effect on poverty will depend on the relative magnitude of the growth and redistribution effects. Classifying the state-wise and all-India decompositions for SC, ST, we find that in rural areas, about half the poverty changes can be classified as (1), the next largest component being case (4). We find instances of case (3), (4) and (5), where rural poverty increased due to the particular magnitudes of the growth and redistribution effect.

For example, the incidence of rural poverty in Orissa increased among the SC and ST in the period of the 1990s. In the case of the SC this was because of a decline in mean consumption in real terms, while for the ST a decline in mean consumption was also accompanied by an increase in within-group inequality. In Assam, there has been an increase in rural poverty among the SC between 1983 and 1999-00, due to an increase in within-group inequality, which has negated the positive growth effect.

So, in general we may say that though growth has been the prime mover of changes in rural poverty among the SC and ST in India in the 1980s and 1990s, within group distributional changes have influenced the magnitude of poverty change and in some cases also influenced its direction. Between-group redistributive policies will have a limited impact on poverty, if it leads to increases in within group inequalities.

So, policies to reduce poverty among the SC and ST may be made more effective by way of a growth driven strategy with special emphasis on the lower quintiles within these groups. The key challenge for the policy maker will lie not only in identifying the policies and institutional structures that will promote equitable growth, but also managing the informational and political-economy constraints that may arise in its implementation.

GROWTH ELASTICITY OF POVERTY FOR SOCIAL GROUPS

As noted earlier, scheduled castes and scheduled tribes are historically excluded groups, scheduled castes by way of social exclusion and scheduled tribes by way of physical or geographical exclusion. It is important to know whether and how far they have been excluded from the benefits of economic growth in the contemporary Indian economy.

We examine this by analysing the extent to which a given rate of economic growth reduces poverty among different social groups, or by examining the 'growth elasticity of poverty' for social groups in India. We define state level economic growth as changes in the per capita net state domestic product at constant prices, and seek to compute the required estimates of growth elasticity of poverty through panel regressions separately for each social group in the rural and urban sector using state-wise data. The model we posit is as follows:

$$\text{Ln HCR it} = a + b \ln \text{PCNSDP it} + c \ln \text{GINI it} + d\ \text{INF i} + e\ \text{it} \quad i=1 \text{ to } 14;\ t=1 \text{ to } 4$$

Here the dependent variable and the three explanatory variables refer to the log of the head count ratio, log of per capita net state domestic product (at constant prices), log of the Gini index and the state level infrastructure index respectively. Our time period is from 1983 to 1999-00, using data from four time points *viz.* 1983, 1987-88, 1993-94 and 1999-00, the years representing the quinquennial rounds of the NSS consumer expenditure survey.

We use data for fourteen major states in India. State-wise estimates of head count ratio and the Gini index for each social group by rural and urban sector are computed using data from these four survey rounds. Data for per capita net state domestic product at constant prices represents the average of the preceding year and the time point under consideration and is computed from the National Accounts Statistics of India. The state level infrastructure index is for the year 1983 and acts as a control variable for the initial conditions in states. This regression is run separately for each social group in the rural and urban sectors, using their respective head count ratio and Gini index. Since scheduled tribes are not present in all states, we have forty-eight observations for scheduled tribes in the rural sector and forty observations in the urban sector. For the panel regression for scheduled castes, Others and in the aggregate we have fifty-six observations each. The panel regression was run separately for each social group and in the aggregate using both fixed effect and random effect models. The infrastructure variable gets dropped in the fixed effect model. The Hausman test was applied to choose between these two models.

The regression coefficient for the log of per capita net state domestic product can be interpreted to be an estimate of the growth elasticity of poverty, controlling for changes in within-group distribution. These indicate the percentage reduction in poverty for a one per cent rate of economic growth. All these estimates are statistically significant at 1% level of significance. The Others are found to have a higher growth elasticity of poverty in both rural and urban sectors.

The scheduled tribes and scheduled castes have the lowest growth elasticity in the rural and urban sectors respectively. The growth elasticity in the aggregate is marginally higher in the urban sector as compared to the rural sector. These results imply that economic growth in the 1980s and the 1990s has not equally benefited the different social groups and the rural and urban sectors, as per evidence from fourteen major states of India.

DETERMINANTS OF AVERAGE CONSUMPTION LEVELS

The presence of social disparities in levels of living, between the SC, ST and Others. It also indicated that the SC and ST are not a homogenous group in terms of levels of living. This part seeks to examine through a cross-section regression analysis the factors underlying differences in levels of living between the SC and ST as compared to Others and for each group separately. We use household level data from the consumer expenditure survey of the 55th round of NSS, which was conducted from July 1999 to June 2000. The survey was conducted by way of an equal sized sample across four subrounds, each of three months duration. The 55th round consumer expenditure survey collected data from 71,385 households in the rural sector and 48,924 households in the urban sector. We use data from the rural sector where 81% of the scheduled caste population and 93% of the scheduled tribe population is concentrated and focus on fourteen major states of India, which reduces the number of sample households to 59, 601.

We seek to provide a profile of the characteristics of rural households by social group, in the fourteen states under consideration. We observe notable differences in the occupational structure, education and land possessed across social groups. More than half of SC households are agricultural labour households, implying that their major source of income is from agricultural labour. 44% of ST households have agricultural labour as their main source of livelihood, but a sizeable proportion (35%) are also selfemployed in agriculture.

Compared to these two social groups, the Others have the least proportion of rural labour households and a larger proportion of cultivators and those engaged in other occupations, which includes regular and salaried employed. These occupational differences are related to the average size of land possessed by each social group. While the ST and Others possess on an average about a hectare of land each, the average size of land possessed by the SC households is only 0.4 hectares, which may indicate a higher proportion of landless households.

The Others are seen to have a higher level of education than the other two groups, both by way of percentage of literates and the maximum level of education (in years) in a household. There does not seem to be much difference across social groups in demographic factors such as average household size and proportion of females in the household, nor in terms of average proportion of workers in the household. We first seek to examine the determinants of monthly per capita expenditure for the rural sector as a whole, consisting of all social groups, and then separately for each social group. The dependent and explanatory variables used in our analysis are along with a discussion of the a-priori expectations on the signs of the regression coefficients.

DEPENDENT VARIABLE

The values of monthly per capita expenditure across states are not strictly comparable due to state specific variations in prices, and therefore we express monthly per capita expenditure at all-India prices, using the state-wise and all-India rural poverty lines, and take the logarithm of the monthly per capita expenditure as the dependent variable.

EXPLANATORY VARIABLES

- Demographic factors:
  - *Household size*: Household size refers to the total number of members in the household, and an increase in the household size may be expected to have a negative effect on the monthly per capita expenditure of the household.
  - *Ratio of workers to household size*: It is expected that larger the proportion of working members in a household, higher would be the MPCE.
  - *Ratio of female members to household size*: Women in India are known to have a lower labour force participation rate as compared to men and there exists evidence for labour market discrimination against women, by way of lower wages. So, an increase in the proportion of female members in a household may lead to a negative effect on MPCE.
  - *Female-headed household*: Dummy variable, which takes the value 1 if the household is a female-headed household and zero otherwise. Households headed by females, such as widows, may be expected to have a lower MPCE than those headed by men and so the expected sign on the regression coefficient would be negative.

- *Area of land possessed*: In the rural economy, a larger area of land possessed may be expected to have a positive effect on the MPCE of a household. As noted earlier, the average size of land possessed by the scheduled tribes and Others is almost equal, but scheduled tribes have a much larger incidence of rural poverty. It would therefore be of policy relevance to examine the impact across social groups, of a marginal increase in the area of land possessed, on the average MPCE.
- *Occupation*: The NSS classifies households into five occupational types *viz.* 'selfemployed in non-agriculture', 'agricultural labour', 'self-employed in agriculture', 'other labour' and 'other occupations', depending on the major source of income of the household. We take dummy variables for these occupational types, with the base category being agricultural labour, known to be the occupational group with the highest incidence of poverty in rural India. So, the regression coefficients for the occupation dummies may be expected to be positive in sign.
- *Seasonal factors*: In a rural economy dependent on agriculture, which is predominantly rain-fed, seasonal variations in average consumption levels may be expected. We take seasonal dummies based on the four sub-rounds with sub-round one (July-September) as the base category since it corresponds to the monsoon season, which is a period of food shortage in the rural economy and when the government public work programmes are also not in operation. However, it is difficult to have any a-priori expectations on the sign of the regression coefficient in this case, since the cultivators and rural labour households may have different consumption patterns in different seasons. But, it would be of interest to examine whether the harvesting season for Kharif (October-December) and Rabi (April-June)

crops would have any impact, with reference to the base period. It would also be of interest to examine whether the scheduled castes and scheduled tribes, which are the poorer social groups, would have a different seasonal variation in consumption levels as compared to the Others.

- *Education*: The survey classifies the level of education attained by each member of the household into thirteen categories, the lowest being illiterate and the highest being graduate and above. We reduce the number of categories to five *viz.* 'literate, but below primary', 'primary, but below secondary', 'secondary, but below graduate', 'graduate and above', and take the maximum education level in the household to be the explanatory variable, with 'illiterate' to be the base category. A-priori, it can be expected that the average income level and hence the average consumption level of the household would increase with the maximum level of education attained and hence we would expect the regression coefficients to be positive in sign and increasing in magnitude, with respect to the base category. In the separate regressions for each social group, we take the maximum education in years attained by any member of the household as the explanatory variable by converting the respective category into the corresponding number of years.
- *Social group and religion*: Social group dummies for scheduled caste and scheduled tribe households, with Others as base category, are used as explanatory variables (only in the combined regression for the rural sector), whose regression coefficients could be expected to be negative in sign. The survey categorizes sample households into eight religions *viz.* Hinduism, Islam, Christianity, Sikhism, Jainism, Buddhism, Zoroastrianism and other religions. We use religion as an explanatory variable with non-Hindus to be the base category. In this context, it

would be of interest to examine whether the non-Hindu scheduled castes and scheduled tribes have higher consumption levels than those within the Hindu religion.

- *Regional characteristics*: The National Sample Survey classifies the country into 78 agro climatic regions. For the fourteen states used in our analysis, we have 56 NSS regions. We use three regional characteristics as explanatory variables *viz.* regions categorized by the concentration of scheduled caste population, by the concentration of scheduled tribe population and by the level of infrastructure.
  - *Scheduled caste region*: We rank the regions in descending order by the composition of scheduled caste population, and define a dummy variable, which takes the value 1, if a household is from any of the first 15 NSS regions defined by the concentration of scheduled caste population, and zero otherwise.
  - *Scheduled tribe region*: We rank the regions in descending order by the composition of scheduled tribe population, and define a dummy variable, which takes the value 1, if a household is from any of the first 15 NSS regions defined by the concentration of scheduled tribe population, and zero otherwise.
  - *Infrastructure*: The National Institute of Rural Development has ranked the NSS regions on the basis of their rural infrastructure, using Census of India, 1991 data. We classify the 56 NSS regions in our dataset into regions with high-ranked (top 28 regions) and low-ranked (bottom 28 regions) rural infrastructure. The dummy variable takes the value 1, if the household is from any of the high-ranked infrastructure regions and zero otherwise.

The scheduled caste and scheduled tribe concentrated regions are mutually exclusive, and these regional dummies are not used in the group specific regressions. The population of these regions comprises about 25% and more of scheduled castes and scheduled tribes respectively. The base category in this case will be the remaining 26 regions with a relatively lower composition of both scheduled tribe and scheduled caste population. Other factors remaining constant, a higher level of infrastructure may be expected to have a positive effect on the monthly per capita expenditure of a household.

DETERMINANTS OF AVERAGE CONSUMPTION LEVELS IN THE RURAL SECTOR

The regression coefficients of demographic factors such as household size, ratio of workers, ratio of females and gender of the household head are statistically significant at 1% level of significance and have correct signs as per our a-priori expectations. An increase in the area of land possessed has a positive and significant impact on the average MPCE of a rural household.

The coefficients of the occupational dummies are also statistically significant and positive in sign, indicating a higher average consumption level for those households in 'other occupations', self-employed in non-agriculture, selfemployed in agriculture and other labour, in that order, as compared to the base category, which is agricultural labour.

The regression coefficients of the seasonal dummies are however found to be statistically insignificant, which does not support our hypothesis of seasonal variations in consumption expenditure in the rural sector as a whole. As expected, the education dummies are statistically significant and positive in sign, with higher education levels leading to an increase in average consumption expenditure.

The coefficients of the social group dummies are negative and statistically significant, indicating that the average monthly per capita expenditure of the SC and ST is significantly lower than the Others, so also with the Hindus as compared to the non- Hindus. An important variation exists with regard to the regional dummies for the scheduled tribes and scheduled castes. Other factors remaining constant, the average consumption expenditure, which we regard as a proxy for the level of living, will be lower in a scheduled tribe concentrated region as compared to regions with a relatively lower composition of both scheduled caste and scheduled tribe population. However, this does not hold true for a scheduled caste concentrated region.

This implies that a scheduled tribe concentrated region may be associated with economic backwardness of the region as a whole, but scheduled castes could be concentrated in number, even in a relatively affluent region. Controlling for other factors, there is a 23% difference in average consumption expenditure between the high-ranked and lowranked regions in terms of rural infrastructure.

DETERMINANTS OF AVERAGE CONSUMPTION LEVELS BY SOCIAL GROUP

As in the regression for the rural sector as a whole, slope coefficients of demographic variables such as household size and proportion of workers are statistically significant with the expected sign. However, there exists a variation across social groups regarding the statistical significance of gender related factors such as the proportion of females, in explaining within-group variations in consumption expenditure.

For instance, the regression coefficient for the proportion of females in a household is not significant in the case of ST but is significant at 10% and 1% level of significance for the SC and Others respectively. This could be due to a higher female labour participation rate among the ST, which needs to be explored further.

In this context, it may be noted that as per Census of India, 1991 data the sex ratio in India is highest among the ST as compared to the SC and Others, who have similar and much lower sex ratios, indicating a comparatively higher social status for women within the ST. The regression coefficients of the seasonal dummies are statistically significant only for the ST group. Controlling for other factors, the average MPCE of the ST in sub-round 2 (October to December) and sub-round 4 (April-June) is respectively 8.50% and 6.40% higher than in the base period, which is sub-round 1 (July-September). It is difficult to explain these seasonal variations in consumption expenditure for a particular group, based on available secondary data, since the empirical result would reflect the aggregated outcome of complex, multifaceted processes at the micro-level.

However, for present purposes, we may note the existence of seasonal variations in consumption expenditure only for the ST, which is the social group with the highest incidence of poverty in rural India, and with higher average consumption expenditure in the period corresponding to the Kharif and Rabi harvest season, as compared to the monsoon season. The coefficients for the occupational dummies, level of education and area of land possessed are statistically significant at 1% level of significance for all groups and with the correct sign, as per theoretical expectations.

Controlling for other factors, the scheduled tribe households in the high-rank infrastructure regions have an average monthly per capita expenditure, which is 23.5% higher than the corresponding households in the low-rank infrastructure regions. The figures for the SC and Others in this regard are 22.31% and 25.54% respectively.

The regression coefficient for the religion dummy is found to be statistically insignificant for the ST group, but significant at 1% level of significance for the SC, with a negative sign. This would imply that being a Hindu or non-Hindu would not lead to differences in the levels of living within the ST, but the non-Hindu SC have a higher level of living than the SC, who are Hindus.

But the result is not robust if we exclude Punjab, where rural poverty levels for the SC are onethird that of the corresponding all-India figure and where scheduled castes comprise 38% of the state's rural population (NSS estimate). The regression results indicate that controlling for other factors, a one per cent increase in the area of land possessed (in hectares) leads to a 12.9% increase in the average monthly per capita expenditure for the ST, the corresponding figures being 17.6% and 21.5% for the SC and Others respectively.

Similarly, a comparison of the partial regression coefficients for the education variable indicates that a one per cent increase in the maximum level of education attained in a household (in years) leads to a 10% increase in the average monthly per capita expenditure of SC, but 12.4% and 17.4% respectively in the case of ST and Others. To examine whether these differences in the regression coefficients across social groups are statistically significant, we introduce social group dummies for SC and ST and separate slope dummies for land and education in the specification of the social group regression.

The results indicate that the regression coefficients of the slope dummies with respect to land and education are negative in sign and statistically significant at 1% level of significance for both the SC and ST group. This implies that a one per cent increase in the area of land possessed, and in the maximum level of education attained in a household, has differential impacts across social groups, with the percentage increase in average MPCE being greater for the Others as compared to the SC and ST.

The interpretation needs to take into consideration the lower average area of land possessed for the SC, and the lower average levels of education for the SC and ST, as compared to Others. Using the estimates of elasticity of average MPCE with respect to land and education, a one hectare increase in the area of land possessed would increase the average MPCE by ₹50.74 for the ST, ₹197.34 for the SC and ₹130.16 for the Others. Similarly, a one year increase in the maximum level of education of a household would increase the average MPCE by ₹13.02 for the ST, ₹10.20 for the SC and ₹16.82 for the Others. For exposition purposes we may refer to these as 'returns to land' and 'returns to education' respectively. So, returns to land are higher for the SC as compared to the Others and are lowest for the ST, while returns to education are lower for both the SC and ST as compared to the Others.

The processes underlying lower returns to education, are however likely to be different for the SC as compared to the ST. These results can be interpreted better keeping in mind the historically rooted different forms of exclusion, which have been faced by the scheduled castes and scheduled tribes *viz.* scheduled castes being socially excluded, but physically being a part of mainstream society, and scheduled tribes being physically or geographically excluded, but not suffering from any social stigma.

That scheduled castes have lower returns to education as compared to the higher caste groups may imply that processes of social discrimination continue to operate in Indian society. The lower returns to land for the ST as compared to the Others can partly be explained by the fact that the scheduled tribes have traditionally been living in difficult terrains such as forests and hilly regions, where the land may not be conducive to cultivation.

To obtain a better understanding of the factors which may affect returns to land, we examine some particulars of cultivation practices by social group, using household level data from the 54th round of the NSS. The data pertains to the agricultural year July 1997-June 1998. The data indicate a marked difference in the cultivation practices of ST as compared to the Others.

More than half of ST households cultivate only in one agricultural season *i.e.* either only a Kharif crop or only a Rabi crop. In contrast two-third of the households from the higher caste groups cultivate in both seasons. The percentage of ST households using some form of irrigation facilities (34.77%) is only half that of the Others (69.98%).

The difference is notable also in cultivation practices such as the use of mechanization, fertilizers, improved seeds and pesticides or weedicides. It can be observed however that the cultivation practices of SC cultivators are very similar to that of the Others. This can again be explained by the fact that the SC live in mainstream society, in close proximity with the Others, but the ST are geographically isolated.

However, in terms of ownership issues such as the percentage of households owning a well, tubewell, diesel pump or electric pump for irrigation, or the average size of land owned, the proportion of scheduled caste households owning any such asset is lower than the scheduled tribes, though both are lower than the Others. This indicates that access to ownership of an asset may be more difficult for the socially excluded groups as compared to the geographically excluded groups.

REGRESSION DECOMPOSITION OF DIFFERENCES IN GROUP MEANS

Given that there are differences in the occupational pattern, level of education and land holding, and returns to education and land across social groups, it would be of interest to examine the relative importance of different factors in explaining higher levels of living for the Others as compared to the SC and ST.

This can be examined by decomposing differences in the group mean of the dependent variable into a part explained by differences in the endowments or levels of different productivity enhancing characteristics (characteristics effect) and a part explained by differences in returns to these characteristics (coefficients effect). There are variations in the precise decomposition techniques employed in the literature, but the standard technique remains the Blinder-Oaxaca decomposition borrowed from the labour economics literature and showed in De Walle and Gunewardena (2001).

In the context of the present document, the decomposition can be explained by the following equations, which show with respect to one explanatory variable X, but can easily be extended to more than one regressor. The left-hand side expression in the two equations represents the difference between the mean of the dependent variable for the Others group and that of SC and ST respectively.

The first expression on the right-hand side represents the difference between the Others and SC, ST in the average value of the characteristic, weighted by the respective regression coefficient of the Others, for whom we expect no 'discrimination' or higher 'returns'. The second expression represents the difference in the regression coefficient of the characteristic, weighted by the average value of the characteristic of the SC, ST group. The difference between intercepts can be regarded as a residual term. We have included decomposition results only for the more policy relevant variables, which are occupation, land, education and infrastructure. The numbers in the percentage share of the respective characteristics effect and coefficients effect in explaining differences in the group means, and can be interpreted to denote the relative importance of different factors considered, in explaining higher levels of living for the Others as compared to the SC and ST.

The results indicate that in explaining lower levels of living for the ST as compared to the Others, it is the characteristics effect of the different policy relevant factors indicated by employment in the rural non-farm sector, level of education and level of infrastructure, which is found to have a larger magnitude than the corresponding coefficients effect, though the coefficients effect for education is also seen to be an important factor.

The notable exception relates to being self-employed in agriculture and size of land holding. The average area of land possessed by the ST is marginally higher than the Others. The proportion of ST households, whose main source of livelihood is being self-employed in agriculture is also comparable to Others.

Therefore, it is clear that with regard to land, it is lower returns to land and not lower area of landholding, which is contributing to the lower levels of living as compared to the Others. Conversely, in explaining lower levels of living for the SC as compared to the Others, it is the coefficients effect that is of larger magnitude than the corresponding characteristics effect for factors such as self-employment in non-agriculture, education and infrastructure.

This may be interpreted to imply lower returns from being self-employed in non-agriculture and from education as compared to the higher caste groups, and a lower social access to infrastructure, as compared to physical access. The results indicate the characteristics effect for education to be an important factor contributing to lower levels of living, though the associated coefficients effect is seen to be of a much larger magnitude. On the other hand, the lower average area of land possessed by the SC, which may be a reflection of the larger proportion of landless households within this social group, explains between-group differences in levels of living vis-à-vis the higher caste groups much more than the corresponding coefficients effect.

SUMMARY AND CONCLUSION

Social group disparities and poverty in India may be viewed as a purely distributional issue and by way of the specific factors underlying these disparities. However, these two ways of looking at the issue are interlinked. Empirical evidence suggests that in terms of absolute poverty, the rate of decline in the extent of poverty has been faster for the Others as compared to the SC and ST, in the overall time period under consideration.

In particular, rural poverty has been virtually stagnant for the scheduled tribes in the 1990s. These trends are reflected in the composition of the rural poor, with poverty tending to get concentrated among the SC and ST. The magnitude of social disparities in India is state-specific in nature. The social group hierarchy in India has remained virtually unchanged and scheduled castes and scheduled tribes remain concentrated in the bottom quintiles of the economy.

Measures of within-group inequality indicate that the SC and ST are not a homogenous group in terms of levels of living. In quantitative terms, withingroup inequalities in the rural sector are of a larger magnitude than between-group disparities, but this does not reflect the social weight on horizontal inequalities.

Changes in rural poverty for the SC and ST have largely been driven by growth, but within-group distributional changes have also affected the magnitude of change and in some cases its direction. Since between-group redistributive policies will have a limited impact on poverty, if it leads to increases in within-group inequalities, a high-growth strategy focusing on the lower quintiles within the SC, ST may be more effective. However, the growth experience in major states of India in the 1980s and 1990s suggests that the growth elasticity of poverty has been lowest for the scheduled tribes in rural India and scheduled castes in urban India. The causes of differing growth elasticities of poverty can be explored through the factors underlying differences in levels of living between social groups, and for each group separately.

Demographic and occupational factors, level of education and land holding, and infrastructural facilities are found to be significant factors determining the levels of living in rural India. Seasonal variations in consumption expenditure are found to be significant only for the scheduled tribes. In addition to the levels of physical and human capital, social group disparities in levels of living are also the result of differences in returns to education and land.

There are contrasting relative magnitudes with regard to scheduled castes and scheduled tribes, of the 'characteristics effect' and 'coefficients effect' of various policy relevant factors in explaining social group disparities, and indicate the distinct nature and causes of poverty among these groups. This in turn is the result of historically rooted 'social disadvantages', by way of social exclusion and physical exclusion respectively, which continue to operate in contemporary Indian society. Overcoming these 'social disadvantages' will constitute the key challenge in any future policy matrix designed for the development of these groups.

5

Poverty and Inequality

AN INTRODUCTION

One of India's most significant accomplishments over the last five decades has been to change the world's image of its poverty. At independence, India was widely regarded as a "poor country" with almost all of its people living in poverty, albeit overlaid by a very thin but rich upper crust of maharajahs and commercial moguls.

The Nizam of Hyderabad and other anachronistic remnants of the pre-colonial era particularly intrigued many people in other countries, who considered such huge personal accumulations of gold and jewels as "real wealth." These extravagant riches and their accompanying regal lifestyles made even less tolerable the contrasting miserable, constrained conditions of most Indians. It represents progress for India to be known and respected now for its large middle class, which is practically as large as the population of the United States. However, the number of Indians who subsist below the poverty line, nearly 400 million in 1992 is greater than India's total population was at independence.

It is also progress that we understand better that the wealth of nations, to use Adam Smith's term, lies not in precious metals and stones but in the capacities of its people, to produce, to invent, and to organize. It is a matter of debate—and more a matter of values than of arithmetic—whether inequality is greater in a country when the vast majority are poor and a few people are very wealthy, with a small middle class—or when there is a considerably larger middle class which has distanced itself from the poor, with the number of rich persons, few of them opulently wealthy, increased by several multiples. The latter situation has a lower Gini coefficient, but it makes more visible to the poor on a continuous and very obvious basis how different are their lives and their life chances from those of the rest of their society.

THOUGHTS ON INDICATORS OF INEQUALITY AND ITS JUSTIFICATION

It is worthwhile to know what are the Gini coefficients and other such measures of inequality discussed in the following stage by Hitzhusen, so that we can assess differences between countries, and over time, in specific and reasonably comparable terms. Having myself undertaken to compare differences in income inequality among 16 Asian countries some years ago as part of an evaluation of their rural development strategies and accomplishments, We have come to favour the ratio of income that is accruing to the highest and lowest quintiles of the population.

Wealth, the stock of income-producing assets, is probably a better indicator than is income, the flow therefrom, but measurement problems are daunting enough to make such figures even less reliable than are income data. This measure of inequality considers the income of the top 20 per cent as a multiple of that which goes to the bottom 20 per cent. This is a comprehensible and meaningful indicator of equality or, conversely, inequality.

It is concrete, not abstract, and moreover, it highlights the most extreme differentials, reflecting the non-linearity that goes with living very far below or very far above the poverty line. Our analysis as Asian experience, which was supported by USAID in the days when it was more concerned with the substance and strategy of development than now, was undertaken to make some objective comparisons among countries that ranged geographically, politically and economically from China and Japan in East Asia to Turkey and Yugoslavia on the western edge of Asia. The analysis was done in the positivist spirit of the time, emphasizing measurement. While income distribution was not a central focus of our research project, it was something that had to be considered. At that time, there was still a strong argument in the literature justifying inequality as good for promoting economic growth. We found, on the contrary, that those countries with the best records in rural development across a wide range of measures also had definitely more equal distributions of income.

Unfortunately, however, the relationships between different development measures and income distribution were too many and too complex for us to attribute which was cause and which effect. Since our research was not intended to illuminate inequality, we reported our findings and left them for readers to consider. What could be concluded from our data, however, was that having a more equal income distribution was not unfavourable for rural development.

Analyses based on a simplistic understanding of the Harrod-Domar model of economic growth had argued that unequal distribution of income should promote economic growth and greater employment because—it seemed logical-

- Richer people would save more than poor people;
- A greater volume of domestic savings will increase the supply of resources available for investment;
- Accelerated capital formation will raise gross domestic product and resulting incomes, a virtuous cycle feeding back into greater savings.

Thus, income inequality, even that reflecting widespread poverty, was regarded as good for development. It would contribute to more savings, investment, and growth of GNP. Already by the mid-1960s, however, at the height of development thinking which equated development with GNP growth, a few economists were already pointing out that this logical construction was not empirically supported by evidence.

Even though these empirical challenges appeared in leading journals at the time, they were ignored. Why? They went against the prevailing paradigm, which seemed so logical. Moreover, they went against predominant economic interests. If development was regarded as depending almost entirely upon capital as the scarcest, and thus as the most valuable factor of production, this justified the owners of capital receiving the largest share of the benefits from development.

About this time, President Julius Nyerere of Tanzania presented in "The Arusha Declaration" a conceptual, not just empirical, challenge to the prevalent view. If poor countries have little capital and an abundance of labour, he asked, why not use whatever capital is available to make the most abundant resource, labour, more productive—rather than use labour, often wastefully and certainly with poor remuneration, to make the resource they had least of, capital, particularly foreigners' capital, more productive? Why should the poor seek to fight their war against poverty with the weapons of the rich? Nyerere asked pointedly.

This was dismissed as ideology rather a legitimate question. There were some stirrings within the economics discipline during the 1960s that questioned the dominant capital-favouring paradigm. But it took another 20 years before the case for more equitable paths to development gained acceptance, though still not dominance. The proponents of "meeting basic human needs" in the 1970s justified this more on grounds of equity and fairness than as a way to raise productivity.

What finally seems to have gained the most ground for equitable distribution of income and wealth was the success of the East Asian "Tigers"—Japan, South Korea, Taiwan and Singapore. By the 1980s, this success was too apparent to overlook, as was their more equal distribution of income. In these countries, policies ranging from land reform and universal basic education to public housing and primary health care had contributed to political-economic systems that sought to contradict the Biblical admonition: "The poor you shall have always with you."

These countries considered poverty to be unacceptable and a drag on their economies. There was also evidence accumulating such as that from Berry and Cline that more equal distributions of land contributed to aggregate agricultural production as well as economic growth. Certainly East Asian land reforms, including that in China, were important impetuses for economic growth in a number of ways.

In recent years, the economic performance of some of the Tigers has flagged. Some might want to attribute this to their relative income equality, since capital formation in Japan and South Korea was only 1.1 per cent and 1.6 per cent during the 1990s. But this was in fact the period in which income distribution in these countries became less equal, with fortunes made in real estate, corporate and other dealings. Since economic behaviour occurs "at the margin" rather than being based on averages, it is difficult to draw definite causal inferences with such complex relationships.

I had the good fortune to have W. Arthur Lewis as a teacher of development economics, and I acquired from him a skepticism about capital formation as the cause of economic growth. He considered it to be in general a consequence of growth, not being persuaded of the validity of neoclassical economics' assumptions and preferring to think along the lines of more classical economic theory.

He did not regard market prices as an infallible equalizer of values, whereby $100 worth of deodorants would be equal to $100 worth of productive land. I share Sir Arthur's reservations, though the current theory and practice of economics is quite happy to equate everything by market prices, even when it is acknowledged that these prices reflect very unequal distributions of income which distort the forces of demand and supply.

The price system, except under unattainable conditions, is better able to maximize profits than to maximize human welfare. It also fails to reflect adequately the needs and interests of future generations. But this is not the time or place for a fundamental debate on economics. In any case, there is enough evidence now accumulated and analysed to assure us that relative income equality is not a necessary drag on growth, and we should know that there is some significant evidence showing positive effects from relative equality. Reducing inequality can thus be seen as a spur to economic growth, reducing poverty by that complex path rather than by a direct process of income redistribution or transfer.

A "LIFE CHANCES" VIEW OF POVERTY

As a social scientist who works on development, rather than an economist who tries to explain all those things that can be denominated in terms of money, I would suggest the following perspective on poverty and inequality. If I were doing today the kind of analysis I undertook with Cornell colleagues 25 years ago, I would still want to look at income distribution data and to compare statistics such as top 20%: bottom 20% ratio to assess magnitudes and trends.

If there are data detailed and extensive enough to use more refined indicators such as the Foster-Greer-Thorbecke measure of inequality, this would be desirable because it maps disparities in income distribution in more precise and meaningful ways. I would also want to have some of the kind of qualitative assessments of poverty that were done for the World Bank by Deepa Narayan and her associates to show the human face of poverty for its 2000-2001 World Development Report on poverty.

But increasingly the most meaningful measure of poverty, in my view, is one not found in the literature. Assessing the lives of people—their present living standards and conditions—is important, but I think poverty is most significant in terms of what it does to people's life chances—their opportunities to get educated, to have food, shelter and clothing that meet basic needs to move not just a little way up the ladder of income distribution but to be able to make some significant jumps and—most important—to give their children greater opportunities.

A life-chances indicator would tell us what is most significant and oppressive about poverty: its stratification of society into relatively static as well as separate groups. This should be of concern to almost everyone, not just those persons who bear the brunt of poverty. To be sure, not everyone loses equally from a social arrangement of group stratification, but the losers, who are more than just the poor, greatly outnumber the gainers from inequality. The poor consume less because they produce fewer goods and services, which are consequently not available to the rest of society.

What is the probability that someone who is born into poverty will in the course of his or her life end up, reasonably stably, above the poverty line? Or put another way, what is the probability that someone born into a family in that lowest 20 per cent of households will eventually head or co-head a household in the next higher 20 per cent, so that her or his children will have definitely "moved up the ladder," even if not out of poverty.

One would like to know this for persons born in the next higher quintile as well. Perhaps the worse thing about poverty is the inescapability it creates from the problems, constraints and insults that are imposed upon the poor, documented by Narayan and her collaborators in the recent World Bank. These deprivations and humiliations are of concern not just within a single generation, but even more, from generation to generation. This raises, of course, "the Lake Woebegone problem."

Not everyone within a country or community can be above average—by definition, a fifth of people must always be in the lowest quintile. So whenever incomes or standards of living are compared, some inequality is unavoidable, though this can be a greater or lesser degree. If one can move from a zero-sum to a positive-sum framework for thinking about wealth and poverty, of course, it is easier to address this problem, both analytically and psychologically.

It is an important question practically and ethically whether persons in the lowest bracket are those who have the least physical and/or mental capacity—or whether they are persons who have, through no action or failing of their own, been deprived of effective opportunities to develop their productive capacities to the fullest and to attain concurrent status and security. The latter situation represents a loss not only for the persons who are so constrained by economic, social, cultural or political circumstances, but also for the whole society. Its aggregate loss may be even greater than that for the poor. All in society remain somewhat poorer when others' productive potential is unfulfilled. Not only are there fewer goods and services to be enjoyed, but there are fewer contributions to the life and culture of a country, fewer songs and poems, less self-respecting friends to enrich social relations, fewer persons of talent and integrity to hold political office, etc.

Poverty reduction is thus not something to be done just to benefit the poor. It is good for everyone except for those persons who derive their wealth from extractive relations that are zero-sum, or worse, negative-sum. If there is one core process that underlies development it is that of creating positive-sum relationships, such as through the production of value-added, through creation of consumer surplus, through economies of scale from market integration and trade, or through broader friendship networks.

Economic relations that are only zero-sum contribute little to development, even though they may add to GNP as conventionally measured. Ironically, some negative-sum transactions, such as waste disposal and pollution abatement, also add to GNP. What truly accelerates development are positive-sum effects. Such an understanding makes issues of poverty and inequality more central to development theory, policy and practice.

Poverty and inequality are not just "a blemish" on the development record of a country, nor are they just "unfinished business" to be taken care of once development has progressed fairly far. Where poverty is of the locked-in variety with stagnant life chances for the poor, it reflects a pattern of development that is not basically driven by positive-sum dynamics. It is a stunted form of development. There are thus some strong practical as well as ethical reasons for "attacking poverty," to use the subtitle of the World Development Report 2000/2001. The conditions of life for the poor can be improved in various ways, directly through assistance, or indirectly but more sustainably, by enhancing people's productivity.

The latter can be accomplished:

- By upgrading the factor endowments of the poor,
- By ensuring them greater access to opportunities through general or specific processes of market integration that enable them to employ their factors more productively,
- By enhancing bargaining power to get more return for factors of production or goods and services, usually through organization,
- By innovative initiatives of entrepreneurship and leadership that alter structures of economic, social and political production in more productive directions Returns to factors of production are affected more by bargaining power than by intrinsic value since the market by itself offers no means to appraise the latter. This "dynamic" view of poverty and inequality should be of interest both to individuals—especially those within categories of "the poor"—and to society as a whole.

Living in poverty has myriad degradations and debilitations, well documented in Narayan but being locked into this status, with its attendant diminutions of life quality, makes a bad situation worse. The prospect that one's children will, through no fault of their own, have not better chances of living a more productive and fulfilled life, adds greatly to the psychological burden of poverty.

From a societal point of view, to the extent that more people and more talent are locked into poverty, their contributions to GNP but also to cultural creations and to political and social life are diminished. "Life chances" can be measured fairly precisely at any point in time, at least retrospectively, by tracking inter-generational mobility in economic and social terms—through interviews with persons just as to some appropriate simple classification or scaling of economic and social status.

The implications for policy are that steps should be taken, and investments made, which most surely increase the probability that people can move to a higher rank, level or category in the future, and particularly that their children will be able to live stably in a higher one.

RELATIVE VS. ABSOLUTE MEASURES

This approach to assessing and attacking poverty leads into some sticky analytical and evaluative terrain. It also argues against my preferred measure of inequality—comparing as a ratio the income going to the top 20 per cent and that to the bottom 20 per cent of households. Such a measure is zero-sum in that it uses a fixed proportion.

The ratio can improve, *i.e.*, move lower, but it can only approach, never reaching, zero; 2:1 or 3:1 ratios would represent a great victory in reducing inequality and alleviating poverty, when the ratio can exceed 25:1 as in Brazil or El Salvador. To assess progress in improving life chances, one would use appropriate poverty line measures, secondarily looking at movement between quintiles of distributed income.

There could be considerable poverty alleviation if all households simply moved up in income level without any change in rank-ordering. However, the creation of greater opportunities for achievement and mobility based on merit will not have been achieved, since one of the few things we know with some certainty in the social sciences is that there is, in inter-generational terms, invariably some "regression towards the mean" in terms of intelligence and other talents.

A "rising tide that lifts all boats" should be welcomed as an unprecedented policy achievement, but it would not represent a full-fledged victory in the war against poverty. While more individuals would be better off, society as a whole would not have gained as much as it could by opening up more opportunities for leadership and responsibility based on talent and innovativeness.

Whether or not persons are in poverty can thus be viewed in either absolute terms or relative terms. Having a high degree of equality in a situation where everyone is poor in terms of their possibilities for consumption and living a good life is hardly satisfactory. For this reason, we are concerned with both poverty and inequality together, even though they can be and should be analysed separately. There is always some tension between the absolute and relative concepts of poverty. "Poverty lines" get conceived and drawn as something absolute, producing certain numbers of persons below them who thus belong in the category of "the poor." Even such lines are, however, relative to some conception of human needs or social acceptability; and the data on which such calculations are based are themselves often very debatable, the products of sampling and surveys that can be contested.

So one should not regard the numbers as being true or real in any absolute sense. Rather, they are constructs, worth knowing, and of special value when they are tracked over time or compared across regions or social groups, using the same standards for derivation.

IMPLICATIONS OF SOCIAL MOBILITY FOR SOCIETAL EFFICIENCY AND EQUITY

For assessing life chances, one needs to ascertain how much socio-economic mobility there is in a society through surveys and observations that do not rely so much on measurement as on simple categorizations, such as job classifications or possession of certain kinds of assets, which are not very ambiguous. Comparing that status of persons with that for their parents can be reasonably objective even if recall must be used because the things being recalled are simple and discrete.

One can put aside the fact that there will always be some persons below average, even way below average; the important question in this kind of analysis is whether they are always the same persons, or always persons from the same families. This "life chances" approach to understanding and evaluating poverty and inequality can be justified by efficiency as well as equity concerns.

One of the few things about human beings known with reasonable certainty is that intelligence, or at least potential intelligence, as well as other talents are distributed quite evenly across all populations, all races, both genders, etc. In a country with a high degree of access to positions of higher income, status and authority based on merit, the offspring of the families in the upper quintile, biologically speaking, have some greater chance of being in that quintile in the next generation simply based on natural talent. This will be augmented by various acquired, as distinguished from innate, characteristics. But this is only a chance, not a certainty. If all of those persons in the top quintile come from parents who themselves have had that status, the country's economic, political and other institutions are being directed by persons who have less than the greatest natural, innate capability.

They may have certain advantages of education and social connections that make them effective in such positions, and this is not to be neglected. But the very highest intelligence and other talents will not be among their endowments. The law of "regression towards the mean" means that most children of the most privileged group in a society will be less capable than their parents were and will deserve to end up in a lower quintile than they were born into.

The converse implication of this law—that persons of highest intelligence can and will be born into any and all social categories—means that, on the basis of merit, there should be many persons, indeed a majority in any generation, in the top category who were born into lower quintiles and on the basis of their talent were able to rise up the socio-economic ladder. In fact, it is unlikely that any social policy aiming to end poverty and inequality can ever succeed fully.

The chances of the "first" really becoming "last" are negligible, even though it can be fruitful to think about the implications of this. The advantages of being brought up in an advantaged family, with social contacts, psychological confidence, role models, etc., cannot be redistributed except by heinous measures that are destructive for everyone in society, as seen from the Khmer Rouge experience in Cambodia which tried to expunge all past privileges by force. What is possible, however, is to have an active policy of investment in developing human capabilities including universal and high quality education and health care, with effective programmes of prenatal maternal as well as childhood nutrition. A progressive inheritance tax that levels the economic playing field between generations could finance a good part of this, offering at the same time the social utility of it becoming easier for persons with talent, imagination, energy and social skills to rise, their way not blocked by less capable persons who had extrinsic inherited advantages.

In India, there is the special problem, which few people are willing to talk about. Even after 50 years, there is still strong residual discrimination against persons born into scheduled-caste or scheduled-tribe families. There are some exceptions, as some of these households have been able to climb up some rungs on the socio-economic ladder.

But this is one of the most glaring sources of poverty and inequality in India: the continuing effect of a caste system several thousand years old. A life-chances approach to evaluating poverty is particularly relevant where we know that there are certain socio-cultural impediments to upward mobility.

ISSUES FOR INDIA TODAY

The good news is that income distribution in India appears to have become more equal over the past 35 years. When calculating the ratio of incomes in India going to the top 20 per cent and the bottom 20 per cent, we found two sets of figures; one was from 1964-65 analysed by Pranab Bardhan, and the other from 1967-68 analysed by K. R. Ranadive. These data sets produced quite different ratios, 6.0:1 and 10.9:1, which we averaged, to consider 8.5:1 as a representative figure for India. The most current figures on income distribution in India give a ratio of 5.7:1, as a result of 46.1 per cent of income going to the top 20 per cent, while 8.1 per cent of income goes to the bottom 20 per cent.

This suggests that India has made some progress in reducing inequality compared to earlier NCAER data, though not with regard to NSS surveys. But what is the vision and strategy of development that the Indian government and its citizens will pursue? Will it be purely incremental, being satisfied to have moved annually some number of individuals or household above the poverty line? Will there be longitudinal tracking to know how this number compares with those who have, in this same time period, fallen below the line? Will we know what kinds of persons are moving out of poverty, and what kind are sinking into it? Aggregate numbers that balance these two groups out, perhaps with little net change, are not very informative.

A life-chances conception of poverty will focus on such data, and on what can be done to create "one-way tickets" out of poverty because that is what "reducing poverty" is taken to mean. Poverty should be seen as bad for everyone, not just for the poor. Looking for ways to help people get themselves out of poverty—note that I did not say, looking for ways to get people out of poverty—would focus on the obstacles for different categories of persons defined as being among the poor. Often these will derive from socioeconomic and sometimes political relationships that are extractive and exploitative, *i.e.*, negative-sum, where the gains of the few are in total less than the losses of the many.

If improvements in life chances are the measure and criterion of success, these relationships become unavoidable focuses of concern, whereas with conventional poverty or inequality measures, any net incremental changes are interpreted as positive, and there is no need to address structural impediments or resistances. What will most improve life chances of the poor in India? Education and health care are the two most obvious measures, which have the advantage of being positive-sum and not requiring anyone else to lose thereby—except those who have been exploiting cheap labour. Having a more educated population is good for the large majority in a country, and having better health has positive payoffs by reducing disease that can harm the better-off.

Programmes for fair hiring and promotion are more difficult to install because they involve some reallocation of opportunities, from less-qualified to more-qualified. But they are not impossible to promote, a kind of fair employment practices system that would benefit employers because they are supported in hiring and promoting on the basis of merit, which should improve the efficiency and profitability of enterprises.

THE SPECIAL ISSUE OF LAND DISTRIBUTION AND ACCESS

A controversial but sound policy would be pursue a kind of land reform or redistribution that is different from the classical "land to the tiller" programme. I call this "universal access to land." It would not try to give every household in the agricultural sector a size of holding sufficient to produce a subsistence income as has been the usual policy objective when such redistribution has been contemplated.

In many places, there is not enough arable land to set up every household wanting to practice agriculture with a so-called "economic unit." This constraint has been a sufficient argument to get land distribution kept off the development agenda for the past several decades. But the image of agriculture that underlies—and is used to discredit—the classical form of land reform is an outmoded one.

In most countries, including India, an increasing share of rural incomes come from non-farm and non-agricultural sources. In part this represents a high degree of desperation as poor rural households find that they must turn to other sources of income to meet their basic needs. But it can also represent modernization and diversification of a rural economy which is no longer solely dependent on agricultural and own-enterprise activities for output and employment.

Two lines of argument support this suggestion, one emphasizing agricultural productivity and the other human productivity. First, as arable land becomes relatively scarcer with population growth, and demand for production continues to rise for this same reason, higher productivity per unit of land becomes critical for further development.

In almost all situations, smaller holdings are more productive per hectare than larger ones because smaller ones are more intensively farmed, while larger ones are farmed more extensively. Mechanized production which substitutes machines for labour raises profits more than it raises production. Only where mechanization increases intensification, as with plowing that permits cultivation of an extra crop, does it increase output. It is true that larger units of production produce higher incomes, but not because of higher output per unit of land. Most of the gains are due to economies of size rather than to technical economies of scale. Gains are based on advantages of bargaining power rather than on real gains in efficiency. Second, there can be very real gains in welfare that contribute to the productivity obtainable from providing poor households with even small holdings.

These units may be considered "sub-economic" by analysts if one expects households to get all their income from agricultural and own-farm pursuits; but they can add to the health, productivity and security which can help households begin moving up out of poverty. This can be seen from two theses done some years ago at Cornell whose findings were ignored because they pointed in a direction that prevailing economic development thinking was not prepared to go.

Research in India by Kumar found that—other things being equal, in other words, for the same level of household income—children's nutritional status was higher if the household owned some, even a small piece of land. This could be easily explained. If a household had an opportunity to produce even a small share of the food that it needed, it had more control over its food supply and would not be as vulnerable to hunger periods.

The land did not even need to be high quality since good management of the soil could improve it sufficiently for growing vegetables and fruits and maybe some staple crop. If a household had only a small plot, it was worthwhile investing labour in raising its productivity. Research in Indonesia by Hart showed that—other things being equal, including controlling for level of education and thus for the inferred level of "human capital"—households that owned even a small amount of land had higher returns for their labour, *i.e.*, they had higher net wages per hour. If a family had even one-quarter acre on which to grow some food to meet its subsistence needs, its workers could hold out for more than the very lowest wages being offered. Those completely landless workers who had no land to fall back on had to accept whatever work was available. These were often jobs to which they had to travel several hours in both directions, being desperate.

The hourly returns for such employment were thus pitifully low. Poor families with even some small amount of land were considered to be more desirable "clients" by the more powerful "patrons" in the village, those persons who had larger landholdings, so these poor families were better able to find employment locally and received better wages for their labour. Also, they were more likely to get benefits like gleaning rights on larger farmers' fields after harvest.

The issue of "land access" should be put on the development agenda, even for a country like India where formal land reform efforts have been mostly a failure and where person:land ratios are in many parts of the country quite high. Two generations of population growth and resulting subdivision of land have accomplished at the upper ends of the land tenure system part of what land reforms intended: the breakup of very huge landholdings But there has been concentration in lower-upper and upper-middle echelons, and the number of landless has continued to grow.

Exclusion from access to land in rural areas, coupled with poor or inaccessible schools, no or non-functioning medical facilities, and social discrimination, means that there are several hundred million Indians who are now—or will in the next generation be—denied the kinds of "life chances" that ought to be a human right. Such life chances are essential for the progress of an economy that is prosperous and dynamic in the modern world.

The absence of life chances will slow an economy due to the inertia of millions of persons who have been marginalized and made dispensable by the economic system. They nevertheless need to meet their survival needs, and they can be adversely affect the economy by becoming, in small or large numbers, strongly negative social and political forces. This perspective on poverty and inequality has various measurement and normative aspects that can be addressed with more or less elegance, but it also has very practical and political implications that need to be addressed with some sense of urgency. A danger of preoccupation with the measurement aspects of poverty and inequality, especially if divorced from normative considerations, is that analysis will have nothing to contribute to the redress of practical needs and political pressures.

POVERTY AND INEQUALITY IN INDIA

Poverty trends in India in the nineties have been a matter of intense controversy. The debate has often generated more heat than light, and confusion still remains about the extent to which poverty has declined during the period. In the absence of conclusive evidence, widely divergent claims have flourished. Some have argued that the nineties have been a period of unprecedented improvement in living standards.

Others have claimed that it has been a time of widespread impoverishment. Against this background, this document presents a reassessment of the evidence on poverty and inequality in the nineties. So far, the debate on poverty in the nineties has focused overwhelmingly on changes in the 'headcount ratio'—the proportion of the population below the poverty line.

We begin with a reassessment of the evidence on headcount ratios and related poverty indexes, based on National Sample Survey data. In particular, we present a new series of internally consistent poverty indexes for the last three 'quinquennial rounds'. The broad picture emerging from these revised estimates is one of sustained poverty decline in most states during the reference period.

It is important to note, however, that the increase in per capita expenditure associated with this decline in poverty is quite modest, e g, 10 per cent or so between 1993-94 and 1999-2000 at the all-India level. We consider related evidence from three additional sources: the Central Statistical Organisation's 'national accounts statistics', the 'employment-unemployment surveys' of the National Sample Survey, and data on agricultural wages. In particular, real agricultural wages in different states have grown at much the same rate as the corresponding NSS-based estimates of per capita expenditure in rural areas. While each of these sources of information, including the National Sample Survey, has important limitations, they tend to corroborate each other as far as poverty decline is concerned, and the combined evidence on this from different sources is quite strong. We focus mainly on the period between 1993-94 and 1999- 2000.

Based on further analysis of National Sample Survey data and related sources, we argue that there has been a marked increase in inequality in the nineties, in several forms. First, there has been strong 'divergence' of per capita expenditure across states, with the already betteroff states growing more rapidly than the poorer states. Second, rural-urban disparities of per capita expenditure have risen. Third, inequality has increased within urban areas in most states.

The combined effects of these different forms of rising inequality are quite large. In the rural areas of some of the poorest states, there has been virtually no increase in per capita expenditure between 1993-94 and 1999- 2000. Meanwhile, the urban populations of most of the better-off states have enjoyed increases of per capita expenditure of 20 to 30 per cent, with even larger increases for high-income groups within these populations.

Some qualifications and concerns. We pay special attention to the apparent decline of cereal consumption in the nineties, which is not obviously consistent with the notion that poverty has steadily declined during that period. We also consider the possibility of impoverishment among specific regions or social groups, in spite of the general improvement in living conditions. Finally, we comment on the unresolved puzzle of the 'thin rounds'.

We argue for supplementing expenditure-based data with other indicators of living standards, focusing for instance on literacy rates, health achievements, nutritional levels, crime rates, and the quality of the environment. This broader approach sheds a different light on poverty trends in the nineties. In particular, it prompts us to acknowledge that social progress has been uneven across the different fields. For instance, the nineties have been a period of fairly rapid increase in literacy and school participation.

On the other hand, there has been a marked slowdown in the rate at which infant mortality has been declining, and a significant increase in economic inequality. An integrated assessment of changes in living conditions has to be alive to these diversities. We also discuss other implications of this broader approach to the evaluation of living standards, going beyond the standard poverty indexes. The concluding part sums up the insights of this enquiry.

POVERTY INDEXES IN THE NINETIES

Official Estimates

We begin with an examination of household per capita consumption and the associated poverty estimates. Consumption is only one element of well-being, but it is an important element, and much interest is rightly attached to the Planning Commission's periodical estimates of poverty-based on National Sample Survey data. The most widely-used poverty indicator is the 'headcount ratio', i e, the proportion of the population below the poverty line.

The latest year for which relatively uncontroversial HCR estimates are available is 1993-94, corresponding to the 50th Round of the National Sample Survey, a 'quinquennial' round. This round was followed by a series of so-called 'thin rounds', involving smaller samples and somewhat different sampling designs; indeed, in the last of these, the 54th Round, the survey was only in the field for six months rather than the customary year and is therefore most unlikely to be comparable with any previous survey.

These thin rounds suggested not only that poverty remained more or less unchanged between 1993-94 and the first six months of 1998 but also that average per capita expenditure stagnated during this period of rapid economic growth. This is very difficult to square with independent evidence, e g, from national accounts statistics. As things stand, we do not have a good understanding of why the thin rounds give what appear to be anomalous results, and until that puzzle is resolved, our confidence in our other results must remain qualified. In contrast to the thin rounds, the official counts from the latest quinquennial round suggest considerable poverty decline between 1993-94 and 1999-2000. Widely relayed, the all-India headcount ratio declined from 36 to 26 per cent over this short period.

As is well known, however, the 55th Round is not directly comparable to the 50th Round, due to changes in questionnaire design. Briefly, the problem is as follows. After the 50th Round, the National Sample Survey introduced an experimental questionnaire with different recall periods for different classes of goods, in addition to the traditional '30-day recall' questionnaire.

The experimental questionnaire used a seven-day recall period for food, pan, and tobacco, as well as a 365-day recall period for less frequently purchased goods such as durables, clothing, footwear, educational and institutional medical expenditures. Prior to 1999-2000, the traditional '30-day recall' questionnaire and the experimental questionnaire were administered to different samples of households.

These alternative questionnaires produced two independent series of expenditure estimates, with a fairly stable 'ratio' of the lower estimates based on the traditional questionnaire to the higher estimates based on the experimental questionnaire. In 1999-2000, the 30-day recall and seven-day recall periods for food, pan and tobacco were used for the same households, in two adjacent columns on the same pages of a single questionnaire.

This effectively 'new' questionnaire design led to a sudden 'reconciliation' of the results obtained from the two different recall periods, perhaps reflecting efforts to achieve 'consistency' on the part of investigators and/or respondents. This reconciliation is likely to boost the expenditure estimates based on 30-day data, and therefore to pull down the official poverty counts, which are based on these 30-day expenditures.

In addition, only the 365- day questionnaire was used for the less frequently purchased items, and this abandonment of the traditional 30-day recall for durables and other items also brings down the poverty count. Indeed, most people report no such purchases over 30 days, but report something over 365 days. The bottom tail of the consumption distribution is thereby pulled up, reducing both poverty and inequality compared with the previous design.

For this reason, as well as because of possible reconciliation between seven-day and 30-day reports, the latest headcount ratios are biased down compared with what would have been obtained on the basis of the traditional questionnaire. There is another, quite different problem with the official estimates, which does not concern the 55th Round specifically.

This relates to the state and sector specific poverty lines that are used by the Planning Commission to compute the poverty estimates. In several cases the poverty lines are implausible, particularly the very much higher urban than rural lines in several states. The source of the problem lies in the use of defective price indexes in adjustments of the poverty line over time and between states. We discuss ways of overcoming this problem and other limitations of the official poverty estimates.

Proposed Adjustments

In this document, we present a new series of consistent poverty estimates for the most recent quinquennial rounds. Essentially, these involve four major departures from the official estimates. First, an attempt is made to 'adjust' the 55th-Round estimates to achieve comparability with the earlier rounds. Second, we use improved price indexes to update the 'poverty line' over time, and to derive state-specific poverty lines from the all-India poverty line.

Third, a similar procedure is used to derive an explicit estimate of the appropriate gap between rural and urban poverty lines. Fourth, in addition to corrected 'headcount ratios', we present estimates of a potentially more informative poverty indicator, the 'poverty-gap index'. Each of these departures calls for further discussion. The possibility of 'adjusting' the 1999- 2000 poverty estimates arises from the fact that the 55th Round questionnaire retained the '30-day recall' approach for a number of items such as fuel and light, non-institutional medical care, and large categories of miscellaneous goods and services. Further, it turns out that expenditure on this intermediate group of commodities is highly correlated with total expenditure.

Expenditures on these comparably surveyed goods can therefore be used to get an idea of trends in total expenditures, and hence, of trends in poverty. This procedure is valid if two assumptions hold. The first is that reported expenditures on the intermediate goods, for which the recall period is unchanged, are unaffected by the changes elsewhere in the questionnaire.

The second is that the relation between intermediate-goods expenditure and total expenditure is much the same in 1999-2000 as in 1993-94. The second assumption would be undermined by a major change in relative prices of the intermediate goods relative to other goods in the late 1990s. It can be checked to some extent by applying the proposed method to the 'thin rounds' instead of the 55th Round, and comparing the predicted distribution of total expenditure with the actual distribution.

These checks suggest that the correction procedure works reasonably well. However, this should not be regarded as a definitive validation of the proposed method, given the ambiguities associated with the thin rounds. There are other possible approaches to adjustment that have not yet been explored, and further work may lead to different conclusions.

Meanwhile, we regard our adjusted figures as the best currently available in terms of dealing with the change in questionnaire design, without pretending that they represent the final word on the topic. Turning to the price adjustments, one limitation of the price indexes that have been traditionally used to update poverty lines over time is that they are based on fixed and frequently outdated commodity 'weights'.

It is possible to calculate alternative price indexes using the information in the consumer expenditure surveys themselves. For more than 170 commodities, households report both quantities and expenditures, and the ratio of the latter to the former provides an estimate of the price paid. These prices can then be combined into consumer price index numbers that allow comparisons across states, and if we use data from different rounds, for states and the whole country at different points in time.

One limitation of these price indexes is that their coverage of commodities is only partial, so that they cannot capture price changes in important items such as transportation, housing, most non-food goods, and services. However, CPIAL data suggest that the inflation rate for the uncovered items is not very different from that applying to the covered items.

The price indexes from the surveys have the advantage of being based on several million actual purchases in each round. They also make it possible to use formulas for superlative indexes, such as the Fisher ideal index or the Törnqvist index, that allow for substitution behaviour as households adapt to relative price changes over time.

The calculated Törnqvist indexes for the 43rd and 50th Rounds are reported in Deaton and Tarozzi, and were updated to the 55th Round by Deaton. These price indexes differ from the official indexes in a number of ways. In particular, they rise somewhat more slowly over time than do the official price indexes, especially in the rural sector.

For example, the all-India rural Törnqvist index rises by 69.8 per cent from 1987-88 to 1993-94 and by a further 54.5 per cent from 1993-94 to 1999-2000, compared with 78.7 per cent and 59.1 per cent for the deflators implicit in the official all-India rural poverty line. For the urban sector over the two periods, the Törnqvist price indexes rise by 73.8 and 57.7 per cent versus 73.5 and 61.4 per cent for the implicit deflator of the urban poverty line.

The price indexes for each state show rather modest differences from one state to another. They also differ from those implicit in the official poverty lines, although the two sets of deflators are correlated. This pattern is consistent with the fact that relative prices across states vary somewhat over time, and that the interstate prices used in the official deflators are outdated. The third departure concerns the gap between rural and urban poverty lines. From the mid-1970s until the early 1990s, there were only two poverty lines for India, one for rural and one for urban. The urban line was around 15 per cent higher than the rural line, and both were held fixed in real terms, with updating on the basis of approximate price indexes such as the Wholesale Price Index or the CSO's private consumption deflator.

The initial ruralurban gap of 15 per cent is anchored in 1973-74 calorie consumption data, but it is essentially arbitrary since the urban and rural 'calorie norms' themselves have a fragile basis. More recently, the Planning Commission has adopted a modified version of the poverty lines recommended by a 1993 Expert Group.

The Expert Group retained the original rural and urban lines, but adjusted them for statewise differences in price levels, separately for urban and rural sectors, using estimates of statewise price differences calculated from NSS data on expenditures and quantities using similar methods to those adopted in this document. The Expert Group lines used the then best-available information on price differences across states, both urban and rural, but the information was outdated, especially for the rural sector. Because the statewise adjustments were done separately for urban and rural households, the price differences between the urban and rural sectors of each state were derived only implicitly, and some are rather implausible, particularly the very much higher urban than rural lines in several states.

For example, the most recent urban poverty lines for Andhra Pradesh and Karnataka are around 70 per cent higher than the corresponding rural lines, with the uncomfortable result that urban poverty is much higher than rural poverty in these two states. In Assam, by contrast, the rural poverty line is actually higher than the urban line, and based on these odd poverty lines, Assam turns out to be one of India's highestpoverty states for rural areas but lowestpoverty states for urban areas. It is hard to accept these and other implications of the Expert Group poverty lines. There are grounds, of course, for questioning whether it is even possible to derive comparable rural and urban poverty lines.

Comparisons of living standards in rural and urban areas are inherently difficult, since there are large intersectoral differences not only in the patterns of consumption but also in lifestyles, public amenities, epidemiological environments, and so on. One way forward is to avoid such comparisons altogether, and to focus on sectorspecific poverty estimates. Yet there is a case for attempting to compare private consumption levels across sectors, bearing in mind that this is at best a partial picture of the relevant differences in living standards.

These comparisons can be made by anchoring poverty estimates in a single poverty line, adjusted where appropriate to take into account rural-urban price differences, using the same method as that described earlier for adjusting poverty lines over time and between states. Based on this procedure, the urban poverty line tends be about 15 per cent higher than the rural poverty line, though there are variations across states. As it turns out, this rural-urban difference in poverty lines is broadly consistent with the original methodology used before the adoption of the Expert Group recommendations.

To recapitulate, the revised poverty lines used in this document. Our starting point is the official rural all-India poverty line for the 43rd Round: 115.70 rupees per person per month. Rural poverty lines for each state for the 43rd Round are obtained by multiplying this base poverty line by the rural price indexes for each state relative to all-India.

The urban poverty lines for the 43rd Round, for each state as well as for all-India, are calculated from the rural poverty lines by scaling up by the respective urban relative to rural price indexes. In all cases, we use the relevant Tornqvist price indexes. To move to the 50th Round, the original all-India rural line, 115.70 rupees, is scaled up by the Tornqvist index for all-India rural for the 50th Round relative to the 43rd Round,

1.698, to give an all-India rural poverty line for the 50th Round. This number is then used to generate rural and then urban poverty lines for each state, following exactly the same procedure as for the 43rd Round. Finally, poverty lines for the 55th Round are calculated in the same way from an all-India rural line, which is the 50th Round all-India rural line scaled up by the value of the Törnqvist index between the two surveys. The motivation for the fourth departure arises from the limitations of the headcount ratio as an indicator of poverty.

The headcount ratio has a straightforward interpretation and is easy to understand. In that sense it has much 'communication value'. Yet, the HCR has serious limitations as a poverty index. For one thing, it ignores the extent to which different households fall short of the poverty line. This leads to some perverse properties. For instance, an income transfer from a very poor person to someone who is closer to the poverty line may lead to a decline in the headcount ratio, if it 'lifts' the recipient above the poverty line.

Similarly, if some poor households get poorer, this has no effect on the headcount ratio. A related issue is that changes in HCRs can be highly sensitive to the number of poor households near the poverty line. If poor households are heavily 'bunched' near the poverty line, a small increase in average per capita income could lead to a misleadingly large decline in the headcount ratio.

This 'density effect' has to be kept firmly in view in the context of comparisons of poverty change, involving questions such as "has there been more poverty decline in Bihar than in Punjab during the nineties", or "has poverty declined faster in the nineties than in the eighties?" Often such questions are answered by looking at, say, the respective changes in headcount ratios.

These changes, however, are difficult to interpret in the absence of further information about the initial density of poor households near the poverty line in each case. One way forward is to use more sophisticated poverty indexes such as the Foster- Greer-Thorbecke indexes or the Sen index. In this document, we focus on the simplest member of the FGT class, the 'poverty gap index'. Essentially, the poverty-gap index is the aggregate shortfall of poor people's consumption from the poverty line, suitably normalised.

The PGI can also be interpreted as the headcount ratio multiplied by the mean percentage shortfall of consumption from the poverty line. This index avoids the main shortcomings of the headcount ratio, is relatively simple to calculate, and has a straightforward interpretation.

Adjusted Estimates

In each panel, the first row gives the official estimates; the second row retains the official poverty lines but adjusts the 1999-2000 estimates for the change in questionnaire design in the way described earlier; the third row gives fully-adjusted poverty estimates, which combine the adjustments for questionnaire design and for price indexes.

As the first two rows of each panel indicate, the official estimates are quite misleading in their own terms: the 1999-2000 poverty estimates are biased downward by the changes in questionnaire design. For headcount ratios, the estimates adjusted for changes in questionnaire design 'confirm' about two-thirds of the official decline in rural poverty between 1993-94 and 1999-2000, and about 90 per cent of the decline in urban poverty.

For poverty-gap indexes, the corresponding proportions are lower, especially for the urban sector. The fully-adjusted estimates in the last row of each panel show somewhat lower rural poverty estimates and much lower urban poverty estimates for 1999-2000 than even the official estimates. Note, however, that because we are recalculating the poverty lines back to the 43rd Round, a good deal of the decrease took place in the six years prior to 1993-94, not only in the six years subsequent to 1993-94.

The fully-adjusted estimates for the headcount ratios and poverty gap indexes suggest that poverty decline has been fairly evenly spread between the two sub-periods in contrast with the pattern of 'acceleration' in the second sub-period associated with the official estimates. The rural-urban gaps in the poverty estimates are also of interest. Looking first at the base year, the rural-urban gap based on adjusted estimates is much larger than that based on official estimates. Indeed, the latter suggest no difference between rural and urban poverty in that year. This is hard to reconcile with independent evidence on living conditions in rural and urban areas, such as a lifeexpectancy gap of about seven years in favour or urban areas around that time.

Our low estimate of the urban headcount ratio relative to the official estimate, and similar differences in 1993-94 and 1999-2000, come from the fact that we take the rural poverty line in 1987-88 as our starting point, and peg the urban poverty lines about 15 per cent higher than the rural poverty lines, in contrast to the much larger differentials embodied in the official lines.

The new estimates of the headcount ratios together with the official estimates going back to 1973-74. The fully adjusted figures are lower throughout because we treat the rural poverty line in the 43rd Round as our baseline so that, with larger rural-urban gaps in the poverty estimates, we estimate lower poverty overall. If instead, we had taken the urban poverty line as base, the adjusted figures would have been higher than the official figures. From 1987-88 to 1993-94, the adjusted headcount ratio falls more rapidly than the official headcount; this is because our price deflators are rising less rapidly than the official ones.

From 1993-94, the adjusted figures fall more slowly because the effects of the price adjustment are more than offset by the correction for questionnaire design. The estimates for the thin rounds—which look very different—are included to remind us of the residual uncertainty about our conclusions.

Regional Contrasts

The same basic structure, except that we jump straight from official to fullyadjusted estimates. The latter suggest that the basic pattern of sustained poverty decline between 1987-88 and 1999-2000, discussed earlier at the all-India level, also applies at the level of individual states in most cases. The main exception is Assam, where poverty has stagnated in both rural and urban areas. In Orissa, there has been very little poverty decline in the second sub-period, with the result that Orissa now has the highest level of rural poverty among all Indian states, just as to the adjusted 1999-2000 estimates. Reassuringly, the 'anomalies' noted earlier with respect to rural-urban gaps in specific states tend to disappear as one moves from official to adjusted estimates.

The corresponding poverty- gap indexes. The general patterns are very much the same as with headcount ratios; indeed the PGI series are highly correlated with the corresponding HCR series, with correlation coefficients of 0.98 for rural and 0.95 for urban. Even the HCR and PGI changes between the 50th and 55th Rounds are highly correlated; the correlation coefficient between changes in HCR and changes in PGI is 0.95 for the rural sector, and 0.96 for the urban sector. Thus, in spite of its theoretical superiority over the headcount ratio, the poverty-gap index gives us very little additional insight in this case.

In interpreting and comparing poverty declines over time, it is useful to supplement the poverty indexes with information on the growth rate of average per capita consumption expenditure. State-specific estimates of APCE growth between 1993-94 and 1999-2000, where states are ranked in ascending order of APCE growth for rural and urban areas combined. Here, a striking regional pattern emerges: except for Jammu and Kashmir, the lowgrowth states form one contiguous region made up of the eastern states, the so-called BIMARU states, and Andhra Pradesh.

The high-growth states, for their part, consist of the southern states, the western states and the northwestern region. Further, it is interesting to note that this pattern is reasonably consistent with independent data on growth rates of per capita 'state domestic product'. With a couple of exceptions on each side, all the states in the 'low APCE growth' set had comparatively low rates of per capita SDP between 1993-94 and 1999-2000, and conversely, all the states in the 'high APCE growth' set had comparatively high annual growth rates of per capita SDP. This broad regional pattern is a matter of concern, because the low-growth states also tend to be states that started off with comparatively low levels of APCE or percapita SDP.

In other words, there has been a growing 'divergence' of per capita expenditure across Indian states in the nineties. It is worth asking to what extent these regional patterns, based on APCE data, are corroborated by regional patterns of poverty decline. One difficulty here is that there is no obvious way of 'comparing' the extent of poverty decline across states. For instance, looking at absolute changes in HCRs would seem to give an unfair 'advantage' to states that start off with high levels of poverty, and where there tends be a large number of households close to the poverty line.

The absolute decline of the rural HCR between 1993-94 and 1999-2000 was about twice as large in Bihar (7.4 percentage points) as in Punjab (3.8 points), yet over the same period APCE grew by only 6.9 per cent in Bihar compared with 20.2 per cent in Punjab, with virtually no change in distribution in either case.

The reason for this contrast is that Bihar starts off in 1993-94 with a very high proportion of households close to the poverty line, so that small increases in APCE can produce relatively large absolute declines in the headcount ratio. An alternative approach is to look at proportionate changes in HCRs or PGIs. These turn out to be highly correlated with the corresponding growth rates of APCE.

The correlation coefficient between the two series is as high as 0.91. This reflects the fact that poverty reduction is overwhelmingly driven by the growth rate of APCE, rather than by changes in distribution. From these observations, it follows that if we accept 'proportionate change in HCR' (or PGI) as an index of poverty reduction, then the broad regional patterns identified earlier for the growth rate of APCE also tend to apply to poverty reduction.

In particular:

- Most of the western and southern states (with the

important exception of Andhra Pradesh) have done comparatively well;

- The eastern region has achieved very little poverty reduction between 1993-94 and 1999-2000;
- There is a strong overall pattern of 'divergence' (states that were poorer to start with had lower rates of poverty reduction).

This reading of the evidence, however, remains somewhat tentative, since there is no compelling reason to accept the proportionate decline in HCR (or PGI) as a definitive measure of poverty decline. It may appear that the 'pace' of poverty decline in the nineties has been fairly rapid.

It is important to note, however, that the associated increases in per capita expenditure have been rather modest in most cases. For instance, the decline of 6.6 percentage points in the all- India HCR (from 29.2 per cent to 22.7 per cent) between 1993-94 and 1999-2000 is driven by an increase of only 10.9 per cent in average per capita expenditure—not exactly a spectacular improvement in living standards.

Similarly, Bihar achieved a large step in poverty reduction in the nineties, with the rural HCR coming down from 49 per cent to 41 per cent. Yet, average APCE in rural Bihar increased by only 7 per cent between 1993-94 and 1999-2000. Why are small increases in APCE associated with substantial declines in poverty indexes?

It is tempting to answer that the distribution of consumer expenditure must have improved in the nineties. However, this is not the case: indeed economic inequality has increased rather than decreased in the nineties.

The correct answer relates to the 'density effect': when many poor households are close to the poverty line, modest increases in APCE can produce substantial declines in standard poverty indexes.

One reason for drawing attention to this is that the official poverty estimates have sometimes been used to claim that the nineties have been a period of spectacular achievements in poverty reduction. In fact, when the relevant adjustments are made, and the poverty indexes are read together with the information on APCE growth, poverty reduction in the nineties appears to be more or less in line with previous rates of progress.

FURTHER EVIDENCE

National Accounts Statistics

There has been much discussion of the consistency between National Sample Survey data and the 'national accounts' published by the Central Statistical Organisation (CSO). The latter include estimates of 'private final consumer expenditure', which is frequently compared with NSS estimates of 'household consumption expenditure'.

Over time, the CSO estimates have tended to grow faster than the NSS estimates, leading some commentators to question the reliability of National Sample Survey data. It is important to note that these two notions of 'consumer expenditure' are not exactly the same, and also that there are major methodological differences between the two sources. The NSS figures are direct estimates of household consumption expenditure. The CSO figures include several items of expenditure that are not collected in the NSS surveys; examples are expenditures by non-profit entreprises, as well as imputed rent by owner occupiers and 'financial intermediation services indirectly measured' (the last item is essentially the net interest earned by financial intermediaries, which is counted as expenditures on intermediation services by households).

Who quote a recent cross-validation study by the National Accounts Department, the last two items account for 22 per cent of the difference in levels between CSO and NSS estimates of consumer expenditure. Further, the CSO estimates are 'residual' figures, obtained after subtracting other items from the national product. Leaving aside these comparability issues, there is indeed a gap between the CSO-based and NSS-based growth rates of consumer expenditure. The per-capita consumer expenditure has grown at much the same rate as per capita GDP between 1993-94 and 1999-2000—about 3.5 per cent per year in real terms. The corresponding NSS-based estimate associated with our 'adjusted' APCE figures is around 2 per cent. This is quite different from the situation that prevailed prior to the 55th Round, when consumer expenditure was hardly growing at all just as to the NSS 'thin rounds' but galloping forward just as to the CSO data.

Today, in the light of more recent estimates, the discrepancy looks much smaller. That discrepancy calls for further scrutiny and resolution, but meanwhile, it can hardly be regarded as an indictment of National Sample Survey data. For one thing, the reference categories are not the same. For another, there is no reason to believe that the CSO estimates are more accurate than the NSS estimates; indeed the cross-validation exercise raised serious questions about a number of the consumption categories in the CSO data.

Agricultural Wages

Agricultural wages provide an important source of further information on poverty. There are, in fact, two ways of thinking about the relevance of this information. First, real agricultural wages are highly correlated with standard poverty indexes such as headcount ratios: where poverty is higher, wages tend to be lower, and vice versa. Based on this statistical association, real wages can be used to provide some information about other poverty indexes.

Second, it is also possible to think about the real wage as a rough poverty indicator in its own right. The idea is that, if the labour market is competitive (at least on the supply side), then the real wage measures the 'reservation wage', i e, the lowest wage at which labourers are prepared to work. This has direct evidential value as an indication of the deprived circumstances in which people live (the more desperate people are, the lower the reservation wage), independently of the indirect evidential value arising from the statistical association between real wages and standard poverty indexes such as the headcount ratio. The data initially come in the form of districtspecific money wages. These are typically aggregated using the numbers of agricultural labourers in different districts as weights, and deflated using the Consumer Price

Index for Agricultural Labourers (CPIAL). The quality of this information is not entirely clear, but available evidence suggests that it is adequate for the purpose of broad comparisons. Real agricultural wages in different states are highly correlated with expenditure-based poverty indexes.

The main 'outlier' is Kerala, where real wages are far above the 'regression line'; it seems that the power of labour unions in Kerala has raised agricultural wages well above the level found in any other Indian states, but that this does not translate into a correspondingly low level of rural poverty, possibly because high wages are partly offset by high unemployment, or because other determinants of rural poverty are also at work.

In 1999-2000, the correlation coefficient between real wages and headcount ratios in different states was 0.79 in absolute value, rising to 0.91 if Kerala is excluded. In 1993-94, the correlation coefficient was 0.87 in absolute value, with or without Kerala. Interestingly, if 'official' HCRs are used instead of our adjusted HCRs, the correlation coefficients come down quite sharply (e g, from 0.91 to 0.73 in 1999-2000 and from 0.87 to 0.54 in 1993-94, without Kerala in both cases).

This can be tentatively regarded as a further indication of the plausibility of the proposed adjustments. Given the close association between real wages and rural poverty, the growth rates of real wages over time provide useful supplementary evidence on poverty trends. Real agricultural wages were growing at about 5 per cent per year in the eighties and 2.5 per cent per year in the nineties.

Thus, real agricultural wages were growing considerably faster in the eighties than in the nineties. But even the reduced growth rate of agricultural wages in the nineties, at 2.5 per cent per year, points to significant growth of per capita expenditure among the poorer parts of the population and reinforces our earlier findings on poverty reduction. In fact, this reduced growth rate is a little higher than the growth rate of average per capita expenditure (1.5 per cent per year) that sustains our estimated declines of rural headcount ratios and headcount indexes between 1993-94 and 1999-2000.

The data on real wages also provide some independent corroboration of the state-specific patterns of poverty decline. We plot state-specific estimates of the growth rate of real agricultural wages in the nineties against the estimated proportionate decline in the headcount ratio (a very similar pattern applies to the poverty-gap index). Here the two main outliers are Punjab and Haryana, where the headcount ratio has declined sharply without a correspondingly sharp increase in real wages (indeed without any such increase, in the case of Punjab).

Leaving out these two outliers, the association between the two series is remarkably close (with a correlation coefficient of 0.88). A healthy growth of real agricultural wages appear to be a 'sufficient' condition for substantial poverty decline in rural areas: all the states where real wages have grown at more than, say, 2.5 per cent per year in the nineties have experienced a comparatively sharp reduction of the rural headcount ratio.

Conversely, in states with low rates of reduction of the headcount ratio (say, 15 per cent or less over six years), real wages have invariably grown at less than 2 per cent per year. This applies in particular to the entire eastern region (Assam, Orissa, West Bengal and Bihar) and also to Andhra Pradesh and Madhya Pradesh. Independent evidence on the growth rates of real wages has recently been presented by K Sundaram (2001a, 2001b), based on the 'employment-unemployment surveys' (EUS) of the National Sample Survey for 1993 94 and 1999-2000.

For the present purpose, these surveys are comparable. Sundaram estimates that the real earnings of agricultural labourers have grown at about 2.5 per cent per year between 1993-94 and 1999-2000. These are tentative estimates, based as they are on data for two years only. Yet it is reassuring to find that they are consistent with the AWI-based estimates.

The Employment-Unemployment Surveys

The National Sample Survey's 1993-94 and 1999-2000 employment-unemployment surveys (EUS) also include consumer expenditure data. These can be used for further scrutiny of poverty trends. This task has been undertaken in a recent document by Sundaram and Tendulkar (2002). They note that the consumption survey in the 1999-2000 EUS uses the traditional 30- day reporting period, but differs from the standard questionnaire by only asking an abbreviated set of questions.

However, the authors find that, in those cases where the questions have comparable coverage, the means from the EUS, using the traditional 30-day reporting period, are typically close to those from the 30-day questionnaire in the main consumption survey. Based on this correspondence, they argue that the 30-day questions in the main 1999-2000 survey were not much distorted by the seven-day questions that were asked alongside them.

In this version of events, the major source of incomparability between the 55th and 50th Rounds is not the contamination of the 30-day questions, but rather the revised treatment of the low frequency items, for which the reporting period was 30 days in the 50th Round and 365 days in the 55th Round. As we have already noted, the 365-day reporting period for these items pulls up the lower tail of the consumption distribution, and thus biases down the headcount ratio compared with earlier methods.

However, Sundaram and Tendulkar note that the 50th Round contained both 30-day and 365-day reporting periods for the low frequency items. Hence, by recalculating the 50th Round headcounts using the 365-day responses, they can put the 50th and 55th Rounds on a roughly comparable basis. When they do this, they find that, in both rural and urban sectors, they can confirm a little more than three-quarters of the official decline in the headcount ratios between the two rounds.

These calculations are not identical to our first-step adjustments but they are close enough to inspire some confidence that both sets of results are in the right range. To sum up, the all-India poverty indexes presented earlier in this document are broadly consistent with independent evidence from the national accounts statistics and the employment-unemployment surveys, as well as with related information on agricultural wages. There is also some congruence between the interstate contrasts emerging from NSS data and independent information on state-specific growth rates of 'state domestic product' and real agricultural wages. The combined evidence from these different sources is fairly strong, even though each individual source has significant limitations.

ECONOMIC INEQUALITY IN THE NINETIES

Growth, Poverty and Inequality

It is possible to think about poverty decline, as captured by standard poverty indexes, in terms of two distinct components: a growth component and a distribution component. The growth component reflects the increase of average per capita expenditure.

The distribution component captures any change that may take place in the distribution of per capita expenditure over households. This decomposition exercise is pursued with reference to the headcount ratio (very similar results apply to the poverty-gap index). The first column repeats the headcount ratio for 1993-94.

The second column (labelled 'derivative with respect to growth') shows our estimate of the percentage-point reduction in HCR associated with a distribution- neutral, 1 per cent increase in APCE in the relevant state. In rural Andhra Pradesh a 1 per cent increase in APCE in 1993-94, with no change in distribution, would have led to a decline of 0.9 percentage points in the rural headcount ratio.

This derivative depends positively on the fraction of people who are at or near the poverty line, which is typically larger in the poorer states. The 1.27 in rural Assam to -0.15 in urban Jammu and Kashmir. If we multiply the second column (the derivative with respect to growth) by the third column (the amount of growth), we get an estimate of the amount of poverty reduction that we would expect from growth alone, in the absence of any change in the shape of the distribution. This is an approximation, because the derivative is likely to change as the headcount ratio falls. In column 4, we report a more precise calculation: an estimate of what the headcount ratio would have been in 1999-2000 if the distributions of consumption in each state were identical to those in 1993-94, but had been shifted upwards by the amount of growth in real per capita expenditure that actually took place. This can be readily calculated by reducing the 1993-94 poverty lines by the amount of growth, and re-estimating the headcount ratios from these adjusted lines and the 1993-94 expenditure data.

These hypothetical changes can then be compared with the actual reductions in the headcount ratios, shown in the final column. The difference between these last two columns is the change in the headcount ratio that is attributable to changes in the shape of the consumption distribution. It is important to note that the last two columns are highly correlated.

The correlation coefficients across the states are 0.97 (rural) and 0.93 (urban), so that growth alone can predict much of the cross-state pattern of reduction in HCRs. Nevertheless, the estimates are far from identical. In particular, the all-India calculations show that 'growth alone' would have reduced the poverty rate by more than actually happened, implying that there was an increase in inequality that offset some of the effects of growth, or put differently, that APCE growth among the poor was less than the average.

These inequality effects vary somewhat from state to state and are much weaker in rural than in urban areas. In urban India, increasing inequality moderated the decline in the headcount ratio in all states except Delhi, Maharashtra, and Jammu and Kashmir. In some cases, such as urban Kerala and Madhya Pradesh, the 'moderating effect' is pronounced, with actual rates of reduction only a little over half those predicted by the growth in the mean.

For the urban sector as a whole, the actual decline in the HCR is one and a half points lower (5.9 versus 7.4 per cent) than would have been the case had growth been equally distributed within each state. This estimate, which is the population-weighted average of the corresponding numbers for each state, calculates what would have happened if each household in each state had experienced the average growth for that state. An alternative, and equally interesting, counterfactual is what would have happened if, between 1993-94 and 1999-2000, each household in the country had experienced the countrywide growth rate of 10.9 per cent. Such a calculation yields an all-India HCR of 21.4 per cent (for rural and urban areas combined), compared with an actual all-India HCR of 22.7 per cent based on the 55th Round. In other words, the all-India HCR in 1999-2000 was 1.3 percentage points higher than it would have been (with the same growth rate of APCE) in the absence of any increase in inequality.

Aspects of Rising Inequality

Three aspects of rising economic inequality in the nineties have come up so far in our story. First, we found strong evidence of 'divergence' in per capita consumption across states. Second, our estimates of the growth rates of per capita expenditure between 1993-94 and 1999- 2000 point to a significant increase in rural-urban inequalities at the all- India level, and also in most individual states.

Third, the decomposition exercise in the preceding part shows that rising inequality within states, particularly in the urban sector, has moderated the effects of growth on poverty reduction. We show the logarithm of the difference of the arithmetic and geometric means (approximately the fraction by which the arithmetic mean exceeds the geometric mean), as well as the variance of the logarithm of per capita expenditure.

The correction for questionnaire design is critical for understanding what has been happening. The direct use of the unit record data in the 55th Round, with no adjustment, shows a substantial reduction in inequality within the rural sectors of most states, with little or no increase in the urban sectors. With the correction, we see that within-state rural inequality has not fallen, and that there have been marked increases in within-state urban inequality. We suspect that the main reason why the unadjusted data are so misleading in this context is the change from 30 to 365 days in the reporting period for the low frequency items (durable goods, clothing and footwear, and institutional medical and educational expenditures). The longer reporting period actually reduces the mean expenditures on those items, but because a much larger fraction of people report something over the longer reporting period, the bottom tail of the consumption distribution is pulled up, and both inequality and poverty are reduced.

Whether 365- days are a better or worse reporting period than 30-days could be argued either way, but the main point here is that the 55th and 50th Rounds are not comparable, and that the former artificially shows too little inequality compared with the latter. Once the corrections are made, we see that, in addition to increasing inequality between states, there has been a marked increase in consumption inequality within the urban sector of nearly all states. Two further pieces of evidence are worth mentioning in this context.

First, our findings on rising economic inequality within the urban sector are consistent with recent work by Banerjee and Piketty (2001), who use income tax records to document very large increases in income among the very highest income earners. They show that, in the 1990s, real incomes among the top one per cent of income earners increased by a half in real terms, while those of the top 1 per cent of 1 per cent increased by a factor of three in real terms.

Second, it is interesting to compare the growth rate of real wages for agricultural labourers with that of public sector salaries. As we saw earlier, real agricultural wages have grown at 2.5 per cent or so in the nineties. Public sector salaries, for their part, have grown at almost 5 per cent per year during the same period. Given that public-sector employees tend to be much better off than agricultural labourers, this can be taken as an instance of rising economic disparities between different occupation groups.

Since agricultural labourers and public sector employees typically reside in rural and urban areas, respectively, this finding may just be another side of the coin of rising ruralurban disparities. Even then, it strengthens the evidence presented earlier on aspects of rising economic inequality in the nineties.

To sum up, except for the absence of clear evidence of rising intra-rural inequality within states, we find strong indications of a pervasive increase in economic inequality in the nineties. This is a new development in the Indian economy: until 1993-94, the all-India Gini coefficients of per capita consumer expenditure in rural and urban areas were fairly stable. Further, it is worth noting that the rate of increase of economic inequality in the nineties is far from negligible.

For instance, the compounding of interstate 'divergence' and rising rural-urban disparities produces very sharp contrasts in APCE growth between the rural sectors of the slow-growing states and the urban sectors of the fast-growing states.

This is further compounded by the accentuation of intra-urban inequality, which is itself quite substantial, bearing in mind that the change is measured over a short period of six years. It might be argued that a temporary increase in economic inequality is to be expected in a liberalising economy, and that this trend is likely to be short-lived. Proponents of the 'Kuznets curve' may even expect it to be reversed in due course.

However, China's experience of sharp and sustained increase in economic inequality over a period of more than 20 years, after market-oriented economic reforms were initiated in the late 1970s, does not inspire much confidence in this prognosis. It is, in fact, an important pointer to the possibility of further accentuation of economic disparities in India in the near future.

QUALIFICATIONS AND CONCERNS

Food Consumption

There have been major changes in India's food economy in the nineties. The eighties were a period of healthy growth in agricultural output, food production, and real agricultural wages. During the nineties, however, productivity increases slowed down in many states. The quantity index of agricultural production grew at a lame 2 per cent per year or so. The growth of real agricultural wages slowed down considerably. And cereal production barely kept pace with population growth. The virtual stagnation of per capita cereal production in the nineties has been accompanied by a gradual switch from net imports to net exports, and also by a massive accumulation of public stocks. Correspondingly, there has been no increase in estimated per capita 'net availability' of cereals. If anything, net availability declined a little, from a peak of about 450 grams per person per day in 1990 to 420 grams or so at the end of the nineties.

This is consistent with independent evidence, from National Sample Survey data, of a decline in per capita cereal consumption in the nineties. Between 1993-94 and 1999- 2000, for instance, average cereal consumption per capita declined from 13.5 kg per month to 12.7 kg per month in rural areas, and from 10.6 to 10.4 kg per month in urban areas. This comparison is based on the 'uncorrected' 55th Round data, and the 'true' decline may be larger still, given the changes in questionnaire design.

The reduction of cereal consumption in the nineties may seem inconsistent with the notion that poverty has declined during the same period. Indeed, this pattern has been widely invoked as evidence of 'impoverishment' in the nineties. If cereal consumption is declining, how can poverty be declining? It is worth noting, however, that the decline of cereal consumption is not new.

A similar decline took place during the seventies and eighties, when poverty was certainly declining. Hanchate and Dyson's (2000) recent comparison of rural food consumption patterns in 1973-74 and 1993-94 sheds some useful light on this matter. As the authors show, during this period per capita cereal consumption in rural areas declined quite sharply on average (from 15.8 to 13.6 kgs per person per month), but rose among the poorest households.

The decline in the average is driven by reduced consumption among the higher expenditure groups. The average decline is unlikely to be driven by changes in relative prices; indeed, there has been little change in food prices, relative to other prices, in the intervening period. Instead, this pattern appears to reflect a substitution away from cereals to other food items as incomes rise (at least beyond a certain threshold).

The consumption of 'superior' food items such as vegetables, milk, fruit, fish and meat did rise quite sharply over the same period, across all expenditure groups. Seen in this light, the decline of average cereal consumption may not be a matter of concern *per se*. Indeed, average cereal consumption is inversely related to per capita income across countries (*e.g.*, it is lower in China than in India, and even lower in the United States), and the same applies across states within India (e g, cereal consumption is higher in Bihar or Orissa than in Punjab or Haryana).

Food intake data collected by the National Nutrition Monitoring Bureau (NNMB) shed further light on this issue. Aside from detailed information on food intake, the NNMB surveys include rough estimates of household incomes. The relation between per-capita income and food intake, for different types of food.

The substitution from cereals towards other food items with rising per-capita income emerges quite clearly. This pattern, if confirmed, would fit quite well with the data on change over time. It also implies that the decline of average cereal consumption in the nineties is not inconsistent with our earlier findings on poverty decline.

Localised Impoverishment and Hidden Costs

The overall decline of poverty in the nineties does not rule out the possibility of impoverishment among specific regions or social groups. That possibility, of course, is not new, but it is worth asking whether its scope has expanded during the last decade.

As the economy gives greater room to market forces, uncertainty and inequality often increase, possibly leading to enhanced economic insecurity among those who are not in a position to benefit from the new opportunities, or whose livelihoods are threatened by the changes in the economy.

The increase of economic inequality in the nineties, noted earlier, suggests that tendencies of this kind may well be at work in India today.

Adverse trends in living standards could take several distinct forms, including:

- Impoverishment among specific regions or social groups,
- Heightened uncertainty in general, and
- Growing 'hidden costs' of economic development.

In connection with the first point, we have already noted that some of the poorer states, notably Orissa and Assam, have not fared well at all in the nineties. It is quite possible that the poorer regions within these states have done even worse, to the point of absolute impoverishment for substantial parts of the population. In the case of Orissa, there is some independent evidence of localised impoverishment in the poorer districts, due inter alia to the destruction of the local environmental base and to the dismal failure of state-sponsored development programmes. Similarly, the overall improvement of living standards may hide instances of impoverishment among specific occupation groups.

The nineties have been a period of rapid structural change in the Indian economy, leading in some cases to considerable disruption of earlier livelihood patterns. Examples include a deep recession in the powerloom sector, a serious crisis in the edible oil industry after import tariffs were slashed, periodic waves of bankruptcy among cotton growers, the displacement of traditional fishing by commercial shrimp farms, and a number of sectoral crises associated with the abrupt lifting of quantitative restrictions on imports in mid-2001. The destruction of local environmental resources is another common cause of disrupted livelihoods in many areas. A related issue is the possibility of 'hidden hardships' associated with recent patterns of economic development. There is much evidence that, in many of the poorer regions of India, further impoverishment has been avoided mainly through seasonal labour migration. The latter often entails significant social costs that are poorly captured, if at all, in standard poverty indexes or for that matter in the other social indicators examined in this document. Examples of such costs include irregular school attendance, the spread of HIV/AIDS, the disruption of family life, and rising urban congestion. Similarly, involuntary displacement of persons affected by large development projects such as dams and mines tends to have enormous human costs.

These, again, are largely hidden from view in income-based analyses of poverty. In fact, the incomes of displaced persons often rise (with 'cash compensation') even as their lives are being shattered. The 'informalisation' of labour markets is another example of economic change with substantial hidden costs (*e.g.*, longer working hours, higher insecurity, lower status, and deteriorating work conditions).

These issues are not new, but it is important to acknowledge the possibility that the hidden costs of economic growth have intensified in the nineties. This acknowledgement helps to reconcile the survey-based evidence reviewed earlier with widespread media reports, in recent years, of sectoral economic crises and localised impoverishment. This issue calls for further scrutiny, based on more focused analysis of survey data as well as on micro-studies.

The 'Thin' Rounds: An Unresolved Puzzle?

We have so far said very little about the 'thin' rounds, and the poverty estimates that can be calculated from them. The recent thin rounds, from the 51st through the 54th Round, generate poverty estimates that are hard to reconcile with the quinquennial 'thick' rounds. If we were to connect up these points with the official HCR estimates, we would get a series in which poverty rose between 1993-94 and 1994-95, fell from 1994-95 to the end of 1997, rose very sharply in the first half of 1998, and then fell with extraordinary rapidity in 1999- 2000.

As we have seen, the official estimate for 1999-2000 is too low, and the last thin round, the 54th Round, ran for only the first six months of 1998, and may therefore not be fully comparable with other rounds. Even so, and with due allowance for corrections, it is very hard to integrate the poverty estimates based on the thin rounds with the picture that emerges from the thick rounds as well as from other sources surveyed in this document. The story is further complicated by the fact that these thin rounds were run in two versions, one of which resembled the standard questionnaire up to and including the 50th Round, and one of which—the experimental questionnaire—had different reporting periods for different goods.

Headcount ratios based on the experimental questionnaire are lower than those from the standard questionnaire, because the experimental questionnaire generated higher reports of per capita expenditure.

However, they also show rising HCRs from the 52nd through the 54th Rounds, and the increase continues into the 55th Round if we use comparable reporting periods from that round. Based on the experimental questionnaire, a case could be made that the all-India HCR has been rising since 1995-96. As we have seen, there are good grounds for distrusting the experimental questionnaire in the 55th Round, because of the juxtaposition of the seven-day recall and 30-day recall data for food-pan and tobacco.

Quite likely, the 'reconciliation effect' pulled down the estimates of per capita expenditure from the experimental questionnaire, thus exaggerating poverty by this count. Even so, if poverty were genuinely falling, there is no obvious explanation why the experimental questionnaire should show a rise in poverty from 1995 through 1998. The Planning Commission has never endorsed poverty counts from the thin rounds. In part, this has been because of the smaller sample sizes.

The Planning Commission needs estimates of HCRs, not just for all-India, but for individual states, and the thin rounds are not large enough to support accurate estimates for some of the smaller (of the major) states. But inadequate sample size generates variance, not bias, and in any case, the thin round sample sizes are perfectly adequate to generate accurate estimates for the all- India HCRs. There are other differences between thick and thin rounds. For example, the sampling frame for the 51st, 53rd, and 54th Rounds was not the census of population, but the 'economic' census. In the population census, each household is asked if it has a family business or enterprise, and only such households are included in the first-stage sampling from the economic census when 'first-stage units' are drawn with probability proportional to size.

This means that a village with few or no such households has only a small or no chance of being selected as a first-stage unit. Even so, when the team reaches the village, all households are listed and have a chance of being in the sample, so it is unclear that this choice of frame makes much difference. Indeed, comparison of various socioeconomic indicators (e g, literacy rates, years of schooling, landholding, or family size) from the surveys suggests no obvious breaks between the 51st and 53rd Rounds on the one hand, and the 52nd Round (which used the population census) on the other. Conversations with NSS and Planning Commission staff sometimes suggest that there may be other (non-documented) differences in the sampling structure of the thin rounds.

Certainly, a tabulation of the population sizes of the first-stage units shows that the 52nd Round contained relatively few large units compared with the 51st, 53rd, 54th, and 55th rounds; this is a different issue from the use of the economic rather than population census (both the 52nd and 55th Rounds use the latter), and the finding suggests that the first-stage units in the 52nd Round were selected differently from other rounds in some way that is not documented.

Moreover, the measurement of consumption is not the main purpose of any of these thin rounds, all of which have some other objective, so it is possible that consumption is not so fully or carefully collected as in the quinquennial rounds. In short, there are grounds for scepticism about the validity of the thin rounds for poverty estimation purposes, and this is all the more so if we remember that aside from indicating no poverty decline in the late nineties, the thin rounds also suggest that average per capita expenditure was stagnating during that period—something that is very hard to reconcile with other evidence. Having said this, we have not been able to identify any 'smoking gun' that would point to a specific problem with any of these rounds and explain their apparently anomalous poverty estimates. Until that puzzle is resolved, we see the evidence from the thin rounds as casting a shadow of doubt over the interpretation of the poverty estimates presented earlier in this document. Perhaps the thin rounds in the next five years will offer some useful clues.

BEYOND POVERTY INDEXES

The decline of poverty in the nineties, as captured in the indicators examined so far, can be seen as an example of continued progress during that period. Whether the rate of progress has been faster or slower than in the eighties is difficult to say, and the answer is likely to depend on how the rate of progress is measured. There is, at any rate, no obvious pattern of "acceleration" or 'slowdown' in this respect.

It is important to supplement the evidence reviewed so far, which essentially relates to purchasing power, with other indicators of well-being relating, for instance to educational achievements, life expectancy, nutritional levels, crime rates, and various aspects of social inequality. This broader perspective reveals that social progress in the nineties has followed very diverse patterns, ranging from accelerated progress in some fields to slowdown and even regression in other respects.

Simple measures of the progress of different social indicators in the nineties are compared with the corresponding achievements in the eighties. Elementary education provides an interesting example of accelerated progress in the nineties. This trend is evident not only from census data on literacy rates, but also from National Family Health Survey data on school participation. School participation among girls aged 6-14 jumped from 59 per cent to 74 per cent between 1992-93 and 1998-99.

The regional patterns are also instructive. It is particularly interesting to note evidence of rapid progress in Madhya Pradesh and Rajasthan, demarcating them clearly from Bihar and Uttar Pradesh, the other two members of the so-called

BIMARU set. There is an important pointer here to the relation between public action and social achievements. Indeed, Madhya Pradesh and Rajasthan are two states where there have been many interesting initiatives in the field of elementary education in the nineties (on the part of government as well as non-government institutions), in contrast with Bihar and Uttar Pradesh where schooling matters continue to be highly neglected.

The fact the literacy rates and school participation have surged in the more 'active' states is an encouraging indication of the possibility of effective public intervention in this field. Turning to instances of 'slowdown', we have already referred to the slackening of the growth rate of real agricultural wages in the nineties. Another important example is the slowdown of infant mortality decline. During the eighties, India achieved a reduction of 30 per cent in the infant mortality rate—from 114 deaths per 1,000 live births in 1980 to 80 per 1,000 in 1990. During the nineties, however, the infant mortality rate declined by only 12.5 per cent—from 80 to 70. In fact, in the second half of the nineties, India's infant mortality rate has remained virtually unchanged.

In some states, notably Rajasthan, the infant mortality rate has stagnated for as long as 10 years. These worrying trends have received astonishingly little attention in policy debates, and even in the debate on 'poverty in the nineties'. Finally, there have also been some areas of 'regression' in the nineties. The increase of economic inequality, discussed earlier, can be seen in those terms. Given the adverse social consequences of economic inequality (ranging from elitist biases in public policy to the reinforcement of other types of inequality), this accentuation of economic disparities is not a trivial matter. Another example of adverse development in the nineties is the decline in the female-male ratio among children, from 945 girls per 1,000 boys (in the 0-6 age group) in 1991 to 927 girls per 1,000 boys in 2001.

This decline appears to be driven by the spread of prenatal sex-determination technology and sexselective abortion, but this does not mean that it is a 'technological' phenomenon, unrelated to other recent economic and social trends. Economic growth, in particular, may facilitate the spread of sexselective abortion, by making the use of sex-determination technology more affordable.

In this connection, it is worth noting that the largest declines of the female-male ratio among children between 1991 and 2001 occurred in five states (Gujarat, Haryana, Himachal Pradesh, Punjab and Delhi) that are relatively well-off economically, and have also experienced comparatively high rates of growth of per capita expenditure in the nineties. A detailed assessment of the progress of development indicators in the nineties is beyond the scope of this document.

However, a few general observations can be made on the basis of these illustrations. First, as noted already, poverty is not unidimensional. The poverty indexes used in the first part of this document are useful indicators of inadequate purchasing power, but on their own do not do justice to the range of deprivations we ought to be concerned with. Following on this, it is important to acknowledge that recent progress in eliminating poverty and deprivation has been quite uneven in different fields.

The debate on 'poverty in the nineties' has often overlooked this basic point. Second, this recognition is also important in assessing the relation between poverty decline and economic growth. As noted earlier, the decline of poverty in the nineties, as captured by conventional indexes such as the headcount ratio or the poverty-gap index, has been overwhelmingly driven by the growth of average per capita expenditure. From this it may seem that the reduction of poverty is mainly a question of economic growth.

However, there is an element of circularity in this argument: if poverty is defined as lack of income, it is not surprising that the growth of income plays a key role in reducing it. When the multidimensional nature of poverty is acknowledged, this relation appears in a different light. Consider child mortality as an aspect of the deprivations associated with poverty. There is, of course, a significant (negative) relation between child mortality and purchasing power. But child mortality is also strongly influenced by other factors such as educational levels, fertility rates, public health provisions (including clean water and vaccinations), and various aspects of gender relations. Looking at interstate contrasts in India, the correlation between child mortality and average per capita expenditure (or even poverty indexes) is actually quite weak.

Other factors, particularly female literacy, are often more important. Similar comments apply in the context of elementary education: the nineties have demonstrated the possibility of rapid progress in this field through public intervention, with or without rapid economic growth. In short, the standard focus on headcount ratios and other expenditurebased poverty indexes tends to foster a simplistic view of the relation between economic growth and poverty decline.

Third, it is also interesting to re-examine the issue of trends in inequality, in the light of this broader perspective. There is much evidence of rising economic inequality in the nineties, in the form of a widening rural-urban gap, enhanced interstate disparities, and also growing inequality wihin urban areas in most states. What about other types of social inequality, involving other dimensions of well-being (*e.g.*, educational levels or life expectancy) and other bases of disadvantage (*e.g.*, gender or caste)?

The decline of the female male ratio among children shows the fact that the phenomenon of rising inequality in the nineties is not confined to standard economic inequalities: 'natality inequality' between males and females is also rising. But this is not to say that inequality has risen across the board. Even within the field of gender inequality, there are changes in the other direction, such as the emergence of a substantial gender gap in life expectancy in favour of women, overturning India's long history of female disadvantage in this respect. Similarly, it is interesting to note that while economic disparities between rural and urban areas have sharply risen in the nineties, there are trends in the opposite direction as well.

The rural-urban gap in life expectancy, for instance, has declined from 10 years or so in the late 1970s to seven years or so today, and ruralurban differentials in school participation have also narrowed. Here again, the picture is more diverse (and more interesting) than it appears on the basis of purchasing-power indicators alone. Fourth, the broad approach explored here calls for a correspondingly broad reading of the causal influences underlying the identified changes.

In the debate on 'poverty in the nineties', there has been a tendency not only to view development trends in unidimensional terms, but also to attribute these trends in a somewhat mechanical manner to the economic reforms initiated around 1991. At one end of the spectrum, it has been claimed that the last decade has been a period of unprecedented improvement in living standards, thanks to liberalisation. At the other end, the nineties have been described as a period of widespread 'impoverishment', attributed to liberalisation.

Clearly, these readings fail to do justice to the diversity of recent trends. But in addition, they ignore the diversity of causal influences that have a bearing on these trends. The accelerated progress of elementary education in the nineties, for instance, has little to do with liberalisation, and the same applies to the slowdown of infant mortality decline, not to speak of the decline of the female-male ratio among children. Much else than liberalisation has happened in the nineties, and while issues of economic reform are of course extremely important, so are other aspects of economic and social policy.

CONCLUDING REMARKS

A number of useful sessions emerge from this reexamination of the evidence on poverty and inequality in the nineties. First, there is consistent evidence of continuing poverty decline in the nineties, in terms of the 'headcount ratio'. The extent of the decline, however, remains somewhat uncertain at this time. Given the methodological changes that took place between the 50th and 55th Rounds of the National

Sample Survey, the official figures (implying a decline from 36 per cent to 26 per cent in the all-India headcount ratio between 1993-94 and 1999-2000) are, strictly speaking, invalid. We have discussed alternative estimates, based on comparable data from the two surveys. As it turns out, these adjusted estimates suggest that a large part of the poverty decline associated with official figures is 'real', rather than driven by methodological changes. While further corroboration and investigation of the adjustment procedure is required, the results have been supported by one independent study using an entirely different methodology.

Further, the adjusted figures fit reasonably well with related evidence from the national accounts statistics, the employment- unemployment surveys, and data on agricultural wages. Second, we have discussed some important limitations of the headcount ratio as an index of poverty (even within the standard expenditure-based approach), and argued for wider adoption of alternative poverty indexes such as the poverty-gap index.

The main argument for using headcount ratios is that they have good 'communication value', in so far as they are relatively easy to understand and interpret. However, this transparency is to some extent deceptive, and much caution is required in interpreting poverty trends on the basis of headcount ratios. For the purpose of the poverty comparisons examined in this document, the headcount ratio turns out to be no less informative than the poverty-gap index. Yet it was important to calculate the PGIs, if only to discover that this refinement does not, after all, make much difference in this particular context.

Third, growth patterns in the nineties are characterised by major regional imbalances. Broadly speaking, the western and southern states (Andhra Pradesh excluded) have tended to do comparatively well. The low growth states, for their part, form a large contiguous region in the north and east. This is a matter of concern, since the northern and eastern regions were poorer to start with. Indeed, National Sample Survey data suggest a strong pattern of inter-regional 'divergence' in average per capita expenditure (APCE): states that started off with higher APCE levels also had higher growth rates of APCE between 1993-94 and 1999-2000. In some of the poorer states, notably Assam and Orissa, there has been virtually zero growth of average per capita expenditure (and very little reduction, if any, in rural poverty) between 1993-94 and 1999-2000.

These regional patterns are at least broadly consistent with independent estimates of the growth rates of state domestic product (SDP). Fourth, the intensification of regional disparities is only one aspect of a broader pattern of increasing economic inequality in the nineties. Two other aspects are rising rural-urban disparities in per capita expenditure, and rising inequality of per capita expenditure within urban areas in most states.

Further, the real wages of agricultural labourers have increased more slowly than per capita GDP, and conversely with public sector employees, suggesting some intensification of economic inequality between occupation groups. Fifth, we have argued for assessing changes in living standards in a broader perspective, going beyond the standard focus on expenditure-based indicators.

In that broader perspective, a more diverse picture emerges, with areas of accelerated progress in the nineties as well as slowdown in other fields. For instance, there is much evidence of rapid progress in the field of elementary education, but the rate of decline of infant mortality has slowed down. These and related trends deserve greater attention than they have received so far in the debate on 'poverty in the nineties'. Sixth, the case for going beyond expenditure- based indicators applies also to the assessment of inequality. While expenditure-based data suggest rising disparities in the nineties, the same need not apply to other social indicators.

For instance, while economic disparities between rural and urban areas have increased in the nineties, there has been some narrowing of the rural-urban gap in terms of life expectancy and school participation. Finally, we have argued against reading these trends simply as evidence of the impact (positive or negative) of 'liberalisation'. For one thing, the impact of liberalisation is a 'counterfactual' question, and much depends on how the alternatives are specified. For another, much else has happened in the nineties, other than liberalisation.

The evidence we have reviewed is of much interest in its own right, independently of the liberalisation debate. Much work remains to be done in terms of identifying the causal relations underlying the trends we have identified.

6

Inequality: Caste and Class

INTRODUCTION

The normative and democratic pillars of institutions and doctrines enshrined in the Constitution of India set the agenda of post-colonial state in India in terms of abolition or at least reduction of social-inequalities. The objective of 'welfare' state was to make a modern caste-less society by reducing centuries old disabilities inflicted upon the 'depressed' and attempt to improve their lot by providing them 'reservations' and 'quotas' in education as well as job market especially in state-bureaucracy and over-sized public sector enterprises.

The Constitution of India requires the state to treat all citizens equally, without regard to birth, gender or religious belief. However, society does not function merely on the basis of formal principles. Enforcement of legal doctrines and attempt to remove social discrimination is a process entangled in the complexities of social formation. The pernicious aspects of jati, varna and class, therefore, still permeate our families, localities and political institutions. In this unit, our focus will be on various aspects of social inequality and their impact on democratic polity and political economy of development in the post-colonial state of India.

NOTION OF SOCIAL-INEQUALITY

Human societies vary in the extent to which social groups as well as individuals have unequal access to advantages. Rousseau had made a distinction between natural and social inequality. The former emerge from the unequal division of physical and mental abilities among the members of a society. The latter arise from the social entitlement of people to wealth or economic resources, political power and status regardless of potential abilities possessed by individuals. Not only economic resources of societies vary just as to the level of development and structural features of society, but also different groups tend to have differential access to these resources. Power enjoyed by the social groups also differ and offers another related social advantage.

Similarly, conventions, rules, customs and laws confer greater prestige and status on certain groups and occupations in most human societies. Hierarchy, stratification, class-divisions are notions used by anthropologists, sociologists and political scientists to describe and denote social-inequality. Anthropologists generally distinguish three types of societies in terms of social-inequality. These are classified as egalitarian, rank and class societies.

Egalitarian societies contain fair amount of equality and no social group enjoys greater access to economic resources, power or prestige. Rank societies do not have unequal access to wealth or power, but they do contain social groups that enjoy greater honour and status. A pre-literate tribal society in which social ranking is based on rules of descent and alliances belong to this category.

The complex class societies have unequal access and entitlement to economic resources, power and status. In many pre-industrial agrarian societies, access to social opportunities and status was determined by birth. The ascribed role or status of individual was assigned by virtue of factors outside his or her own control such as birth, sex, age, kinship relations, and caste. This assigned role was rationalised as divinely ordained and natural.

The estates or orders of medieval Europe were unequally ranked and this hierarchy of ranks was legally recognised and approved by religious-normative order of the society. Indian caste system was another type of validation of social hierarchy. The individual's professional or occupational role came to depend on individual effort and ability in the modern industrial and democratic society. This new role was emphasised in the political discourse of modernity and was seen as consonant with the democratic ideal. It involved an exercise of effort and choice as well as a fair deal of competition to occupy a given position. The society moved from the principle of hierarchy to stratification. Hierarchy prevailed in societies based on castes or estates and social-inequalities were legitimated as naturally given.

Stratification, on the other hand, is a feature of modern industrial societies in which inequalities do exist but are not considered as a part of natural or divine order. In this process of social change, inequality did not vanish or reduce, but changed its nature. Now class boundaries became more porous and permeable, individual mobility is possible and society's normative order is based on formal equality.

However, there is still a large area of industrial society where roles are allocated by virtue of being male or female, black or white and so on. G.D. Berreman suggests that out of 'differentiation' of persons, which is a natural and universal phenomenon, inequality or social evaluation of differences arises. He terms the behavioural expression of inequality as 'dominance' and combination of inequality and dominance is socialinequality.

Dominance and status in egalitarian societies is often negotiable and contextual whereas in ranked or inegalitarian societies, inequality is institutionalised. It is embedded in a hierarchy of statuses and is not linked to individual differences of ability. Marxists generally tend to view gradations of power and status as correlated to the distinctions of class defined by economic position and accessibility of economic entitlements. In the Weberian paradigm, however, status and power are not entirely governed by economic divisions or control over economic entitlements.

Although the term stratification reminds us of a geological image which signifies a sort of vertical layering or arrangement of social strata, social organisation is much more fluid and complex. A multiple set of factors affect a particular social formation and it is never a simple vertical or hierarchical arrangement of layers like the earth's crust. Political thinkers like Pareto, Mosca and Michels assigned primacy to power as the real source of inequality in society. Power is the ability to make others do what they do not want to do and the elite groups exercise this power as they occupy the top positions within the institutions of a given society.

Similarly, French scholar Bourdieu employs terms symbolic capital and distinction to identify social groups who enjoy more prestige and honour in society simply because they are endowed with more symbolic capital reflected in their pattern of behaviour and taste. The notion of social-capital also has similar connotations. It demonstrates how certain social groups have greater capacity to form social-relations and competence to associate with others. They indicate that differences in terms of esteem, prestige and status rather than neat economic or political hierarchy may play the dominant role in some systems of stratifications.

THE NATURE OF CASTE-INEQUALITIES IN INDIA

Caste is the most contentious issue that has fascinated and divided scholars who have wished to study this system of stratified social-hierarchy in India. There is an enormous body of academic writing and political polemic on the issue. These are basically the part of debate on the transformation of Indian society under the impact of colonialism and its administrative mechanisms.

Some argue for the continuities of pre-colonial social-structures including caste. Others stress the basic qualitative changes introduced by the colonial rulers. Louis Dumont, the French scholar and writer of a famous book on caste, Homo-Hierarchicus, constructed a textually-informed image of caste. Two opposing conceptual categories of purity and pollution are the core elements of caste-structure.

These unique core principles of caste-hierarchy are observed in scriptural formulation as well as the every-day life of all Hindus. In other words, these values separate Indians culturally from the Western civilization, making India a land of static, unchangeable, 'oriental' Brahmanical values. This notion of caste has been challenged by Nicholas Dirks and others. Dumont's notion was criticised as it failed to explain the social change, dynamism and individualistic strivings even within the traditional Indian society. Gerald Berreman pointed out that the principle of Brahmanical hierarchy was not uniformly followed by all Hindus. He also criticised the Dumontian notion that power and economic factors are distinct and epiphenomenal to caste. It has been pointed out by others that caste hierarchy is not a fixed hierarchy; rather it is context-specific and fluid and contains seeds of contestation among various castes.

Nicholas Dirks cites ethnographic and textual evidence to demonstrate that Brahmins and their texts were not so central to the social fabric of Indian life. Power relations and command over men and resources were more important. Brahmins were merely ritual specialists, often subordinate to powerful ruling families. The caste-based scriptural or Brahmanical model of traditional India was an invention of the British Orientalists and ethnographers. However, caste played a very critical role in the Indian social-reformers' and nationalists' perception of caste. It was certainly not a mere product of British imagination.

CASTE AS THE INVENTION OF COLONIAL MODERNITY

Two opposing viewpoints see caste differently. Some view it as an unchanged survival of Brahmanical traditions of India. Brahmanism represents a core civilizational value and caste is the central symbol of this value. It is the basic expression of the pre-colonial traditions of India. Contrary to this view, Nicolas Dirks, in his Castes of Mind, argues that caste is a product of colonial modernity.

By this he does not mean that caste did not exist before the advent of British. He is simply suggesting that caste became a single, unique category under the British rule that expressed and provided the sole index of understanding India. Earlier there were diverse forms of social-identity and community in India. The British reduced everything to a single explanatory category of caste. It was the colonial state and its administrators who made caste into a uniform, all-encompassing and ideologically consistent organism. They made caste a measure of all things and the most important emblem of traditions. Colonialism reconstructed cultural forms and social-institutions like caste to create a line of difference and demarcation between themselves as European modern and the colonised Asian traditional subjects.

In other words, British colonialism played a critical role in both the identification and production of Indian 'tradition'. The colonial modernity devalued the so called Indian traditions. Simultaneously, it also transformed them. Caste was recast as the spiritual essence of India that regulated and mediated the private domain. Caste-ridden Indian society was different from the European civil society because caste was opposed to the basic premises of individualism as well as the collective identity of a nation.

The salience of this pre-colonial identity and sense of loyalty could easily be used to justify the rule by the colonial modern administrators. So, it was the colonial rule of India that organised the 'social difference and deference' solely in terms of caste. The attempts to downplay or dismiss the significance of Brahmins and Brahmanical order is not in accordance with familiar historical records and persistence of caste-identities even in the contemporary Indian social life. Caste-terms and principles were certainly not in universal use in pre-colonial periods. Caste in its various manifestations and forms was also not an immutable entity.

However, starting from the Vedas and the Great Epics, from Manu and other dharmasastras, from puranas, from ritual practices, the penal system of Peshwa rulers who punished culprits just as to caste-principles, to the denunciations of anti-Brahmanical 'reformers' of all ages, everything points towards the legacy of pre-colonial times. It is true that there were also non-caste affiliations and identities such as networks of settlements connected by matrimonial alliances, trade, commerce and state service in the pre-colonial times. However, caste was also a characteristic marker of identity and a prevailing socialmetaphor. Caste was not merely a fabrication of British rulers designed to demean and subjugate Indians. It did serve the colonial interests by condemning the 'Brahmanical tyranny', colonial administration could easily justify their codes to 'civilise' and 'improve' the 'fallen people'. Moreover, strengthening of the caste-hierarchy could also act as a bulwark against anarchy.

NATURE OF CLASS INEQUALITY IN INDIA

Class societies are characterised by the horizontal division of society into strata. In Marxist terms, classes are defined by their differential access to the means of production. The dominant classes appropriate the'surplus' produced by other classes through their control of means of production, and thus exploit their labour. The actual configuration of social classes varies from one society to another.

The rise and growth of Indian social classes was organically linked to the basic structure of colonialism and bore the imprint of that association. What constitutes the dominant proprietary class in the urban-areas is marked by plurality and heterogeneity in its composition. A clear-cut demarcation along the lines of merchant, industrial and finance capital is not possible in case of India.

The Indian business classes exhibit a complex intertwir ıg of functions. Under the colonial rule, the Indian businessmen were initially relegated to small private trade, money lending and acted as agents of foreign British Capital. The British capitalists and merchants controlled the upper layer of Indian economy represented by the big joint stock companies, managing houses, banking and insurance and major exportimport firms.

Despite obstacles and constraints, the Indian capitalist class grew slowly and steadily and breached white 'collective monopoly'. With all structural constraints, colonialism also guaranteed the security of private property and sanctity of contract, the basic legal elements required for a market-led growth. The expansion of foreign trade and commercialisation eased the capital shortage and accelerated the growth of sectors where cost of raw-materials was low such as cotton textiles, sugar, leather, cement, tobacco and steel. Certain groups of Parsis, Marwaris, the Khojas, the Bhatias and Gujarati traders benefited from their collaboration with the European companies and pumped their resources into the manufacturing sector. This Indian capitalist class grew, diversified to some extent and acquired important position by 1940s. This class thrived during Independence under the government's policy of importsubstitution and quantitative controls.

The 'Public- Sector' units provided the infrastructure and the intermediate and capital goods to this 'protected' class while the public lending institutions provided it with cheap sources of finances. The assets of the biggest 20 industrial houses increased from ₹500 crores in 1851 to Rs 23,200 crores in 1986. This was the result of benefits derived from state-developed infrastructural facilities, subsidised energy inputs, cheap capital goods and long-term finance made available to these by big monopoly industrial houses under the planning. On the other hand, almost 70% of the people exist on merely subsistence level and 76.6 million agricultural labourers earn only one-tenth of what an organised sector worker in the city earns. In the 1980s, unemployment reached about 10% of total active population.

In the urban centres, the bulk of labourers are working in unorganised informal sectors. The vast army of pavement vendors, domestic servants, porters and street hawkers represent a kind of disguised urban unemployment. The class-composition in the rural areas also bears the stamp of colonialism. The older group of rural gentry, although its wings were clipped away by the British colonial regime, was retained and transformed into a kind of rentier class of landlords invested with newly defined property rights on land. This was especially true of permanently settled Zamindari areas of Bengal and Taluqdari areas of Awadh. This landlord-rentier class generally emerged from the pre-existing groups' of Zamindars and Taluqdars who had enjoyed the rights of revenuecollection under the pre-British regimes. They exercised "extra-economic" feudal coercion over their small marginal share-croppers. Since the Congress Party favoured a bureaucratic rather than mobilisational form for carrying out a gradual social transformation after Independence, the power and privileges of these semi-feudal agrarian magnates remained intact in some areas.

These classes now managed the new democratic polity. The failure to implement radical agrarian reforms meant that the availability of resources and accessibility to spaces within the new polity to the socially marginal groups remained limited. The rich farmers, however, are numerically the most important proprietary class in the rural areas. In areas outside Zamindari settled areas of Bengal, the colonial state settled land revenue with dominant cultivating groups.

A class of rich farmers emerged from these groups. They took advantage of the expanding market networks under the colonial economy and they had resources like sufficient arable land, livestock, implements and better access to credit. They also became less dependent on money lenders and they took to usury themselves. The Jat peasants of Punjab and the Upper Doab, the Vellalas in Tamilnadu, the Kanbi-Patidars of South Gujarat, the Lingayats of Karnataka and the Kamma-Reddy farmers of Andhra constituted this group.

The tenancy legislation under colonialism and after Independence initiated the process of transfer of landed resources from non-cultivating, absentee landlords to the enterprising rich farmers. Some older groups of rentier landlords also converted themselves into this class. The political clout of this class grew as it drew encouragement from state's policy of providing price-supports to agricultural produce and from liberal provisions of subsidised inputs such as water, power, fertilizers, diesel, credit and agricultural machinery.

This class is easily identifiable by the ownership of landed and other agricultural resources. In 1970s, about 20% households of the rich farmers owned about 63% of rural assets such as land, livestock, building, and implements. This disproportionate access to rural assets is combined by its control over wage labour which is used to produce a sizeable marketable surplus by this class. The other pole of rural social-structure is the world of semi-proletariat having little or no control over productive resources. The agricultural labourers are a predominant group with little or no guarantee of a regular employment, often burdened by coercive domination of rich farmers. The bureaucratic-managerial elite also constitute a significant class in India as the relatively weak capitalist class at the time of India's Independence was not in a position to completely subordinate the highly developed administrative state apparatus.

The growth of non-market mechanisms and planning in the allocation of resources and economic patronage also resulted in the expansion of bureaucracy. This class expanded in the post-colonial phase with the spreading out of education and need for professional and white-collar jobs involving new skills and expertise. This is not merely an auxiliary class of bourgeois as there are conflicts of interests between the public sector professionals and private capital. The command over knowledge, skills, tastes and networks of relationships are notable features of this class.

INTERRELATION OF CASTE AND CLASS HIERARCHIES

Caste and class point towards inequality and hierarchy. In both the cases, however, the principle of organisation differs. The core features of caste are: endogamy or marriage within caste, occupational differentiation and hereditary specialisation of occupations, notion of pollution and a ritual hierarchy in which Brahmins are generally at the top. Classes, on the other hand, broadly refer to economic basis of ownership or non-ownership relation to the means of production. But how does caste and class correlate to each other? Classes are sub-divided in terms of types of ownership and control of economic resources and the type of services contributed to the process of production.

The Brahmanical ritual hierarchy of the caste is also not universally applicable and upheld by all. In many cases, ritual hierarchy is only contextual. The prosperous Jats in North

India enjoy social and political dominance without equivalent ritual status. In most popular renditions of caste, hierarchy alone is emphasised and that too from Brahmanical point of view. Sometimes, however, caste works as a discrete community, without hierarchical relationship to other segments of society. Our conceptual categories do not always recapture the existing social reality.

For instance, a conceptual distinction is often made between sharecroppers and agricultural labourers. In actual life, however, there is a high degree of overlap and they do not constitute discrete entities. Similar overlap is found in the rentier-landlord and cultivator-owner categories. The picture becomes hazier when we turn to caste-class configuration.

Caste and class resemble each other in certain respects and differ in others. Castes constitute the status groups or communities that can be defined in terms of ownership of property, occupation and style of life. Social honour is closely linked to ritual values in this closed system. Class positions also tend to be associated with social honour; however, they are defined more in terms of ownership or non-ownership of means of production.

The classes are much more open and fluid and have scope of individual upward social mobility. In caste system, only an entire segment can move upward, and hence, the mobility is much slower. Although there is considerable divergence between the hierarchy of caste and that of class, the top and bottom segments of the class system are largely subsumed under the caste structure. The upper castes own means of production and act as rentiers.

The landless agrarian proletarian coincides with the lower castes or dalits who provide labour services for the rentier upper caste people as well as rich prosperous farmers of intermediate level. At the intermediate level, articulation of class-identities is more complex. The process of differentiation of communities dislocates class-relations from the caste-structure. If caste and class show a fair degree of overlap at the top and bottom level and in some cases appear almost co-terminus, the picture is quite ambiguous at the intermediate level of caste hierarchy. Similarly, the processes of modernisation especially urbanisation, acquisition of education and new skills act as the forces of dislocation that puncture the forces of social inertia and modify caste-rigidity.

SOCIAL INEQUALITIES, DEVELOPMENT AND PARTICIPATORY POLITICS

If social inequalities are so deeply entrenched, then how do they affect the developmental process and participation of deprived parts of society in a democratic polity? This key question has been answered in different ways. Kothari, while analysing the intrusions of caste into politics and politics into caste, distinguishes three stages in the progression of political modernisation after Independence. In the first stage, he says the struggle for political power was limited to the entrenched and the ascendant castes.

In the second phase, competitions within these castes for power led to factionalism and in the third stage, lower castes have been mobilised and are asserting themselves in the political domain. In his words "It is not-politics that gets caste-ridden; it is the caste that gets politicised". With the extension of franchise in the post-colonial India, each social group and sub-group got mobilised for a share in the developmental process and competed for positions in the state-bureaucracy. The Indian polity is, thus, governed both by vertical mobilisation by the dominant castes and horisontal alliances in the name of jati and varna.

The political parties exacerbate the existing cleavages in a developing society like India. The salience of primordial ties of kinship, caste and community play significant role in hindering the establishment of civil society. Moreover, there is never a set chronology of mobilisation and political modernisation, especially any pre-ordained and unconditional progression along a set path. In the rural hinterlands, cleavages of caste and community and articulation of kinship and territorial affinities work against implementation of a piece of redistributive land-reforms. The rich prosperous farmers use the existing social networks in the multi-class agrarian mobilisation in the electoral arena to mobilise and harness marginal and small farmers for their own economic interests such as lower taxes, higher prices for agricultural produce, better subsidies and cheaper credit facilities.

So, despite the egalitarian ideal of post-colonial Indian state, there are still disproportionate access to resources, power and entitlements between different social classes and castes. The relationships between the upper and lower castes in the rural areas are still governed by the ideology of caste. Professionalisation and specialisation of modern service sector in the post-colonial Indian society has increased the role of formal education, technical skills and training; 'family' and not caste plays critical role in the social reproduction of inequality, especially in urban areas.

However, it is still a debatable point whether the increasing bureaucratisation of professional activities *per se* enhances the chances of social mobility and equality of opportunities. Although, there may be no legal barriers to entry into new occupation, the unequal distribution of life chances, status and power on the grounds of birth determine the social and political trajectories that accord positions, ranks and power to the individuals.

The establishment of a formal democracy in itself is no guarantee that all citizens will enjoy equal access and participation in the political processes. Political privileges are retained and ingrained in many non-elective institutions, the civil bureaucracy and the police in particular. They protect the interests of the dominant proprietary classes and the upper castes.

The lower castes and classes are not yet sufficiently empowered to shape and mould the political processes or the state's social and economic policies. The powerful landed magnates of upper castes in the countryside and the industrial and business classes of urban rich make use of authoritarian streak inherent in the non-elective institutions to deny genuine democratisation of polity. The apparent assertion of their rights and mobilising capacity by the backwards and scheduled castes is used by the crafty politicians to augment their power and wealth. Such mobilisations, thus serve the interests of a spoils system and a thoroughly corrupt and inefficient bureaucracy instead of articulating a programme of equitable development and social empowerment.

Apart from other institutional constraints, the failure of democracy to grant substantive democratic rights and deliver the promise of redistributive justice is rooted in the class and caste-based inequalities in India. Dreze found evidence of subtle forms of deprivation in the rural areas of the Eastern U.P. in terms of accessibility of the disadvantaged groups to schooling, health services and exclusion of marginal parts of population from effective participation in the political processes.

7

Social Determinants of Health Inequalities

Social inequality refers to a situation in which individuals in a society do not have equal social status. Areas of potential social inequality include voting rights, freedom of speech and assembly, the extent of property rights and access to education, health care, quality housing and other social goods.

CAUSES

Social inequality is different from economic inequality, though the two are linked. Economic inequality refers to disparities in the distribution of economic assets and income. While economic inequality is caused by the unequal distribution of wealth, social inequality exists because the lack of wealth in certain areas prohibits these people from obtaining the same housing, health care, etc. as the wealthy, in societies where access to these social goods depends on wealth.

Social inequality is linked to racial inequality and wealth inequality. The way people behave socially, through racism and other forms of discrimination, tends to trickle down and affect the opportunities and wealth individuals can generate for themselves. Thomas M. Shapiro, The Hidden Cost of Being African American, in which he tries to demonstrate the level of inequality on the "playing field for blacks and whites". One example he presents reports how a black family was denied a bank loan to use for housing, while a white family was approved. As being a homeowner is an important method in acquiring wealth, this situation created fewer opportunities for the black family to acquire wealth, producing social inequality.

OBESITY, DIETS, AND SOCIAL INEQUALITIES

Rising rates of obesity in industrialized societies have been blamed on increased consumption of sweetened beverages and energy-dense foods. Published research has variously linked rising obesity rates in the United States to the consumption of refined grains, added sugars, added fats, snacks, beverages, fast foods, and eating away from home. One way to change dietary behaviours is by modifying the obesogenic food environment. Reducing consumer access to palatable sweet and high-fat foods seems to be the main goal of many nutrition policies and programmes .

Minorities and the poor are clearly at a disadvantage when it comes to the adoption of healthier eating habits. Simply put, fats and sweets cost less, whereas many healthier foods cost more. Researchers have shown that low-income neighbourhoods attract more fast-food outlets and convenience stores as opposed to full-service supermarkets and grocery stores. By contrast, more affluent areas generally have access to better restaurants, fresher produce, and more opportunities for physical activity.

Such studies merely demonstrate that socioeconomic factors, including inequitable access to healthy foods, have a profound effect on weight and health. It is economic deprivation that is obesogenic, and one key predictor of weight gain may be low diet cost. The obesity debate in the United States has steered clear of the complex issue of social class. Instead, much time has been spent on genetics, physiology, race/ethnicity, personal responsibility, and freedom of choice. Some in public health nutrition have adopted the view that most Americans could follow a healthy diet but simply choose not to. Attempts to improve population dietary habits have therefore emphasized the food-choice behaviour of individuals. The emphasis has been on psychosocial factors, self-efficacy, and readiness to change. The unspoken assumption has been that healthful foods are inexpensive and that all American households, regardless of income, have access to a healthy diet. It may be time to point out that obesity is an economic issue. Many segments of society have limited resources and are unable to resist powerful economic forces that are largely beyond their control. Americans spend the lowest proportion of disposable income on food (~12%) and have the lowest-cost food supply in the world. Until recently, no one seriously questioned the benefits of low-cost foods or indeed the freedom to choose. Official recommendations and guidelines, including the 2005 Dietary Guidelines for Americans, exhorted consumers to "choose" healthful diets as opposed to unhealthful ones.

Other documents recommended that obese consumers replace white bread, bologna, and mayonnaise with fresh salads, mangos, and star fruit. The rapid rise in food prices has helped demonstrate that healthier diets are no longer merely a matter of choice. Food choices are made on the basis of taste, cost, convenience, and, to a lesser extent, healthfulness and variety. Refined grains, added sugars, and added fats are good tasting, readily accessible, and inexpensive.

Lowcost foods and low-cost diets tend to be energy dense and nutrient poor. On one hand they are associated with overeating; on the other hand they are preferentially selected by the low-income consumer. The low cost and high palatability of energy-dense foods—mainly sugars and fats—along with the easy access to such foods can help explain why the highest obesity rates are found among the most disadvantaged groups. The key variable, however, is not the macronutrient composition of the diet; rather, what may predict obesity is low diet cost.

POVERTY AND OBESITY ARE LINKED

The rates of obesity and type 2 diabetes in the United States follow a socioeconomic gradient, with the highest rates observed among racial/ethnic minorities and the poor. At the individual level, obesity rates are linked to low income, low education, minority status, and a higher incidence of poverty. Among women, higher obesity rates tend to be associated with low incomes and low education; the association of obesity with low socioeconomic status has been less consistent among men. At the environmental level, obesity rates are higher in lower income neighbourhoods, legislative districts, and states. 8,9 Although obesity rates have continued to increase steadily in both sexes, across all ages and all races, and at all educational levels, the highest rates occur among the most disadvantaged groups.

Obesity and food insecurity, defined as the limited or uncertain availability of nutritionally acceptable or safe foods, also appear to be linked, at least among female recipients of food assistance programmes .

ENERGY-DENSE FOODS COST LESS

Developments in agriculture and food technology have made energy-dense foods accessible to the consumer at a very low cost.

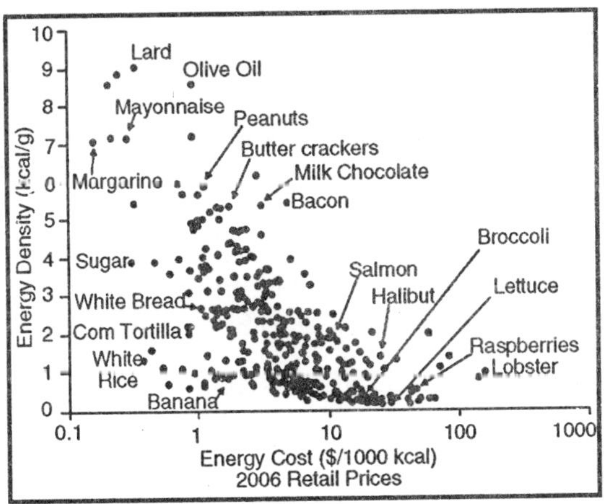

The inverse relationship between the energy density (kcal/g) of foods and the energy cost (US$/1,000 kcal). Food prices were obtained in 2006 from supermarkets in Seattle. The energy cost of fresh produce was 10 times as much as that of vegetable oils and sugars. As indicated by the logarithmic scale, the difference in energy costs between the healthy and unhealthy foods was several thousand per cent. The energy cost of soft drinks was, on average, 30 cents per megajoule (MJ), whereas that of orange juice from concentrate was 143 cents/MJ. Fats and oils, sugar, refined grains, potatoes, and beans provided dietary energy at minimum cost. Dry foods with a stable shelf life are generally less costly (per MJ) than perishable meats, fish, dairy products, or fresh produce. The selection of refined grains, added sugars, and vegetable fats may represent a deliberate strategy to save money. Lower food costs may be associated with more energy-dense diets, and total energy intake may actually increase.

This means that, paradoxically, it is possible to spend less and eat more, provided that the extra energy comes in the form of added sugar and added fat. The association between poverty and obesity may be mediated, in part, by the low cost and high palatability of energy-dense foods. In fact, the foods implicated in promoting obesity, like snacks, fast foods, sweets, and refined grains, are those that provide dietary energy at a very low cost.

The standard dietary advice is to replace fats and sweets with more fruit, vegetables, whole grains, poultry, and fish. However, these more healthful foods are also more expensive and beyond the reach of many. Some low-income families limit their food budget to $100 for four people per week, or less than $4 per person per day. The only foods that can be obtained for this amount of money are high in refined grains, added sugars, and added fats, and the healthful, recommended foods are separated by an immense gap in energy costs.

HEALTHIER DIETS COST MORE

Not only do healthier diets cost more, they are also consumed by more affluent persons. Diet quality in the United States is very much a function of socioeconomic status. People who are older, wealthier, and better educated are both thinner and have better diets than do the poor. The impact of socioeconomic status variables on diet quality has normally been ascribed to a higher educational level or a greater awareness of health issues among higher-income groups. One less-explored hypothesis is that food choices are driven by the relative differences in cost between high-quality and low-quality foods. This observation is not restricted to the United States: similar associations between higher incomes and higherquality diets were also found in Canada, France, the United Kingdom, and other countries of the European Union. A study of the relationship between energy density and the cost of freely chosen diets in a French community11 showed that dietary energy density was associated with higher energy intakes. More energy-dense diets were associated with a higher consumption of grains, fats, and sweets; there was a negative association between energy-dense diets and consumption of fruits and vegetables. In addition, the energy density of the diet was inversely linked to the energy cost.

Replacing fats and sweets with more vegetables and fruits was associated with higher diet costs: each 100 g increment in additional fruit and vegetable consumption increased diet costs. In contrast, higher consumption of fats and sweets was associated with a net savings in diet costs. These data showed that sweets and fats cost less, while low-energy-density diets high in vegetables and fruits cost more. In Western societies, lower energy costs are generally associated with higher energy intakes.

OBESITY: AN ECONOMIC HYPOTHESIS

Food choices by the obese have been explained in terms of abnormalities in biology, physiology, and behaviour. The biological explanation has been that the observed cravings for fats and sweets are driven by central metabolic events, a serotonin or dopamine imbalance, altered leptin levels, or the endogenous opiate peptide system. Physiological explanations have invoked the glycemic index of foods, individual differences in fructose metabolism, satiety deficits, or insulin resistance.

Psychological explanations have addressed an addictive personality, a cortisol-mediated response to stress, or simply the seeking of comfort in high-fat foods. Environmental approaches have blamed the susceptibility of individuals to external cues provided by fast foods or snacks and the inability to regulate calories following the consumption of soft drinks.

Fewer studies have made the link between the low cost of energy-dense foods and the obesity epidemic. The present hypothesis is that the links seen between poverty and obesity are primarily attributable to economic variables. Unhealthy diets cost less, while the recommended healthier diets cost more. As consumers reduce food expenditures, their diet becomes increasingly energy rich but nutrient poor. Whereas increasing food expenditures does not guarantee a healthy diet, reducing food spending below a certain limit virtually guarantees that the resulting diet will be nutrient poor and energy dense.

Households on a limited budget will find it difficult to eat more healthfully unless they adopt unfamiliar eating habits, depart from social norms, or eat mostly unpalatable foods. Public policies to promote dietary change should take into account food preferences and usual eating habits. The growing price gap between healthy and unhealthy foods also supports the causal link between poverty and obesity. The foods that have been found to maintain their price are fats and sweets, which could accentuate disparities in the access that people with lower incomes have to healthy diets.

8

Health Inequality in India

Recent research has witnessed considerable engagement with the task of comprehending the crucial determinants of health outcomes. It is observed that the burden of ill health is borne disproportionately by different population subgroups and that people of lower socio-economic status consistently experience poor health outcomes. Several empirical studies have also acknowledged such incomerelated inequalities in health, propounded as the absolute income hypothesis. In view of such findings, health promotion of the poor has emerged worldwide as a vital area for policy research and action.

Policy initiatives and programmes strongly perceive that inequalities in the health outcomes of different population subgroups are characterised by certain systematic deprivations. Apparently, some of the Indian health policies and programmes also attempt to eliminate deprivation in the provisioning of healthcare and achieve the objective of health equity. In order to achieve this objective, it is important to steer policymaking through timely and systematic assessment of prevailing health inequality, 2 a task that so far does not seem to have received serious attention. Although a few studies have presented regionspecific or population-subgroup-related health profiles for India, they are at best able only to reflect on disparities and not inequalities.

While disparities are evaluated based on the positioning around aggregate outcome, inequalities have to be adjudged just as to specific ethical or economic ideals. Moreover, for ensuring equitable and efficient allocation of public health resources, it is imperative to unravel the depth and the varied dimensions of health outcomes, especially through measures sensitised for equity concerns. Apart from these considerations, it is also of analytical interest to examine whether income inequality itself poses as a public health hazard. This question has gained much academic attention but most of the findings of studies3 on the topic have remained inconclusive. The literature on health economics, which identifies this question as the relative income hypothesis states that the distribution of income in a society has a larger impact on population's health than absolute income.

Since most of the studies on relative income hypothesis are undertaken in the context of developed countries, it would be worthwhile to gather some insights from the Indian experience to further our understanding of the income-health nexus. We employ widely accepted measurement techniques to assess inequities in child health across different Indian states and draw some interesting conclusions on the relationship between income inequality and health inequality in the country.

As we all know, health of children assumes significance for human and economic development of any country; but what is more important is to regard it as their right to survival, protection, participation and development as ratified by the government of India in 1989 through the Convention on the Rights of the Child drafted by the United Nations Commission on Human Rights. Unfortunately, most of the deaths rampant among children in India are preventable and are caused by a combination of under-nourishment and onslaught of infectious diseases.

Although, child health and welfare has been a prime item in the agenda of the central and the state governments, their intent cannot proceed very far in the absence of a prior assessment of the magnitude and varied dimensions of the problem. With the motivation to fill this void, the rest of the document is organised as follows. The measurement techniques employed to measure the magnitude of disparities in child health status. The data sources and the variables identified for the analysis. The empirical findings obtained for the income-related dimension of health inequality and attempts to interpret the results theoretically. The discussion and presents a few policy suggestions.

METHODS

As we already argued, the assessment of health status could be improved by adopting certain distribution-sensitised measures along the identified dimensions. In order to examine incomerelated inequality, we adopt the standard technique of employing concentration curves and concentration indices. Underlying this technique is a simple but interesting principle of defining equity.

The principle involved stipulates that the cumulative proportions of ill health must match with the cumulative population shares and any mismatch between the two sets is defined as inequity. The concentration curve (CC) and concentration index (CI) have certain attractive properties compared to certain other measures of health disparities and are employed here as a means for quantifying the degree of income-related inequality in certain specific health variables. The CC plots the cumulative proportions of the population along the x-axis against the cumulative proportions of ill health plotted on the y-axis.

For interpretative purposes, if the burden of ill health were equally distributed across socio-economic groups, the CC would coincide with the diagonal. If poor health is concentrated in the lower socio-economic groups, the health CC would lie above the diagonal and the farther the CC lies from the diagonal, the greater would be the degree of inequality. The CI is defined as twice the area between the CC and the diagonal. The CI provides a measure of the extent of inequalities in health status that are systematically associated with socio-economic status.

The CI can be easily computed by making use of the convenient covariance result as follows: CI = 2 cov(Hi, Ri)/?, where H is the health variable whose inequality is being measured,? is its mean, Ri is the ith individual's fractional rank in the socio-economic distribution and cov(Hi, Ri.) is the covariance. The CI ranges between +1 and -1 and takes negative values when the CC lies above the line of equality, indicating disproportionate concentration of the ill health outcome among the poor.

DATA AND VARIABLES

Notwithstanding the measurement techniques, availability of health information disaggregated by population groups becomes crucial in evaluating health inequities. Prior to the advent of the National Family Health Surveys, health information was restricted to aggregate measures and it had been difficult to study the distribution pattern of health in the population. The genesis of the NFHS, its wide coverage and the nature of information collected offer an exclusive opportunity to employ robust measures to comprehend health disparities across the Indian union.

In order to portray the status of health deprivation in India and its spatial and group related dispersal, we utilise the unit level records of the third and the latest round of NFHS, conducted by the International Institute for Population Sciences and ORC Macro. To retain the sensitivity of the health outcome indicators, the domain of child health has been taken as a major criterion as it allows for better interventions right from the preliminary stages of life.

Therefore, in our analysis we engage ourselves with child health outcome variables, across different states of the Indian union. As the key indicators of child health, this document employs the information available on under-five mortalities, immunisation status and nutritional performance of the child population of the different states.

For measuring the inequities in child undernutrition, we use the NFHS 3 information provided on the basis of the new international reference population released by World Health Organisation in April 2006 and accepted by the government of India. To focus attention on issues of association and causation, we have obtained information also on three other economic variables: One, the state-wise net state domestic product 2004-05 at factor cost, which is obtained through the statistics published by Central Statistics Organisation. The second is the information on public spending on health as a share of total health spending, which is taken from Rao *et al.* In addition to these variables we also required information on the income inequality levels across different Indian states. For this purpose we have used the unit level records of National Sample Survey's 61st round on consumer expenditure. Here, the consumption expenditure of the households is taken as a proxy for income and we have computed the Gini coefficient of inequality in per capita monthly consumption expenditure for all the states of India.

INTERSTATE DIFFERENCES IN HEALTH INEQUALITIES

We examine the magnitude of income-related inequalities in health, across the different Indian states. For this purpose, we have computed the CI for the selected indicators of child health across all the Indian states. The CI values for a range of child health indicators for the country as a whole are negative, confirming the prevalence of income-related health inequalities that are manifest primarily among the poor.

On comparison of these inequalities across varied indicators of child health, inequalities are more pronounced in the case of the underfive mortalities, in undernutrition and the receipt of basic vaccinations for immunisation. The under-five mortality CC for all-India as well as for three other major states with higher health inequality levels. All these CCs lie above the diagonal and thus, indicate a greater concentration of health eventualities among the poorer groups.

While the CI value for under-five mortality at the national level is computed to be, it presents a reasonably wide range across various states with the minimum of in West Bengal and maximum of in Uttaranchal. Among the other major states, Maharashtra, Madhya Pradesh, Gujarat, Tamil Nadu and Punjab experience greater income-related inequalities in underfive mortality as against the states of Uttar Pradesh, Rajasthan and Bihar, which show much lower levels of inequalities. Apart from the differences in the magnitude of inequalities across the board, the negative values indicate vulnerabilities among the poor. Other than under-five mortality, similar inequality is assessed for a set of child health indicators, which include nutritional make-up, anaemia and child immunisation. As regards nutritional make-up, the two dimensions namely stunting and the underweight manifest inequalities at the all-India level ranging between (-0.1249) and (-0.1600).

The all-India level inequality in weight-for-age based nutritional assessment being the largest depicts a similar pattern across states as well. Compared with stunting, the inequality in nutrition just as to the underweight criterion has a wider range between (-0.0835) in Madhya Pradesh and (-0.3063) in Goa. The level of overall prevalence of the same could also condition a moderate range of inequality across states for the alternative nutritional measures.

This is obvious from the fact that prevalence of under nutrition just as to the underweight criterion is by far the largest when contrasted with the same evaluated on an alternative criterion like stunting. Further, weight-forage in its own construct has a propensity for larger variation during childhood. As regards stunting the all-India concentration index value is (-0.1249) with a variation range of (-0.0325) in Meghalaya and (-0.2867) in Goa.

Not only is the range of variation in this inequality measure relatively lower compared to the same just as to the underweight criterion but also the high inequality magnitudes are lesser in this case. For the indicator of anaemia the all-India CI value of (-0.0518) is observably lower and could be due to the widespread prevalence of anaemia across the population but still the poorer parts are found to remain at a higher disadvantage.

The inequities in child-anaemia do not vary significantly across the major states. However, the states of Mizoram (-0.1,363), Goa (-0.1,126), West Bengal (-0.0919) and Orissa (-0.0851) are found to be more inequitable. In addition to these health outcome indicators, we have also tried to examine whether income-related inequities are present in the attainment of basic vaccinations, which is provided through the public health machinery. Apart from the problem of lower rates of complete immunisation, there are evidently higher income-related inequities inherent in the distribution of non-immunised children across different states. Even in states with better coverage of primary healthcare, children belonging to poorer parts of the population are at a greater disadvantage as the concentration of these incomplete immunisations is higher among them.

Undoubtedly, apart from income, inequality in such outcomes is arising due to the interplay of several factors including education and health awareness and it would be an important and challenging task to probe into inequalities obtained due to reasons other than the elementary issue of income deprivation. After providing a preliminary account of income-related child health inequality in India, we now turn to discuss the relationship between health inequalities and income across different Indian states.

To facilitate the discussion, we have classified the different states into four categories. Employing the all-India figures of per capita NSDP and CI for under-five mortalities as a cut-off level, the states are classified into "low income—low health inequality", "low income—high health inequality", "high income—low health inequality" and "high income—high health inequality" ones depending on whether their respective values exceed or fall short of the cut-off level.

On this basis we are able to obtain vital insights into the relationship between the magnitudes of inequalities in health and the state's income profile. States like Punjab, Maharashtra and Gujarat demonstrate the coexistence of higher levels of income along with higher levels of inequalities in under-five mortalities and states such as Uttar Pradesh, Bihar and Orissa which have lower income levels are also found to have lower levels of inequalities in under-five mortalities.

These states suggest, that there is a straightforward relationship between income levels and health inequality. But there are other states such as Madhya Pradesh, Karnataka and Kerala, which are exceptions to such a relationship and suggest there is no such clear-cut relation. To probe further, we bring in the element of income inequalities to comprehend the observed health inequities across these states. Inclusion of income inequality5 into the analysis would signify that the health inequality in a state is not only dependent on the overall level of income but also on its distribution.

This too is not sufficient to explain the observed pattern of health inequalities across different states. For example, consider major states such as Kerala and Madhya Pradesh, which are exception to any such direct relationship. Both these states have higher levels of income inequalities coupled with varying levels of income and health inequality. Therefore, without asserting association any further, we present a simple model to better elucidate the expected relationship between the two.

INCOME INEQUALITY AND HEALTH INEQUALITY

To understand health inequality through the income domain, we adopt a simple model discussed in Wagstaff. In this model, the relationship between health and medical care is assumed to be concave, meaning that medical care is subject to diminishing returns in the production of health. It suggests that richer individuals are likely to end up with higher levels of health and that increases in income inequality result in higher levels of health inequality.

Further, it is inferred that if medical care is subsidised through public spending, it helps to lower the levels of health inequality. It also suggests increases in health inequality if rising incomes are accompanied by technological improvements in healthcare. In order to verify these predictions from the model, an empirical analysis has also been attempted.

This exercise shows that neither income inequality nor the public share of health spending proves to be a significant determinant of health inequities but that average income of the population is significant in determining the same. However, such findings raise the question as to why these empirical findings differ from the theoretical insights offered by the model. For instance, why are rising levels of income inequalities not accompanied with higher levels of health inequality? In fact, the interstate analysis to be discussed later also provides us with similar results. Does it imply that the supposedly strict concave relationship between health and medical care is weak? To explore further, we modify the assumption of a strictly concave relationship between income and health and instead work with a convex-concave relationship between income and health. This modified assumption helps to elucidate relationship between health and medical care expenditure—particularly in a developing country—by capturing the indivisible nature of health expenditure and to comprehend health inequality in a striking manner. What motivated us to engage with such a relationship are the facts that in a developing country whenever an individual decides to seek medical care, his first task would be to arrange for an array of healthcare-related expenses beginning from travelling cost and medical fees.

Also, during the initial phases of the treatment process, often, the individual is advised to undergo a few diagnostic tests, which undoubtedly help detect the ailment accurately but importantly require additional expenditure. It must be noticed that many such expenses are indivisible and unavoidable under conditions of feeble health systems as is the case in many developing countries.

Such specific difficulties in accessing quality medical care provide inadequate returns to health at low levels of income. Under such a framework, richer individuals are likely to end up with higher levels of health but it also suggests that individual incomes have to exceed a certain threshold to able to meet the initial expenditure requirements for medical care in order to reap greater health benefits.

In the absolute sense, both these incomes are low and thus, lead to low levels of health. But still, there exists a certain degree of income inequality between these individuals that leads to health inequalities. It is important to note that the inequalities in health, both in absolute and relative senses, are smaller than the inequalities observed in the income distribution and suggest that at lower levels of income, health inequalities are also low. But if individuals are around the threshold income level beyond which they would be able to afford better healthcare, then the relationship between income and health inequalities worsens. To demonstrate this fact, consider two individuals with incomes Y3 and Y4 respectively and allow for a considerable degree of income inequality between them. Here, unlike in the earlier case, we observe that despite similar degrees of income inequalities, the level of health inequality has increased with increase in incomes.

In a nutshell, the modification of the income-health function allows one to infer that for a given level of income inequality, if overall income levels are lower then health inequalities are also lower. It also suggests that the levels of income inequality also have significant bearing upon the extent of health inequality but that the impact becomes more observable if the income inequalities are associated with higher levels of income.

More importantly, under conditions of lower incomes and high-income inequality, the health inequality levels would get enhanced whereas if income levels are higher and income inequality levels are low, they would have a moderating impact on health inequality levels. Another related discussion that is relevant here is the impact of public health spending upon health inequality.

Although it is desirable that such facilities should be distributed more evenly across the population, the actual result may be undesirable as health facilities provided through public health spending often tend to be concentrated in particular regions such as urban areas or certain other targetlocations thereby, often failing in guaranteeing universal access and opportunity.

Any such bias in the provisioning of public health could thus worsen the distribution of health across individuals. In order to quickly verify the predictions of these two different frameworks in the Indian context, a simple regression exercise is undertaken here. This analysis could also be viewed as a preliminary attempt to comprehend the differences in health inequality across the different states of India in terms of income inequality, per capita income and share of public health spending. We have selected the negative of the under-five mortality CI as an indicator of child health inequality. As explanatory variables, the Gini measure of inequality in per capita monthly consumption expenditure is taken as a proxy for income inequality, per capita NSDP at factor cost is utilised to represent the state per capita income and public spending on health as a share of total health spending is taken to represent the role of subsidies in healthcare.

The R-squared value suggests that hardly 2 per cent of the variations in health inequality are actually explained by the differences in income inequalities. This finding is similar to what Wagstaff finds while comprehending the differences in health inequality across developing countries. Given the inability of income inequality alone to capture the variations in health inequality, we add other important variables to comprehend the causation.

Specifically, in model 2 we control for income inequality and public health spending levels and thereby attempt to elicit the role of per capita income in determining health inequalities. The results endorse the view that increases in average income also increase the levels of health inequality as indicated by the positive and significant coefficient of NSDP per capita. The theoretical framework discussed earlier has predicted this relationship.

However, it is also observed that the coefficient obtained for the variable of public health spending as a proportion of total health spending possesses a negative sign, suggesting its favourable effect for reducing health inequalities. However, the effect turns out to be statistically insignificant. The overall results obtained here, especially in relation to income inequality and average income, are partly in agreement with the framework but do not lend any concrete support to the relative income hypothesis. In other words, it may also be opined that the concave relationship between income and health is somewhat unable to capture the conditions prevalent in developing countries. Hence, now we go on to test the alternate framework namely of the convex-concave relationship between health and income. What is necessary here is to conceive of a variable, which should be sensitive to both, average income levels as well as income inequality levels.

For this purpose we develop a simple composite index of income and income inequality in two small steps as follows. Firstly, we normalise the NSDP per capita across the states in such a way that the state with the highest income obtains a value of one and the lowest-income state is assigned a value of zero.

In the second step, we obtain the composite index for each state, by taking a simple average of the Gini coefficient for the state and the normalised NSDP per capita values for the respective states obtained through the previous step. This new index represents the relative levels of both income and income inequality and is used as an explanatory variable in the analysis to comprehend health inequality. Model 3 finds that this new composite index measure given by the average of the Gini and normalised NSDP per capita turns out to be a statistically significant factor explaining the variations in health inequality with an explanatory power of 27 per cent, greater than that of the previous two models. Besides, the coefficient value too is higher (0.211) which is statistically significant at the 1 per cent level of significance.

This result supports the theoretical prediction that if higher levels of average incomes are accompanied by higher income inequalities then it leads to increase in health inequality. Further, effects on health inequality get cushioned if either the distribution of income is more equitable or if the average income levels are lower.

Although here we have not performed a rigorous analysis of the said framework, this exercise could be considered as a preliminary attempt at gauging the proposed health-income relationship. Undoubtedly, a more comprehensive examination would be able to help draw further insights because income alone is insufficient to describe the larger variations observed in health inequity, as is evident from the explanatory power of the regression.

POLICY NOTES AND CONCLUSION

We shall begin this concluding part by reiterating the motivation behind this present engagement. The concern beneath this empirical exercise is the sheer urgency to unravel the inadequacies of the summary measures in vogue of health outcomes and to evoke policy concerns pertaining to social justice and equity. It is disconcerting to witness, especially from an ethical perspective, that poorer populations in India are bearing the brunt of health disadvantages.

Although certain policy interventions are in place to deal with such adversities, greater attention needs to be directed towards the assessment of health deprivation and inequities in India. Also, we would like to stress upon the recognition of differential constraints in accessing medical care across regions. For instance, for some, availability may be an issue while for others it may not actually be the major worry. Similarly, availability alone may not be sufficient; unless it is supported by a policy of greater subsidisation of health facilities through special schemes for maternal and child healthcare.

The problem may as well be one of poor levels of awareness for some others. Given such possibilities, the social planner has to acquire more complete information with regard to the sources of inequality and identification of the vulnerable groups. Undoubtedly, such an exercise would go a long way to optimise resource allocation and enhance the targeting efficiency of such interventions. The present analysis pursues this thinking and endeavours to enhance the informational base for policymaking, by incorporating into the summary measures, a slightly more elaborate account of health inequality caused by a factor such as income inadequacy.

While analysing the income component, it was observed that poorer parts of the population were beleaguered with ill-health whether it be their efforts for child survival or anxieties pertaining to child nutrition. Another highlight worth mentioning here relates to the inequality levels being higher with higher levels of the event as against lower levels. Undoubtedly from a policy perspective, focused attention needs to be paid towards improving the mortality situation in backward states and perhaps inequality aversion measures need to be promoted in states like Maharashtra and Gujarat with lower under-five mortality rates (of 47 and 61 per 1,000 live births respectively) in order to obviate the concentration of this misfortune among the poor. Further, a simple theoretical model was resorted to comprehend associational and causational factors.

The analysis revealed that the degree of health inequalities escalates when the rising average income levels of the population are accompanied by greater income inequalities. On the one hand, such an association does reflect that the product of economic growth in the form of rising average income and income inequalities presents certain impediments to attaining equitable health by allowing the better-off population to secure greater benefits of the growth process. On the other hand, it is also evident that the summary measures of health also improve with the betterment of the income profile of a region. The interplay of these two impacts may actually help policymakers trade off a little bit of health inequality for gaining higher health levels. However, a social planner needs to sail through such quandaries and should arrive at prudent mechanisms to utilise the resources and technology obtained through economic growth, by allocating greater resources towards those parts of the population who have been excluded from the growth process.

Even the countries with the shallowest health gradients, such as Sweden and England, have viewed their own health inequalities as unacceptable and have initiated policy measures to mitigate those. We now turn to the larger question, namely, the one relating to the type of social policies that could be pursued by the state to reduce health inequalities. Scholars have advocated for a policy matrix, which not only accommodates immediate or direct health interventions such as medical facilities but also consists of basic interventions indirectly related with the health of individuals. Such investments are largely sought in the form of investment in basic education, better housing, water and sanitary conditions as well as the introduction of programmes to provide income security. By suggesting a holistic policy matrix, our contention here is not as much to argue for allocation of resources but rather to suggest an exercise that would integrate these basic investments, at least, at an analytical level while arriving at resource allocation decisions for the health sector itself.

Decisions on resource allocations for public health, taken in isolation from other pertinent factors, may actually affect the efficacy of the policy matrix in toto. Perhaps the state should acknowledge the fact that social sector expenditures, particularly on health and education, are complementary in nature and if put together do produce large individual as well as social benefits.

9

Educational Inequalities

INTRODUCTION

Between-group economic inequality is a common phenomenon in mutli-ethnic societies. Such inequalities often reflect persistent differences in the capacity of individuals from different social groups to seize market opportunities, either due to discrimination or market constraints. A society with unequal opportunities is said to be characterized by a low degree of social mobility, in that individuals' economic success/status is largely predictable in terms of family background such as caste and religion.

This immobility leads to intergenerational persistence in poverty, with serious implications for the process of development. What is needed is to promote a distribution of human capital where schooling varies along with individuals' level of effort instead of family background and other characteristics for which they cannot be held responsible. In recent years, attempts were made to measure equality of educational opportunity in terms of schooling mobility using comparable household datasets with information on individuals' family background.

Two studies—Dahan and Gaviria and Behrman, Birdsall and Szekely—adopt a regression-model approach to measure schooling mobility using data on children's schooling from Latin America. Educational mobility in these studies is modelled in terms of inter-generational persistence in schooling. Similarly, Schütz, Ursprung and Wobmann use comparable data on students from the TIMSS survey and develop a regression-based index of the inequality of educational opportunity in 54 countries. However, even if we focus exclusively on the instrumental value of education as productivity enhancer, intergenerational correlations serve as imperfect indices of the inequality of educational opportunity for at least two reasons. Firstly, they relate a limited set of circumstances beyond the individual's control to his/her wellbeing outcome. Thereby, by construction, attributing too much of welfare inequality to characteristics for which individuals should be held accountable.

In the inequality of opportunity literature the idea is to account for as many circumstances beyond the individual's control as possible. Secondly, consider the distributions of well-being conditioned by circumstances beyond individuals' control. If their dissimilarities are deemed to contribute to inequality of opportunity then intergenerational correlations are inappropriate to measure inequality of opportunity even in hypothetical societies where just one single parental attribute constitutes the set of circumstances beyond the individual's control.

As Yalonetzky shows, several joint distributions of parental and offspring's well-being can produce the same intergenerational correlations. By contrast studies like Gasparini, Checci and Peragine, Lefranc *et al.*, Ferreira and Gignoux and Barros *et al.* have developed and implemented indices of inequality of opportunity that handle multivariate sets of circumstances, which is a minimum methodological requirement for quantifying inequality of opportunity. In this study, we follow an approach similar to that of Ferreira and Gignoux. The key challenge in empirically assessing the degree of inequality of opportunity is to find data on exogenous circumstance factor for adults and their parents. The most widely referred circumstance factor is parental education. However, no nationally representative large scale datasets for India provides this information for adults. In the absence of such data, our study focuses on two other commonly studied "circumstance factors", namely, gender and religion of the individual. Using data on caste, gender and religion, the objective of this document is to look at the interplay between social origins and gender in the determination of educational opportunity in contemporary India.

The key questions that we address are:

- Are educational opportunities in India becoming more equal?
- Are there intra- and inter-regional disparities in educational opportunities?
- If so, how much mobility is there over time-do states that were less equal in the past have remained so today? To explore the Indian experience of progress in equalizing educational opportunities, we use National Sample Survey data spanning the time period 1983-2004. We calculate three indices—a Pearson-Cramer index, an overlap index and a special Gini index—in order to measure inequality of educational opportunity across Indian states.

The PC index is related to one of Roemer's definitions of equality of opportunity. It takes the value of zero if and only if conditional distributions of well-being are identical across social groups and it takes its maximum value of one if and only if there is complete, or absolute, association between social group partitions and values of the outcome. We also estimate a multivariate, multiplegroup version of the overlap index originally proposed by Weitzman.

The overlap index is also equal to zero if and only if conditional distributions are identical across groups. Both indices share the benchmark of perfect equality of opportunity. However while the PC index is sensitive to different group sizes, the overlap index compares "representative agents" from each and every group independently of size. Therefore, with these indices, we offer results that are consistent with both approaches to group size.

In addition, we estimate Lefranc *et al.*'s Gini of opportunity. It is an interesting index based on a definition of inequality of opportunity different to Roemer's. It measures Gini-inequality over Sen's welfare metric across social groups. Because the study is based on household datasets, we can describe the trends in inequality of opportunity between states and regions. In addition, we study exchange mobility of Indian states and regions in terms of decline in inequality of educational opportunity over time.

Irrespective of the index used, the state of Kerala stands out as the least unequal in terms of educational opportunities. However, even after excluding Kerala, significant interstate divergence persists amongst the remaining states. Transition matrix analysis confirms substantial exchange mobility in inequality of opportunity across India states. Rajasthan and Gujarat in the West and Uttar Pradesh and Bihar in the Centre experienced large falls in the ranking of inequality of opportunities.

However, despite being home to a large number of poor people, Eastern states of West Bengal and Orissa made significant progress in reducing inequality of opportunity whilst the situation worsened in Bihar. At a region level, Southern, North-eastern and Eastern regions experienced upward mobility in terms of decline in inequality of opportunity, whereas the Central region experienced downward mobility.

STUDY BACKGROUND

India has made significant progress in increasing enrolment and school completion over the past decades. Enrolment in primary schools has increased from 19.2 million in 1950- 51 to 113.6 million in 2001. Gross primary school enrolment is nearing 100%. Overall enrolment of children in all stages of education in India has improved over the years. Such increase in school participation has been also associated with a significant jump in the literacy rate which rose from 18% in 1951 to 65% in 2001.

On the one hand, the growth in enrolment has taken place in the backdrop of introduction of various centrally sponsored educational interventions. Examples of such schemes include Sarva Shiksha Abhiyan, the Non-formal Education Programme, Operation Blackboard for small rural schools, Total Literacy Campaigns, District Primary School Education

Programme and more recently the mid-day meal schemes. Between 1950 and 1990, the number of schools increased more than three-fold, outpacing the growth of the school age population. School participation may have responded to these supply-side changes. On the other hand, the growth in school participation has coincided with the era of economic reform and liberalization which also saw high rates of economic growth by historical standards. Between 1983 and 2004, rural poverty declined from 46.9% to 28.4%, at a rate of one percentage point a year.

Economic growth may have enabled previously poorer families to enrol children in school thereby reducing inequalities in educational opportunities. Indeed the post-reform era of the nineties has been a period of fairly rapid increase in literacy and school participation. Nonetheless, substantial gaps remain in educational outcomes across gender, caste, religion and between urban and rural inhabitants.

Altogether these explain a large part of educational inequality in India; which is not only one of the highest in the world, but it has not declined much in the last three decades. Recent research using multiple rounds of nationally representative data documents the persistence of gender, caste and religion gaps in school participation and attainment. A comparison of data from 1980s with that from 2000s reveals that even the later years of liberalization have not been accompanied by a complete closure of social gaps in schooling, an important premarket factor.

Overall, these trends in inequality of educational outcomes are not conclusive of a reduction in inequalities of educational opportunities. For instance, there is evidence of continued importance of other "circumstance factors" such as parental wealth and education, which is suggestive of persistent inequality in educational opportunities. Indeed, India hosts a large part of the world's out-of -school children, mostly belonging to poor households. Whilst the country has made sizable progress in bringing these children to school, there remains striking contrasts in educational achievements at the state level. To this end, considerable educational investment has been made in past decades by state governments. Examples of state sponsored schemes include Lok Jumbish and Shiksha Karmi programmes in Rajasthan, Education Guarantee Scheme in Madhya Pradesh, Balyam programme of Andhra Pradesh and Basic Education Programme in Uttar Pradesh.

Andhra Pradesh is also home to one of the largest Anganwadi systems in India which brought children from particularly poor households into schools. Whilst in some states such initiatives have led to significant growth in school enrolment, there exist large disparities in educational achievement across states in India—about two-thirds of the children who do not attend school are in five of the poorest states: Bihar, Uttar Pradesh, West Bengal, Madhya Pradesh, and Rajasthan.

Persistence of schooling inequalities in some states raises concerns regarding the extent to which educational investment has translated into greater equality of educational opportunities. Dreze and Sen attribute existing inequality in educational achievement to variation in efforts to expand basic education in different states. If inequality in the access to education continues to restrict the benefit of investment in education to children from higher social class and the majority group, educational opportunities are unlikely to equalize.

It is of policy interest to study the degree of inequality of educational opportunity across Indian states. The country's federal structure and multi-ethnic nature provides an ideal setting to investigate this issue. Yet, there is no published study for India. In the absence of a lack of a statistical measure, past research on this topic has focused on the broader question of between-group inequality.

A closely related study is Deshpande, who examines between-group socio-economic inequalities in India. Deshpande constructs a gendercaste adjusted HDI for Indian states. However, this approach is rather ad-hoc as it has no explicit link to well-established theories and concepts of inequality of opportunities. In this document, we build on recent developments in the literature that has operationalized concepts in the inequality of opportunity theory and construct three indices of inequality of educational opportunity using data on an adult sample. To the best of our knowledge, this is the first study that attempts to empirically investigate the extent and correlates of equality of educational opportunity across states in India.

Therefore, our study fills an important gap in the otherwise rich literature on the between-region differences in human development in India. The personal distribution of schooling described in this document is based on a representative sample of households drawn from two periods spanning the year when the Indian economy was formally liberalized. The two time periods of the NSS chosen mark the pre- and postliberalization era in India.

This presents an interesting setting to study equality of opportunity to acquire education, an important pre-market factor. Market liberalization has brought important changes in the distribution of background factors that matter for schooling success. The liberalisation of the Indian economy in 1991 was followed by significant economic growth and fall in poverty. However, growth patterns in the nineties are characterised by major regional imbalances.

As a matter of fact, regional disparities increased in the 1990s, with the southern and western regions doing much better than the northern and eastern regions. Broadly speaking, western and southern states have tended to do comparatively well. The low growth states, on the other hand, form a large contiguous region in the north and east. This is a matter of concern, since the northern and eastern regions were poorer to start with. In some of the poorer states, notably Assam and Orissa, there has been very little poverty reduction during the 90s. These patterns have implications for equality of educational opportunity at the state level.

Therefore, we go beyond documenting the progress made in equalizing educational opportunities by additionally exploring its link with poverty reduction and economic growth in a given state.

METHODOLOGY AND DATA

In this part, we briefly introduce the three indices used for tracking changes in inequality of opportunity of education in India from 1983 to 2004. We first present the general framework of circumstances and outcomes; and then explain the PC index, followed by the overlap index, and finally the Gini index of inequality of opportunity.

DATA

The data used come from the NSS 1983 and 2004 rounds. Our analysis is based on individual's school completion. Since these data are censored for children, we restrict our analysis to adults aged at least 25 years old. The indices relate data on school completion to a variety of circumstances such as religion and gender. Because for certain states, sample size was too small, we further restricted our data to 25 states. This yields a total of four comparable circumstance sets: Hindu male, Hindu female, non-Hindu male, non-Hindu female. For some of the analyses we also compute inequality of opportunity allowing states to differ in their circumstance sets. The latter include gender, religious affiliation and belonging to scheduled tribes or to scheduled castes.

RESULTS

The indices for the whole India over adults 25 years or older. In all cases, the point estimates are surrounded by narrow confidence intervals as is to be expected from the large sample size. This confirms the statistically significant difference of our estimates of Inequality of opportunity indices from 1983 to 2004. The plot of the PC index suggests a modest decline in inequality of opportunity whilst the opposite is true for estimate of GIO index. National averages of the PC index and the GIO index can mask important between-state differences in educational opportunities.

FIRST

In the case of primary and secondary education, significant progress has been made between 1983 and 2004.

In 1983, none of the states had more than 20% of the population with up to or above secondary level education. By 2004, this increased by 2-3 folds in all states except Andhra Pradesh, Rajasthan, Orissa and Tripura. Because of the low base, the fraction of population with secondary education increased by more than 100% in the Northern state of Uttar Pradesh as well as in the Southern state of Kerala. Similarly, the fraction of population with primary education almost doubled in almost all states between 1983 and 2004. Once again Northern states such as Uttar Pradesh and Bihar saw 100% increases in the percentage of primary educated population. States that had invested heavily in primary education in the past also saw modest growth in primary educated population.

SECOND

There is some disagreement between the GIO and PC indices over the ranking of states in 1983, less so between the other two possible comparisons. However, the three indices pairwise correlate highly for 2004 data. Moreover, the Friedman test of rank independence strongly rejects in both years the null hypothesis that the three rankings are independent from each other. The differences on the indices between the two years are statistically significant, which is reasonable considering the sample size. However the difference may not be large enough to be economically significant. In addition, the opposing trends espoused by the indices, for some states and at regional and national levels, are possible since they do not measure the same concept of inequality of opportunity. The PC and the overlap indices measure inequality as distances across multinomial distributions, which in turn are related to the degree of association between population groups and outcomes. By contrast the GIO is a Gini index of Sen's metrics, W(x), for each group in which I(x) is estimated using the intra-group Gini coefficient.

THIRD

In 2004, there is also a negative link between level of educational attainment in the population and inequality of opportunity. For instance, in that year, 76% of the population completed primary schooling in the least unequal state of Kerala whilst the figure for Uttar Pradesh, the most unequal state, was 44%. However, the correlations are far from perfect and seldom significant at 5% level.

FOURTH

The pace of improvement in inequality of opportunity has been quite uneven between states within India. To highlight the extent and direction of movement of states in terms of inequality of opportunity. The Y-axis corresponds to position in 1983 whilst the X-axis indicates position in 2004. If a state is above and further from the 45 degree line, it indicates increasing inequality of opportunity. Reassuringly, irrespective of the index used, Uttar Pradesh and Bihar are located above the 45 degree line and experienced significant decline in their original rank in 1983.

FIFTH

Both the PC and GIO indices are sensitive to different group sizes. In order to consider an alternative assessment insensitive to group sizes, comparing "representative agents" from each and every group. Reassuringly, our key conclusions regarding changes in inequality of opportunity do not change when we use the overlap index.

The index ranks Kerala as the most equal and notes large gains for West Bengal and Orissa during 1983 and 2004. Estimates for Uttar Pradesh, Bihar and Rajasthan on the other hand show significant deterioration in ranking. This remarkable similarity in results is also confirmed by high positive association between rank estimates obtained from overlap and the other two indices.

Therefore, our discussion in the remaining part of the document is largely based on estimates of GIO and PC indices. For comparability purposes, we continue reporting the overlap index. To examine movement in inequality of opportunity rankings more formally, we construct a transition matrix of the PC index for 25 Indian states. The calculated value of the underlying immobility indices, as measured by the trace index is close to unity implying substantial mobility in inequality of opportunity across India states. A problem in transition matrix analysis is that with only 25 observations, some cells have no observations at all. To partially circumvent the problem, we disaggregate state data by rural and urban areas and re-calculate the transition matrices using the resultant dataset which now contains 45 observations in total.

Once again, the calculated value of the trace index remains high confirming that several states changed ranks so that many of those with relatively high inequality of opportunities in 1983 are not in the same category by 2004. To what extent are observed interstate differences in inequality of opportunity mirroring between-region inequality in educational opportunity? To answer this question, we re-produce the scatter-plot of state rankings showing the region of each state in the plot.

We find that:

- Western states were equally divided above and below the 45 degree line-Rajasthan and Gujarat saw a worsening of equality of opportunity whilst Maharashtra and Goa an improvement.
- Eastern states rank consistently amongst states that have succeeded in reducing inequality of opportunity.
- Southern states all gained in terms of ranks. However, when assessed in terms of the PC index, 2 states fell below the 45 degree line but both remained very close to the line.
- North/North-Eastern states have equal share above and below the 45 degree line
- Central states are mostly above the 45 degree line.

Once again, to examine how much mobility there is across regions, we compute quartile transition matrix and immobility indices. Given only 6 regions in India, we further disaggregated the data by rural/urban location of the households to enlarge the sample size. The value of trace index is once again close to unity implying substantial mobility in inequality of opportunity across India regions. The Pearson chi-square statistic however is only marginally significant which likely owes to the small number observations. To better understand the movements in the position of regions across the distribution of inequality of opportunity. It is easy to trace changes in inequality of opportunity in education across Indian regions using the graphs.

Several patterns are noteworthy:

- Irrespective of the index used, the central region saw a rise in inequality of opportunities;
- Irrespective of the index used, the southern, eastern and north-eastern regions saw a decrease in inequality of opportunities;
- Compared to the GIO index, there is more movements across regions in terms of the PC index.

Lastly, our preceding analysis only allowed for similar types across states. The positive correlation between educational attainment and equality of opportunity in 2004 is robust to this change in type definitions. On the other hand, whilst all the three indices remain significantly correlated, the correlation is far from perfect highlighting the fact that they measure different aspect of the notion of inequality of opportunity.

POLICY ORIGIN OF INEQUALITY OF OPPORTUNITY

What can explain the large-scale fall in the ranking of Rajasthan and Gujarat in the West and Uttar Pradesh and Bihar in the Centre? On the other hand, what explanation is there for reductions in inequality of opportunity in the Eastern states of Orissa and West Bengal that are much poorer? These questions are interesting because in the last two decades, India has experienced significant economic growth at a sustained rate.

The 1990s saw significant fall in poverty, a significant source of disadvantage for children born into Muslim and other minority social groups. Overbearing poverty has been a significant cause of withdrawal of children from schools. GDP growth and poverty reduction has been achieved in the backdrop of 1990s market liberalization which has also led to changes in economic structure and organization. These changes may have relaxed household credit constraints and altered household returns to investment in education. However, gains in poverty reduction following economic growth have not been equally divided across states. In a federal state like India, provision of public goods is the responsibility of individual states. The importance of state-level policy choice is well documented in the literature.

In a seminal study, Dreze and Sen demonstrate how differences in entitlement to basic services between Uttar Pradesh and Kerala are related to differences in the scope and quality of public services such as school facilities which in Uttar Pradesh are often non-existent. Relevant factors, among others, are the importance of social movements and public action, and the lack of political power of socially disadvantaged groups. Between-state differences in policies and institutions can lead to differences in inequality of educational opportunity for a number of reasons.

First, certain states in India display a poor record in terms of gender gaps in the labour market which can distort household investment decisions in female schooling. For instance, the northern Indian state of Uttar Pradesh has a long history of oppressive gender relations. Other states such as Punjab and Haryana have some of the lowest sex ratios. On the other hand, women's economic participation has been active in the Southern state of Kerala for a long time, which is arguably responsible for a wide range of social achievements. Kerala and Tamil Nadu also have high sex ratios.

Second, there is significant difference in access to public infrastructure by various social groups in India. The Sachar Commission report 2006, Muslims in India are frequently found in relatively unbanked villages, and access to credit matters for human capital acquisition. Therefore, differences in financial provisions across states can influence educational attainment by gender and religious membership. Third, Indian states differ in terms of overall spending on education as well as educational policies/interventions. Higher spending *per se* may not be enough to equalize opportunities. Some states have policies targeting disadvantaged and/or difficult-to-reach social groups. These states can be expected to succeed in equalizing educational opportunities.

Lastly, more accountable states may have affirmative action policies that attenuate the adverse effect of discriminatory factors such as caste and religion. For all these reasons, it is of policy interest to document why inequality of educational opportunity varies across Indian states. We go beyond documenting state-rankings in inequality of opportunity by examining the reasons for the divergence in state-level experience of equalizing educational opportunities. In order to delve a little deeper into the state-level policy factors and experiences with economic growth and poverty reduction, we build on Besley.

It ranks 16 Indian states by percentage change in inequality of opportunity and their growth elasticity of poverty, GDP growth rates, rates of poverty reduction, and performance in four areas of policy: voice and accountability; access to finance; human capital investment and gender inclusion. All variables relating to economic growth, poverty and policies are in lagged form.

The informal look at how policy performance such as gains in GDP growth and poverty reduction are linked to the changes in inequality of educational opportunity. The next column ranks the states in terms of economic growth and poverty reduction. These states have tended to have fast growth rates and high growth elasticities of poverty. Poverty reduction is greatest in states like Kerala, Punjab, and Andhra Pradesh whilst it is lowest in states like Bihar, Assam, and Madhya Pradesh.

On the whole, there is a statistically significant, positive correlation between inequality of opportunity and poverty reduction. States that have been more successful in reducing poverty are also those who have been more successful at reducing inequality of opportunity between 1983 and 2004. Similar positive correlations also exist with respect to GDP growth rate and growth elasticity of poverty. However, the rank correlation coefficients are smaller in size suggesting the relative importance of poverty reduction over the other two variables in equalizing educational opportunity. The remaining columns correlate inequality of opportunity indices with four selected policy indicators.

In the column on voice and accountability, a higher newspaper circulation per capita is associated with a higher growth elasticity of poverty, a higher growth rate, a higher overall reduction in poverty and a higher percentage reduction in inequality of opportunity. A similar pattern is found in the access to finance column, where states are ranked by per capita credit extended by commercial banks. States with greater access to finance have higher ranks in all three indices.

The pattern of correlations between human capital, proxied by state education expenditures per capita, and changes in inequality of opportunity is recorded in the next column. The correlation of this variable with changes in inequality of opportunity indices is insignificant, and not always positive. In other words, states that have spent more on education are not always successful in reducing inequality of opportunity.

Finally, in the column on gender, inclusion of women in the labour force, as proxied by the ratio of female-to-male workers, is positively correlated with changes in inequality of opportunity rankings irrespective of the index used. Lastly, our preceding analysis was based on common types across states. Our major conclusions appear significantly robust to this alternative. Changes in inequality indices are almost always positively correlated with our policy indicators and these remain statistically significant in most cases.

As before, educational expenditure stands out for its lack of correlation with changes in inequality. To summarize, states with more accountable governments, greater access to finance, greater reduction in poverty, and greater inclusion of women in economic growth emerged as those that also succeeded in reducing inequality of opportunity. The positive correlations between policy variables, poverty reduction, growth elasticities of poverty, growth rates and inequality of opportunity are descriptive—they do not imply causality. Nonetheless, they help clarify the variables' overall effect on inequality of opportunity. The policies we have identified may be reducing inequality of opportunity because they positively affect growth and enhance the poverty effect of growth.

CONCLUSION

Our results show that India's record in reducing inequality of educational opportunity in postliberalization is characterized by considerable variation across states and regions. The state of Kerala stands out as the least unequal in terms of educational opportunities irrespective of the index used. In general, Southern states experienced lower inequality in educational opportunity when compared to Northern states.

This finding is consistent with observed North-South divide in social outcomes in India—numerous earlier studies have pointed out how Southern states such as Kerala and Tamil Nadu differ from Uttar Pradesh and Bihar in education and health outcomes. In addition, even after excluding the single success story, Kerala, significant interstate divergence remains amongst the remaining states.

Our findings show that different kinds of problem arise in different parts of India. The incidence of rural poverty is high in the Eastern states of Bihar, Orissa, and West Bengal. Yet both West Bengal and Orissa made significant progress in reducing inequality of opportunity whilst the situation worsened in Bihar.

On average, states with more accountable governments, greater access to finance, greater reduction in poverty, and greater inclusion of women in economic growth emerged as those that also succeeded in reducing inequality of educational opportunities. In other words, although not causal, significant positive associations were found between policy variables, poverty reduction, GDP growth elasticity of poverty, growth rates and reduction in inequality of educational opportunities. The policies we have identified may be reducing inequality of opportunity because they positively affect economic growth and enhance the poverty effect of such growth. Because the study period provides with both pre- and post-reform data on India, it is tempting to attribute the rising inequality of opportunities in some states and in some measures of opportunity to market reforms. The last decade has been a period of unprecedented improvement in living standards, thanks to liberalisation.

The accelerated progress of elementary education in the nineties in some states may have been a response to weakening of credit constraints and increasing market returns to education which followed economic reforms and liberalisation of 1990s. Therefore the finding of a positive correlation between reduction of inequality of educational opportunity and poverty reduction and growth is reassuring. If true, this suggests that social inequality does not matter as long as economic growth and poverty reduction is in place.

However, as argued by Dreze and Deaton, "Much else than liberalisation has happened in the nineties, and while issues of economic reform are of course extremely important, so are other aspects of economic and social policy". Lastly, it will be interesting to follow up this study using more recent data in the near future.

The last couple of years have seen marked improvement in school participation which is arguably due to the Sarva Shiksha Abhiyan "education for all" initiative. SSA aimed at achieving five years of primary schooling for all children by 2007. Nonetheless, completion rates for grade 5 had only reached 70% by 2005-6 with significant variations across states.

Similarly, although the SSA scheme aimed at achieving eight years of schooling for children aged 14-17 years, only slightly more than 50% of all 15-year-olds had completed eight years of schooling in 2004. Even then, considerable cross-state differences remained. Moreover, attention needs to be given to circumstance factors such as childhood poverty that affect schooling directly and are common across some social groups.

10

Social Inequality in Land Ownership in India

INTRODUCTION

The policies of stabilisation and structural adjustment implemented by the Government of India since 1991 have had a profound impact on agriculture, rural development and the living standards of the poor in rural India. One aspect of the new policy internationally is the attempt to replace classical land reform—which involves "the dispossession of a class of landlords, and the distribution of land to, and the enhancement of the freedom of, classes of the peasantry and agricultural workers hitherto dispossessed and exploited by landlordism"—with what has come to be known as "market-driven land reform".

However, studies have shown that in a capital constrained economy, the scope for achieving equitable distribution of resources through market operations is limited. Redistributive land reform not only enhances production and reduces poverty but is also a part of a democratic revolution that frees the people of the countryside from the fetters of landlordism. An important requirement of genuine land reforms is that the State intervene to ensure access to productive resources, mainly land, to social classes and groups that traditionally have not had access to land and free these classes from social and economic oppression. This document deals with an important form of discrimination in the countryside, the lack of access of Dalit and Adivasi households to ownership and operational holdings of land in rural India. It includes a case study of the impact of land reforms in one State of India, West Bengal, on land holding among Dalit and Adivasi households. Dalits and Adivasis have been subjected to various forms of deprivation historically. In many places Dalits are still subjected to the criminal practice of untouchability and other atrocities. Dalits also face various forms of deprivation and inequality with respect to education, health, and access to different kinds of jobs.

Access to land in an agriculture-based rural economy is important because land is a primary means and instrument of production. The social distribution of land in a village economy determines the economic position and power relations between different social groups in the village. Chakrabarty and Ghosh using NSS data on ownership holdings of land, showed that in most States of India the proportion of land owned by SC households was much lower than their share in total population.

However, in rural India the proportion of land owned by SC households had increased in the period between 1982 and 1992. Thorat noted that in 1993-94 only 19 per cent of all Dalit households were self employed in agriculture while the comparable statistic for non-Dalit/Adivasi households was 42 per cent. Thorat, "the limited access to agricultural land and capital assets is both due to the historical legacy associated with restrictions imposed by the caste system and the ongoing discrimination in land market and capital market and other related economic spheres".

In this context it is important to distinguish land used for productive purposes from land that is not used directly for agricultural production. Land used for income bearing activities, for example cropland, plantations and orchards constitute productive agricultural land, while housesite land, fallow and barren lands are categories of land not used directly for productive purposes. Our aim in this document is to determine Dalit households' access to land for production, and compare this access with that of other social groups. This document is in seven parts. A brief description of secondary sources of data on land holdings in India. We present some findings from secondary data on the differential access to land by different social groups in India. The document uses primary data from seven villages in the State to examine the access to land by different social groups in West Bengal. We analyse the role of government intervention through redistribution of land in improving access to land among under-privileged groups in West Bengal. The participation of different social groups in land markets in the same seven villages of West Bengal and a concluding part.

SECONDARY DATA SOURCES ON LAND HOLDINGS IN INDIA

There are three major sources of secondary data on land holdings in India: the National Sample Survey Land and Livestock Holdings surveys, NSS Employment and Unemployment surveys and the World Agricultural Census. The L&LH surveys of the NSS were initiated in 1954-55 as part of the World Agricultural Census and since 1970-71 these surveys have been carried out decennially. The NSSO conducted its most recent L&LH survey in 2002-03.

In these surveys, the NSSO deals with two kinds of land holding, household ownership holdings and household operational holdings. Household ownership holdings include all land owned or held in owner-like possession by households. The definition of household ownership holdings includes all kinds of land owned by households, including homestead land and non-agricultural land.

The published reports of the NSS provide data on households that do not own land disaggregated by social groups. However, as the preceeding definition indicates, households that have no land for production are nevertheless not counted as "landless" when they own homesteads or other types of land.

The data published by the NSS reports disaggregate total household ownership holdings into two sub-categories: homesteads and land other than homestead land. NSS reports provide data on aggregate household ownership holdings separately for different social groups. The data on homestead and non-homestead land are not disaggregated by social group. The household operational holding is the extent of land managed—whether the land be owned, leased or otherwise possessed—as a techno-economic unit of production in which some agricultural production had been carried out in the reference period. Operational holdings are thus a better measure of access to land for production than ownership holdings. The NSS Reports do not publish data on operational holdings of land disaggregated by social group.

The NSS E&U surveys provide data on "land possessed" and "land cultivated" by rural households. The published Reports present the data disaggregated by social groups. "Land possessed" by households includes all land owned and occupied by households. It includes all types of land: agricultural land, homestead land and non-agricultural land.

As in the case of ownership holdings in L&LH surveys, this kind of classification of land tends to underestimate the incidence of landlessness with respect to productive land. "Land cultivated" includes all cropland, plantations and orchards cultivated by households. It excludes homestead land and non-agricultural land. This category includes land owned and selfcultivated, land occupied and land leased in. It excludes land leased out by households. It is equivalent to an operational holding of agricultural land.

The L&LH surveys, only 6.6 per cent of the rural households in India did not own any land in 2003. The incidence of landlessness declined between 1992 and 2003. E&U surveys, 2 per cent of households in rural India did not possess any land in 2004-05. There has also been a very sharp decline in the proportion of households without land between 1993-94 and 2004-05.

These figures are such because of the inclusion of homestead land in the definition of ownership holding. At the same time, landlessness with respect to the control of cropland and other productive land appears to have increased. Studies on landlessness often use the percentage of landless agricultural labour households in the total workforce from NSS

E&U surveys to measure the extent of landlessness in India. Landless agricultural labour households are households that are engaged in agriculture but do not have access to land for purposes of production.

The percentage of landless agricultural labour households increased in the 1990s, which constitutes strong circumstantial evidence of an increase in landlessness itself in rural India. An Agricultural Census in India was initiated in 1950 as part of the World Agricultural Census programme organised by the Food and Agriculture Organisation. Until 1960, the Agricultural Census of India was carried out by the NSSO. From 1970 the Agricultural Census has been carried out every five years by the Department of Agriculture.

The Agricultural Censuses are censuses of land holdings, and provide data on the distribution of operational holdings of land. The available published data are disaggregated by social groups. In States where plot-wise land records are revised annually, the Agricultural Census is simply a retabulation of the existing land records. In the States that do not have plot-wise land records, the Agricultural Census is a sample survey of households that operate land. In any case, being a survey of holdings rather than households, the Agricultural Census does not provide us with estimates of landlessness among households.

SOME RESULTS FROM SECONDARY DATA

We have used two indicators to assess access to land. Absolute deprivation of access to productive land is measured by the incidence of landlessness. Inequality in access to land is measured by an index of access to land for cultivation. The definition of ownership and operational holdings in the Reports of the NSSO on the L&LH surveys. A further note is necessary on the changes in the definition of ownership holdings at the L&LH surveys in the 48th round and the 59th round.

In 1992, a household ownership holding was divided into the following subcategories:

- Homestead

- All land other than homestead

In 2003, a household ownership holding was divided into the following subcategories:

- *Homestead*: Uncultivated part; and homestead: cultivated part
- All land other than homestead

The sub-category of the 2003 survey represents land that could have been either in or in 1992. Thus, sub-category of 1992 does not correspond either with sub-category in 2003 or the sum of sub-categories and in 2003. The E&U surveys provide us with comparable serial data on rural households that do not cultivate land, that is, households that are landless with respect to operational holdings of productive land.

First, I present the data on households that were landless with respect to ownership holdings from the L&LH 59th Round survey of 2003. These data cannot be used to compute rates of change in landlessness between the 48th Round and 59th Round. Secondly, I present NSS data on rural households that did not cultivate land and discuss the changes that occurred in the levels of landlessness over these two surveys. Thirdly, I use NSS data from Employment and Unemployment surveys to calculate an Index of Access of rural households belonging to different social groups to productive agricultural land.

LANDLESSNESS IN THE NSS LAND AND LIVESTOCK HOLDING SURVEY, 2003

We have used NSS data on Land and Livestock Holdings Survey, 2003 by States and social groups in order to make an initial estimate of the proportion of rural households that do not own agricultural land. The proportion of households that do not hold any land other than homesteads by States and social group in 2003, that is, category in the preceeding discussion on the 59th round data. By NSS 2003 data, 41.6 per cent of rural households in rural India did not own any land other than homesteads. The incidence of landlessness was higher among Dalit households than among Adivasi households and non Dalit/Adivasi households. While 56.5 per cent Dalit households did not own non-homestead land, 35.5 per cent Adivasi households and 37.8 per cent non Dalit/ Adivasi households did not own non-homestead land. The data generally substantiate the impression that while Dalit households are landless, Adivasi households have small plots of land of low productivity.

The proportion of Dalit households that do not own any land other than homesteads is highest in Punjab, Kerala and Haryana, where above 80 per cent Dalit households do not own any land other than homesteads. The States with lowest incidence of landlessness are Jammu and Kashmir and Himachal Pradesh. In West Bengal, 46.5 per cent households do not own land other than homesteads.

This is slightly higher than the national average. However, the proportion of landless Dalit households is below the national average in West Bengal by both the definitions of land holdings. The proportion of Adivasi households that do not own land other than homesteads is much higher in West Bengal than in India as a whole.

HOUSEHOLDS WITH NO OPERATIONAL HOLDINGS: NSS DATA 1993-94 AND 2004-05

For any time series analysis of the incidence of landlessness based on consistent concepts and definitions, the only data source available is the NSS E&U surveys. NSS E&U surveys allow us to estimate the incidence of landlessness in terms of operational holdings of land. The change in the proportion of households that did not cultivate land in the period between 1993-94 and 2004-05. The proportion of rural households that did not have access to land for cultivation in India has increased by 10.6 per cent between 1993-94 and 2004-05. The data show that the incidence of households that do not cultivate land has increased in almost all Indian States in the previous decade, Kerala, Jammu and Kashmir and Assam being the only exceptions. The decline in the incidence of landlessness in Kerala and Assam can to some extent be attributed to the extension of cultivation of plantation crops like rubber within the homestead. Homesteads are also included in 'cultivated land' in these States, since orchards and plantations are considered as 'cultivated land' by the NSS definition, thus bringing down the proportion of households who do not cultivate land, without an actual change in land holding structures. The highest increase in the incidence of landlessness was experienced in the States of Himachal Pradesh, Rajasthan, Madhya Pradesh, and Uttar Pradesh.

The increase in the share of households without access to land for cultivation in India between 1992-93 and 2004-05 is higher for Adivasi households and non SC/ST households than for Dalit households. In six States, Jammu and Kashmir, Kerala, Assam, Tripura, Bihar and Punjab, landlessness among Dalits has declined. Landlessness among Adivasis has also declined in seven States, namely Jammu and Kashmir, Kerala, Assam, Tripura, Bihar, Gujarat and Haryana.

It is however important to note that in Himachal Pradesh and Rajasthan which have witnessed the highest increase in landlessness, it is mainly the Dalits and Adivasis who have lost land. In these two States landlessness among Dalits has increased by more than 60 per cent. The increase in landlessness among Dalits is very low in West Bengal. It is mostly the Adivasi households and non-Dalit/Adivasi households who have lost land in West Bengal in this period.

SOME RESULTS FROM PRIMARY DATA IN WEST BENGAL

West Bengal is a State where policy efforts have been directed to distribute land to the landless and the poor, and specifically to Dalits, Adivasis and other deprived social groups, and also to issue joint title deeds to men and women. Some of the social-distributive effects of the land reform programme show up in recent village-based research and analyses of secondary data.

These show that West Bengal is a ahead of other States with respect to the distribution of agricultural and homestead land to Dalit and Adivasi households, and also with respect to the purchase of agricultural land by the rural poor, including Dalit households. We shall examine specific features of the ownership of agricultural and homestead land by Dalit, Adivasi and other households from village-level data collected from different parts of West Bengal. The village-level data come mainly from a series of village surveys in seven villages in different agro-climatic zones in West Bengal conducted in May-June 2005. Dalkati is located in the red laterite zone of West Medinipur District. Its population is predominantly Adivasi. The levels of agricultural productivity are low, and, since the village is situated in the fringes of a forest, the collection of forest produce forms a important source of livelihood.

Bidyanidhi and Kalinagar are in Barddhaman District, where paddy yields have traditionally been high. Kalmandasguri in Koch Bihar District and Amarsinghi in Malda District are villages where paddy and jute cultivation predominates, and where mechanisation is low. Thuthipakar is a village in Uttar Dinajpur where the cropping pattern has recently shifted from paddy to tea and pineapple. Tentultala, in the estuarine region of North 24 Parganas, has also witnessed major changes in cropping pattern in recent years. Cultivation has shifted from paddy to prawn cultivation in the village.

Dalkati village in West Medinipur district did not have a Dalit population. In the other villages Dalits constituted over 30 per cent of all households. Tentultala and Kalmandasguri each had a significant Muslim population, and Thuthipakar and Kalinagar each had a significant Adivasi population. In three of these seven villages, the Index of Access to agricultural land of Dalit households was greater than one. The Index value was 1.49, 1.28 and 1.41 in Tentultala, Thuthipakar and Kalmandasguri repectively. In other words, in these villages, the share of Dalits in land ownership was greater than their share in the population. In the two villages of Barddhaman district, the index values for Dalits were as low as 0.2 and 0.3.

In Tentultala, Kalmandasguri and Bidyanidhi, Muslim households constitute a substantial part of the population, but the index value for Muslims was low. In each village, the index value for operational holdings for Dalit households is marginally higher than the corresponding index for ownership holdings. This indicates that land tenancies have helped Dalit households gain access to operational holdings of land. The case of Tentultala is an interesting one. In Tentultala, extension of prawn cultivation has had a striking effect on the pattern of land distribution. Operational holdings in Tentultala are highly concentrated in the hands of a few prawn tank owners who lease in most of the village land for prawn cultivation. The tank owners living in the village belong to Dalit and Muslim households and that is reflected in the new position of these two social groups with respect to land. To sum up, in three of the six villages with a Dalit population, the value of the access index for Dalits is greater than one.

LAND REFORMS

West Bengal is well known for its land reform, a policy on which there is a large literature. Till 2005, 445,503 hectares of agricultural land were redistributed in West Bengal to 2,817,179 beneficiaries. In a State in which 23 per cent of the population is Dalit and 5.5 per cent is Adivasi of the new title-holders, 37 per cent were Dalits and 19 per cent were Adivasis. The social-distributive effects of the land reform programme are well acknowledged. The West Bengal Human Development Report 2004 states that "the di' proportionate granting of patta rights to Scheduled Castes and Tribes is likely to have led not just to some degree of economic empowerment, but also a greater sense of social dignity as well".

The land reform programme of the Left Front Government in West Bengal brought land to new parts of the peasantry. Land reforms in West Bengal had three components: tenancy reforms, redistribution of ceiling surplus land to the landless and the poor and distribution of homestead land. Our analysis deals with the distribution of ceiling surplus land and of homestead land. First, let us consider the redistribution of crop land to the landless and rural poor. The implementation of land reforms varied across the seven villages. In Dalkati almost 60 per cent of the households received agricultural land, while in Thuthipakar only 7 per cent of the households benefited from redistribution of agricultural land. This includes households that obtained pattas directly, and households that inherited assigned land. In terms of the area redistributed, the highest was in Dalkati, where 32 per cent of the total area of household ownership holdings in the village was acquired in the course of land reform. The area of redistributed land was lowest in Bidyanidhi, where only 1.9 per cent of total agricultural land owned was redistributed land. It is interesting also to note that not one of the study villages was untouched by land reforms.

The major beneficiaries of the distribution of agricultural land in our study villages have been Dalit and Adivasi households and in Kalmandasguri, Muslim households. In Dalkati, Tentultala, Kalinagar and Bidyanidhi more than 70 per cent of the agricultural land redistributed was assigned to Dalit and Adivasi households. In Kalmandasguri, 40 per cent of the redistributed agricultural land was assigned to Muslim households and another 43 per cent to Dalit and Adivasi households.

In two of the villages, Thuthipakar and Amarsinghi, where major beneficiaries were non-Dalits, most of the non-Dalit households who were assigned land belonged to the Other Backward Classes group. Secondly, let us consider the distribution of house-site or homestead land, which is an important component of land reform in West Bengal. Access to homestead land is also an important aspect of land ownership in India.

Ownership of homestead land means not only a place to live and a changed position in society, but also represents access to a new source of potential nutrition and livelihood support as a result of kitchen-garden cultivation. The absence of ownership of a house-site is often a key factor in the unfreedom of peasant and agricultural worker households in India.

In all seven study villages, Muslim, Dalit and Adivasi households were the major beneficiaries of homestead land distribution. Out of 210 households that gained homestead land, 21 per cent were Dalit, 46 per cent were Adivasi, 24 per cent were Muslim, and 10 per cent belonged to other caste groups. Of the last group, a majority belonged to the Other Backward Classes. An important feature of the distribution of homestead land in Kalmandasguri, Thuthipakar and Dalkati was the larger size of homesteads compared to the other villages.

In these villages, the average size of homesteads distributed per household was 0.13 acres, 0.15 acres and 0.17 acres respectively. Larger homesteads allow for kitchen garden cultivation and rearing backyard poultry, both a common phenomenon in these villages. Such activities enhance household incomes and nutritional standards.

PARTICIPATION IN LAND MARKETS

In a 2001 study, Vikas Rawal showed that while empirical studies in parts of Uttar Pradesh and Punjab had found that the net buyers of cultivable land were large landowners and that the net sellers of land were small landowners, the trend was quite the opposite in the two villages of West Bengal he studied. The major buyers of land in the period 1977 to 1995 in these two villages of Bankura District were landless households and small landowners.

The document attributed the ability to purchase land to the increased purchasing power among the poor in Bengal facilitated by land distribution, tenancy reform, higher wage rates, and access to credit. The present study confirms and adds a new dimension to this conclusion. In the survey of seven villages, information was collected from households on the purchase and sale of all types of land between 1990 and 2005. Five of the seven villages have significant Dalit populations. In four of them, Dalit and Muslim households were net buyers of land, while caste Hindu households were net sellers.

The only exception to the rule was Amarsinghi, where both Dalit and non-Dalit households were net sellers of land and Tentultala, where caste Hindus were net purchasers of land. The acquisition of ceiling-surplus land by the Government of West Bengal for redistribution was and still remains a major disincentive for landowners with relatively large holdings to purchase land. The case of Bidyanidhi is a striking example of how large land owning households have sold their rural property and have moved to urban areas for new types of employment. In this village, 13 acres of land was acquired for redistribution from the largest land owning household and the household owned roughly 16 acres of land during the 2005 survey. On my subsequent visit to the village in June 2006, I found that the household had sold another 5 acres of land.

The head of the household informed me that most of the household members now lived outside the village and they had decided to sell the land before the State acquired any more land. In a State where control over land by old-style landowners have ceased to be a source of social and political power as in the past, large landowning households that are not mainly dependent on agricultural incomes for their livelihoods have not hesitated to sell their land.

CONCLUSION

The exclusion faced by Dalits in India in terms of access to basic economic resources remains a reality in contemporary India. In particular, the right of the Dalit masses to productive resources such as land has generally been left unattended, if not grossly violated, since access to land demands deep and radical changes in social structure. West Bengal is one State in India where efforts have been made to grant land rights to landless households, especially Dalit and Adivasi households.

The impact of land reforms in West Bengal is reflected in the national level statistics on land holdings. Secondary data show that Dalit households in West Bengal have better access to land compared to other States. This is indicated by the fact that the proportion of landless Dalit households in terms of ownership holdings is lower in West Bengal that the national average and the Index of Access to agricultural land is higher than the national average.

There has been very little increase in the incidence of landlessness among Dalits in West Bengal between 1993-94 and 2004-05. Village level data show that Dalit, Adivasi and

Muslim households have been major beneficiaries of land reforms in West Bengal. These social groups have gained access to agricultural and homestead land through the process of land reforms.

The policy of land reform implemented by the Government of West Bengal has thus contributed though in a limited way to lowering inequalities across social groups in the State. Village level data show that Dalit and Muslim households were net buyers of land in recent years. This has also increased their access and control over this very crucial economic resource

11

Stigma, Social Inequality, Alcohol and Drug Use

INTRODUCTION

This document discusses stigma and marginalization in connection with psychoactive substance use, and how these affect patterns by social class and other social inequalities. The document starts from the point that adverse outcomes from heavy alcohol and drug use are much more strongly related to lower social class position than the patterns of heavy alcohol and drug use themselves.

As will be discussed, there are certainly mechanisms by which poor people can suffer worse outcomes than more affluent people for the same behaviour. My argument is that, in the case of alcohol and drug problems, an extra factor has been relatively neglected: that alcohol and drug use and problems are heavily moralized territories, often resulting in stigma and marginalization, and that these factors are important in the adverse outcomes.

SUBSTANCE USE CONTEXT, POVERTY AND MARGINALIZATION ARE NOT NECESSARILY CAUSALLY PRIOR

While the term 'social inequality' encompasses differences on other social differentiations such as gender, age or ethnoreligious category, the main emphasis in public health usage has been on socio-economic differentiations. Even here, it is well recognized that there are definitional and measurement choices to be made: poverty can be defined in absolute or in relative terms; and the variables often included in measures of socio-economic status, such as education, income and occupational and neighbourhood status, differ both conceptually and also often in their relationship to health outcomes.

By and large, the public health literature takes the attribute of being disadvantaged as causally prior in considering its relation to life-style factors such as substance use and to health outcomes. There is a certain logic to this, where the kind of outcome being considered is a death from heart attack, liver cirrhosis or AIDS.

Even in the sphere of physical health, however, the model becomes more questionable when the outcome in question is shifted from death to illness or disability; the existence of the illness or disability may bring a downward drift in socioeconomic status.

To the extent that the illness is caused by substance use, the causal arrow between the use and the socio-economic status is then potentially bidirectional. When consideration extends beyond physical to include mental health, there are further complications.

In the first place, an aspect of the substance use now becomes potentially the end-point, rather than an intermediator, in the form of alcohol and drug dependence and other substance use disorders. Secondly, with mental disorders the issue of the element of social definition in the end-point becomes inescapable.

While there is an element of social construction and definition in all illness, the threshold of what becomes defined as a mental disorder is often set by the reactions of others to behaviours which they are defining as 'strange and odd'. The element of social construction is particularly important when it comes to substance use disorders, and for that matter such partly medicalized social categories as 'substance abuser'. More generally, the use of alcohol and drugs is strongly moralized, and those transgressing moral norms are subject to stigma and social marginalization.

STIGMA, POVERTY AND ALCOHOL AND DRUG PROBLEMS

We may take as a working definition of stigma, in the context of alcohol and drug use, the one used in the law of a US state, Wisconsin: 'Stigma' means disqualification from social acceptance, derogation, marginalization and ostracism encountered by... persons who abuse alcohol or other drugs as the result of societal negative attitudes, feelings, perceptions, representations and acts of discrimination.

Those who are stigmatized or marginalized are often poor, and otherwise lacking social resources; but there is no necessary relation between stigmatization and poverty or other social inequalities. The empirical overlap between those who are marginalized and those who are poor has long been recognized to be partial; Shaw's distinction between the 'deserving' and the 'undeserving poor' in Major Barbara reflected the common social welfare distinction of the time. On the other hand, it is also possible to be rich and stigmatized and marginalized, although the affluent are ipso facto better able to purchase protection from this.

There is also no necessary relation between psychoactive substance use and stigma or marginalization. In the developed countries today this is most obvious for alcohol, where drinking is closely associated with many positively valued and highprestige activities and statuses-we have only to mention champagne for a wedding reception, or complimentary drinks for first-class passengers.

It is also now true, at least in some youth subcultures, for some forms of illicit substance use-*e.g.* ecstasy at a rave, or cannabis at a student party. On the other hand, as we shall discuss, some aspects of psychoactive substance use seem to attract near-universal stigma and marginalization.

SOURCES OF SOCIAL VALUE AND DEROGATION

What are the properties of psychoactive substances which are relevant to social valuation or derogation? In the first place, psychoactive substances are valued physical goods. Their status as physical goods renders them subject to commodification, and indeed globalization in use and trade. Given their positive valuation, possession and use has often been a symbol of power and domination or at least of access to resources beyond subsistence.

Secondly, using psychoactive substances is a behaviour, and very often a social behaviour. There are thus many social and cultural associations, mostly positive, around the use of the substance. Toasting in champagne as a symbol of celebration, the cannabis joint passing around the circle of users, the wine circulating at a family holiday meal, the sense of community that may be engendered at a rave, are all contemporary images which conjure up the social meanings which become attached to the use and which extend beyond the psychoactive effect *per se* of the substance.

Use of the substances socially means that the use often serves to demarcate the boundaries of inclusion and exclusion in a social grouping-so that the use of a psychoactive substance in itself can signal social exclusion and marginalization. Thirdly, psychoactive substance use is a peculiarly intimate behaviour, in that the substance is taken into the body. Any such substance is a potential source of contamination and poison, as well as of nutrition, pleasure or solace.

In this respect, psychoactive substances are a part of the more general category of foodstuffs and drinks, and carry at least their share of the complex of prescriptions and taboos which surround what is ingested. Fourthly, by definition psychoactive substances affect thinking and feeling, and are often expected to affect behaviour-even to the extent that the substance may be seen as possessing the user, submerging the true self.

The psychoactive qualities of the substances is what makes them both 'prized' and feared as 'dangerous', as Steele and Josephs put it. The psychoactivity accounts both for much of the positive valuation on the substances and for much of the moral loading that commonly surrounds their use. For all these reasons, a heavy load of symbolism thus often attaches to the use or non-use of psychoactive substances. The use may be a positive signal of power or status, may be heavily derogated or stigmatized, or may simply be an expression of difference without strong implications for power or status.

PSYCHOACTIVE SUBSTANCES AND SOCIAL INSTITUTIONS AND RUBRICS

Psychoactive substance use and its risks are influenced or governed by social institutions and professions. In many countries, for instance, alcohol can only be sold with a government licence, carrying with it limits on the circumstances of sale. By international agreement, some psychoactive substances are available only when permitted by a prescription from a physician, with a licensed pharmacist usually actually providing the substance.

Use of psychoactive substances results in a variety of social and health consequences, both immediate and chronic. Included are not only chronic and acute health consequences to the substance user, but also injury and other harm to others and problems in work and family roles. The full range of social institutions and professions which respond to and handle health, casualty and social problems are involved in responding to psychoactive substance problems.

Each of the professions and institutions tends to be associated with a particular governing image or rubric of the problems with which it deals. Physician and hospitals deal with illness, psychiatrists and mental illness clinics specifically with mental illness, police and judges with crime, welfare workers and social welfare with disability or destitution, priests and churches with sin.

Problems from alcohol or drugs sometimes fall between these jurisdictions, but more commonly fall into areas of shared jurisdiction. It is thus not obvious which institutional system should be assigned the primary jurisdiction, and there are considerable differences from one society to another, and sometimes from one substance to another, in this. Thus the health system has primary jurisdiction for alcohol problems in Italy and Denmark, while the welfare system has traditionally had primary responsibility in Sweden and Finland. In Denmark, on the other hand, drugs are handled by the welfare system. Responsibility can be shifted between systems, sometimes abruptly; thus, for a couple of years in California in the late 1960s, alcoholism was shifted from being a health disorder to being a vocational disability; for that period, if a Californian did not need help with getting or keeping work, he or she was not eligible for alcoholism treatment.

A primarily US-based sociological literature, using 'deviance' as its general term for problems considered to need social handling, has emphasized a general shift in the 20th century from crime to illness models of deviance. On the other hand, the literature has acknowledged that the trend had been in the opposite direction in the first half of the 20th century for illicit drugs in the United States.

The general perception, in a US context, has been that more stigma is associated with crime or vice than with disease, so that the alcoholism movement, for instance, dedicated itself to persuading the society that changing the conceptualization of alcohol problems from vice or crime to illness would diminish the stigmatization of those with the problems.

THE GENERALIZED AND UBIQUITOUS STIGMA OF ALCOHOLISM AND ADDICTION

The question of how much the stigmatization of those with a particular problem is affected by changing its rubric, or even its social handling procedures, remains open. For one thing it has long been recognized that, in the minds of many in the general population, the rubrics are not mutually exclusive: those who subscribe to a disease model of alcoholism are also ready to think of it as a vice or moral weakness. Thus the intent of the alcoholism movement in putting forward the disease concept of alcoholism, that it should replace the 'old moral model', has not been realized.

As a recent US discussion put it, 'in spite of two centuries of claims that addiction is a disease, and more recently that it is similar to other chronic diseases, the idea that addiction is rooted in repeated bad choices remains widely compelling'. Alcoholism and drug addiction are, on the one hand, from the perspective of medical nosology and public health, categories in the international classification of health disorders, under their professional names of alcohol and drug dependence. On the other hand, in social terms both alcoholism and drug addiction are thoroughly moralized and derogated categories. Both 'alcoholism' and 'drug addiction' ranked near the top, in terms of degree of social disapproval or stigma reported by local key informants, in a list of 18 conditions ranked for 14 different countries in a WHO study in all but two countries, for instance, above being 'dirty and unkempt'; while in all but three being a drug addict was reported to be more disapproved or stigmatized than having a criminal record for burglary.

An individual's patterns of psychoactive substance use, in a great many societies, are thus not only a matter of public health interest, but are also a subject of social evaluation in terms of approval or disapproval, of honour or stigma, in everyday life. The evaluations attached to a particular pattern of substance use vary over time and between cultures, and often vary also within a culture just as to circumstances and who is using. Disapproval may be expressed in the form of state sanctions, up to and including being deprived of life, liberty or property. Whatever we may think of these moral evaluations, an analysis which takes into account social realities cannot ignore them.

In this sense, patterns of psychoactive substance use, particularly through the social evaluations of them, become involved in the creation of marginalization, social exclusion and stigma. This is a familiar territory for sociologists and criminologists. In sociological theories of labelling and deviance the pattern of substance use becomes the 'primary deviance', the negative social evaluation of which initially potentially sets the user on the road to marginalization and exclusion.

In the classic scenario, the marginalized users then find each other, and form a mutually supportive counterculture which cements its members into a further marginalization through 'secondary deviance'. At the end-point of this process, the deviant substance user is fully marginalized and socially excluded, indeed extruded from respectable society. The universality and inevitability of this scenario has been challenged empirically, at least for mental illness. However, by whatever mechanism, there is no doubt that some patterns of substance use-archetypally, the patterns of drinking which become defined as 'alcoholism'-entail a process of social degradation and exclusion, a process described in classic Alcoholics Anonymous language as ending in the drinker 'hitting bottom'.

A glimpse of the processes of social devaluation directly relevant to health outcome can be seen in the literature on public opinion about which personal characteristics should be taken into account in setting health priorities. Summarizing six studies from Britain, the United States and Australia, Olsen report that respondents felt that tobacco smokers, 'high' alcohol users and illegal drug users should all receive less priority in health care. Often the justification given is the belief that the users' behaviour contributed to their own illness. Along the same lines, the 14-country WHO study found that, in responses on scenarios involving alcohol or heroin problems, the 'theme of personal responsibility became vividly apparent'. Studies in health services show that the care given is in fact likely to be inferior if the patient is seen as a skid-row drinker or a similarly derogated category.

Santana found that among nine categories of 'disadvantaged people' interviewed in a population sample in deprived districts in Portugal, those identified as alcoholics were, along with the homeless, the least likely to have used health services, despite 100% having less than good health, and the most likely to have a 'bad' or 'very bad' opinion of the health services. To the extent access to good health care affects health status, these findings show a direct path by which exclusion and marginalization can affect health status.

SOURCES AND OBJECTS OF SUBSTANCE USE-RELATED STIGMATIZATION

If we focus on processes in an ongoing society, we can conceive of stigmatization and marginalization as proceeding from three main sources: There are the intimate processes of social control and censure among family and friends which are frequently effective, but which may also result at length in the family and friends becoming fed up and pushing the user out of the family or into treatment.

There are the decisions by social agents and agencies, which tend to focus attention on the most problematic cases and to amplify their marginalization. Even official actions intended as positive steps towards social reintegration may result in marginalization if the case does not 'succeed'. There are also policy decisions at the local or national level which result in marginalization.

For example, the US law that a family should be evicted from public housing if any member of the family is associated with drug dealing has the result of increasing marginalization. More generally, policy decisions to be 'tough on drugs' always carry the potential to stigmatize and marginalize those who do not conform. Marginalization of those defined as having alcohol or drug problems is thus a process which can have both elements which are personal and interactional and elements which are institutional and structural.

Underlying the process is the heavy moralization and stigmatization of substance use which is defined as problematic-not least by other substance users, who often define themselves in contrast to the problematic category. The underlying determinant of what is problematic is the occurrence of problems which are ascribed to the substance use: illness, violence, casualties, and failure in major social roles, particularly at work and in the family.

Part of modernity, starting in the early 19th century, seems to have been an increased willingness to see first alcohol, and later other psychoactive substances, as causal agents in these calamities and failures in responsibility. From the point of view of the substance user, this fundamental and minimum level of moralization of substance use operates in terms of 'getting caught'. In the company of other heavy drinkers, there may be little or no moral loading on the drinking behaviour itself. The ideal of the 'competent drinker', as Gusfield describes it among the heavy drinkers he studied, is not defined in terms of characteristics of the drinking behaviour, but instead simply in terms of the drinker's 'self-judgement of his state of risk acceptance', *i.e.* the ability to handle himself without adverse consequences.

But if the drinker misjudges-or if he simply gets caught out in a situation where the risk may have been low but not zero-then moral disapproval descends on him, not only from society in general but also from other heavy drinkers, to whom he now appears as an incompetent drinker, one who has 'let the side down'.

Similar conceptual mechanisms can be seen at work for use of other drugs, for instance in Slavin's study of socially integrated methedrine injectors, who-far out on the distribution of drug use as they themselves were-distinguished themselves from 'junkies' in terms of their own sense of 'control' of their risks. Slavin notes his own discomfort at the 'pejorative language' of his informants concerning the 'junkies', but also notes that the distinction they make 'works in some ways to reduce drug related harms for these men and keep them "functional".

We may see three other areas of moralization and stigmatization built on this fundamental understanding of adverse events and consequences of the substance use. The first is the moralization of intoxication itself. At a minimum, to be stoned or drunk in specific circumstances-*e.g.* when about to drive a car, or as a parent looking after small children-is unacceptable to nearly everyone.

For those who do accept getting intoxicated or high at all, it should be in periods and circumstances of 'time out' when the risks are limited and those in attendance are presumably assuming the attached risks. But acceptance of intoxication as a desirable or morally acceptable state is rare in 'serious' public discourse in many modern societies, inhabiting instead the realm of literary and other artistic works. The proportion of key informants in each of 14 countries reporting that 'people would think it was wrong' for a person with each of 10 named conditions to appear in public. Overall, the conditions most likely to be socially excluded were 'someone who is visibly drunk' and 'someone who is visibly under the influence of drugs'. The moralization of intoxication means that advocates of the argument that alcohol problems are best controlled by integration of drinking in cultural practices specify carefully that they do not include intoxication, however culturally integrated it may be.

Thus, for instance, Morris Chafetz, long a leading exponent of this position, specified that anyone who 'has been intoxicated four times in a year' should be considered a problem drinker. Similarly, those touting the advantages of drinking have been careful to specify that it is moderate drinking, and not intoxication, which they favour: 'Citizens for Moderation the interests of who consume responsibly and in good health'.

Conflating intoxicated bad behaviour with addiction, and arguing for a 'moral vision of addiction', Stanton Peele called for inculcating 'values that are incompatible with addiction and with drug- and alcohol-induced misbehaviour', contrasting 'values towards health, moderation and selfcontrol' with 'the immorality of addictive behaviour'. Those on the 'wetter' side of debates about drinking practices and policies have thus been at pains to differentiate controlled or moderate drinking from intoxication, and to assign opposite moral valences to them-negative for intoxication, but positive for controlled or moderate drinking.

Intoxication has thus remained morally reprehensible or at least questionable in most public discourse throughout the modern period. The stigma on intoxication is so taken for granted that what exactly is wrong with it is not often spelled out. There seem to be three related elements. A person under the influence of alcohol or drugs is seen as unpredictable, and thus anxiety-provoking for those in the vicinity.

The intoxication is seen as disinhibiting, and thus as potentially resulting in bad or injurious behaviour. And to be intoxicated is also to abandon the norm of 'sober attention as the normative mode of consciousness for every waking minute', in the modern world of exacting machinery and intellectual work. A second area of moralization and stigmatization is in terms of addiction or dependence. The high level of stigma around alcoholism and addiction. A loss of control-over the substance use and over one's life-has always been the central element in modern cultural understandings of the nature of alcoholism and addiction, so that they have often been characterized as 'diseases of the will'. Half a century ago, Edwin Lemert collected a number of statements of American attitudes towards the alcoholic, and noted that the 'general theme underlying' them 'has to do with lack of self-control on the part of the drinker'.

Lemert went on to note the stigmatization that this theme inevitably involved: 'This societal symbolism of the deviation as a sign of character weakness is one of the most vivid and isolating distinctions which can be made in a culture which attributes morality, success, and respectability to the power of a disciplined will'. A third potential area of moralization and stigmatization is less universally applied: stigmatization in terms of substance use *per se*.

For alcohol, the general stigmatization applies only in certain cultural milieux, *e.g.* for Mormons or for Moslems, although there are statuses or circumstances-a pregnant woman or an on-duty bus driver, for instance-where any use tends to be stigmatized. For tobacco, cigarette smoking has increasingly taken on a somewhat stigmatized status; as might be predicted, it is lung cancer patients, those who have been 'caught' in adverse consequences from the smoking, who feel the stigma most keenly.

The aim of 'just say no' policies on drugs is generally to render use of the drugs socially unacceptable, that is to stigmatize use, and users in fact report that they do experience some stigma.

STUDYING STIGMA

There are two literatures on stigma, operating on very different premises. One literature, oriented primarily around illness, mental illness and disability, focuses on those who are already in a stigmatized status or condition; stigma is taken for given as a discriminatory social evil. The studies often consider the negative effects of stigma on the stigmatized person or on the professional—patient interaction from the perspective of how the stigma or these effects can be neutralized.

Aligned with this literature are substantial public policy initiatives, like the Wisconsin legislation quoted at the start of this document, which provides that the state agency may 'develop and implement a comprehensive strategy to reduce stigma of and discrimination against persons with mental illness, alcoholics and drug dependent persons'. The other literature, oriented primarily around crime, generally views stigmatization as a form of social control, either as an aspect of judicial punishment of crime or as social norms which potentially deter even without formal punishment.

In the context of this literature, stigma is often viewed benignly, as an effective way of deterring bad corporate conduct or as a less harsh alternative to punishment by the state. The argument against harsh punishments too liberally applied becomes that they lose their effectiveness through 'stigma saturation', *i.e.* a reduction in their power to stigmatize. Aligned with this literature, too, are public policy initiatives, including those which frequently justify their provisions by the need to 'send a message' about what is and is not considered tolerable behaviour.

The two literatures thus examine two ends of a common process. One considers the deterrent value of stigma as a means of social control-where the ideal result might be universal primary deterrence so that no one was actually stigmatized. The other considers the real-life circumstance where the ideal has not been attained, and the effects of stigma on those who have not been successfully deterred. In general, the studies of stigma as a means of social control recognize that the result may not in fact always be social control and conformity. A whole sociological literature on 'secondary deviance' is devoted to studying processes which may be construed as failures of stigma to result in conformity. In contrast, the literature on stigmatization and mental health seems generally to be less alive to the possibility that efforts to reduce stigma may also have unintended effects. One example where this was found, however, is the classic evaluation of the effects of a positive mental health campaign in the 1950s, Closed Ranks, which found that efforts to persuade a community to see mental health was a continuum, as opposed to seeing mental illness as a separate state, were strongly resisted, putatively because the continuum model threatened the community's toleration of its more 'eccentric' citizens.

The alcohol and drug field falls into and overlaps the field both of mental health and of crime. Some parts of the field are usually considered under a crime rubric-drinking driving is a good example-and easily subsumed in the stigma-associal-control literature. Thus Blume discusses 'stigmatizing drunk drivers' in approving terms in his concluding argument. On the other hand, cases under treatment for alcohol and drug problems are easily subsumed into discussions of stigma and mental illness.

However, as a matter of cultural politics, it is difficult to extend either framing of stigma to cover the whole alcohol and drug field. On the one hand, it is unusual nowadays to find direct arguments for the stigmatization of those who have a history of alcohol or drug problems, but who are now sobre. For that matter, to the extent alcohol or drug addiction is construed as a disease, it is legally impermissible as 'cruel and unusual punishment' in the United States to punish an addict for exhibiting the signs of the disease.

On the other hand, policies against stigma usually carefully exclude from their scope those who are at the time under the influence of alcohol or using drugs. Discussions of stigma in the alcohol and drug field have primarily been clinically-orientated considerations of the stigma on those treated for alcohol or drug problems, from the perspectives of stigma as a barrier to coming to treatment managing the stigma post-treatment or documenting or decrying public attitudes. One study considers empirical evidence on the adverse effects of post treatment stigma.

SOCIAL INEQUALITY, MARGINALIZATION, ALCOHOL AND DRUG PROBLEMS

Some problems from alcohol and drug use are a direct physiological effect of the accumulation of use-usually relatively heavy use-over a long time. These notably include chronic physical harm such as liver cirrhosis or lung cancer. The relation here may be relatively uncomplicated by the social evaluation of the behaviour, so that marginalization and stigma may play only a small role.

More important in the relation between poverty and the harm may be market factors in terms of the price and promotion of products containing the substance. As the very poor in China move into the cash economy, cigarettes become available to them as a regular consumption item for the first time; the eventual result will be rising rates of lung cancer at the bottom as well as top of the socio-economic ladder in China. Similarly, the relatively high taxes on alcohol in the United Kingdom for most of the 20th century meant that liver cirrhosis used to be a disease of the relatively well-off in Britain.

The fall in the price of alcoholic beverages relative to spending power has now put cirrhosis within reach of the poor in Britain; thus the index of inequality in male cirrhosis mortality by social class in England and Wales rose from 0.88 in 1961 to 1.40 in 1981. An analogous shift was found in Sweden from the 1960s to the 1990s in the relative class positions for heavier drinking and for alcohol specific hospitalizations. Even for chronic health problems, however, poverty may increase the harm from a given level of substance use. For example, nutritional deficiencies may interact with alcohol in raising the risk of cirrhosis. Moral considerations and stigma may also play a role in the handling and chances of the individual case.

An example is the conditions which the medical system may set for a liver transplant for cirrhosis or a lung transplant for lung cancer. Abstinence from alcohol for a considerable time is usually a precondition for one and abstinence from nicotine for the other, under conditions which cannot be justified on purely medical grounds, and which clearly include a moral element. The poor and particularly the marginalized are likely to be disadvantaged in these processes. Other problems from alcohol and drug use are a result of a single occasion of substance use. These include overdoses, injuries from accidents or violence, and infections, as well as such social reactions as police arrests. Here poverty is likely to play a part in increasing the risk of harm from a given occasion of use.

A poor drinker or drug user will have fewer resources to reduce risks by hiring a taxi or buying an unused needle, and often will be less secluded or protected from risks in the environment and the reactions from others. However, it is surprisingly difficult to find comparable data which quantifies the effects of social inequality on the harm resulting from equivalent behaviour.

Studies in the United States looking for police bias by social class or race in drinking-driving arrests, for instance, have not necessarily found it. A Stockholm County study gives a sense of the combined effect for chronic and acute alcohol-specific harms to health. Comparing rates of relatively heavy drinking among manual workers in 1984 with those among higher level non-manual workers, the rates for manual workers were about 1.5 times higher for men, and about equal for women.

But hospitalization rates for alcohol-specific causes were more skewed between the social classes: rates for manual workers in the county in 1980—84 were 3.6 times as high for men and 2.5 times as high for women as for the higher level nonmanual workers. A third class of problems are adverse social consequences of the substance use-effects of drinking in such areas as family relationships, friendships, and work performance and standing.

Both specific occasions of use and the cumulation of a use pattern over time are likely to be involved in the occurrence of these problems, although it is clear that the likelihood of the problems occurring is much greater when enough use to get high or intoxicated is involved. In Sweden from the 1960s to the 1990s in the relative class positions for heavier drinking and for alcohol-specific hospitalizations. Even for chronic health problems, however, poverty may increase the harm from a given level of substance use. For example, nutritional deficiencies may interact with alcohol in raising the risk of cirrhosis. Moral considerations and stigma may also play a role in the handling and chances of the individual case. An example is the conditions which the medical system may set for a liver transplant for cirrhosis or a lung transplant for lung cancer.

Abstinence from alcohol for a considerable time is usually a precondition for one and abstinence from nicotine for the other, under conditions which cannot be justified on purely medical grounds, and which clearly include a moral element. The poor and particularly the marginalized are likely to be disadvantaged in these processes. Other problems from alcohol and drug use are a result of a single occasion of substance use.

These include overdoses, injuries from accidents or violence, and infections, as well as such social reactions as police arrests. Here poverty is likely to play a part in increasing the risk of harm from a given occasion of use. A poor drinker or drug user will have fewer resources to reduce risks by hiring a taxi or buying an unused needle, and often will be less secluded or protected from risks in the environment and the reactions from others.

However, it is surprisingly difficult to find comparable data which quantifies the effects of social inequality on the harm resulting from equivalent behaviour. Studies in the United States looking for police bias by social class or race in drinking-driving arrests, for instance, have not necessarily found it. A Stockholm County study gives a sense of the combined effect for chronic and acute alcohol-specific harms to health.

Comparing rates of relatively heavy drinking among manual workers in 1984 with those among higher level non-manual workers, the rates for manual workers were about 1.5 times higher for men, and about equal for women. But hospitalization rates for alcohol-specific causes were more skewed between the social classes: rates for manual workers in the county in 1980-84 were 3.6 times as high for men and 2.5 times as high for women as for the higher level nonmanual workers. A third class of problems are adverse social consequences of the substance use-effects of drinking in such areas as family relationships, friendships, and work performance and standing.

Both specific occasions of use and the cumulation of a use pattern over time are likely to be involved in the occurrence of these problems, although it is clear that the likelihood of the problems occurring is much greater when enough use to get high or intoxicated is involved.

These divergences between the pictures from general population studies and from clinical populations led me to suggest that we can talk of the 'two worlds of alcohol problems'. The salient feature of the clinical picture is the marginalization of many of the clients- the high rates of 'spare and awkward people', without ties to a family, a continuing home, or a steady job.

'We may suspect that the process of entering treatment is to some extent a process of extrusion from the general population, that many clients come to treatment after having exhausted their moral credit with employers and families'. The years since this sketchy account was written have seen a number of studies which fill in more of the picture, but we still know too little about what goes on in the hinterland between the two worlds-about how and under what circumstances some of those with heavy substance use and occasional problems from it move on into the more marginalized and stigmatized world of the clinical populations.

SOME CONCLUSIONS ABOUT RESEARCH DIRECTIONS

Psychoactive substance use occurs in a highly charged field of moral forces. Outlawing a drug and punishing those caught using it may be intended to 'send a message' about standards of behaviour. Alcohol and drug use can serve as a demonstration to the user and to others about highly valued personal qualities such as self-control. Adverse consequences of use can be regarded as evidence of moral iniquity. Entering treatment for alcohol or drug problems is potentially humiliating evidence of failure in self-management. In these and many other ways, substance use can serve as an instrument of social inclusion or social exclusion. In terms of social exclusion the user may be stigmatized, and the result may be social marginalization.

These processes are separate from issues of the division of resources in society and social inequality. On the other hand, access to resources gives the user greater opportunities to insulate behaviour from social reactions and from potential stigma and marginalization.

Social inequality, stigmatization and marginalization around substance use interact in complex ways, which need to be better understood. There is a high degree of marginalization and stigmatization among those who end up in treatment for alcohol or drug problems, even in well-developed welfare societies.

Improving the social reintegration of such treated populations, or implementing effective interventions short of tertiary treatment, will require a better understanding of how and under what conditions the marginalization and stigmatization happens. Quantitative and qualitative studies are needed of the extent and mechanics of marginalization and social stigmatization of substance users and those with substance use problems in different societies and milieux. These studies should include attention to the potential preventive effects of stigmatization, on one hand, and to the potential deviance-amplifying and other adverse effects on the other hand.

General studies are needed in different societies and milieux of the relationship between components of social class and social inequality and, conversely, of marginalization and stigmatization. Again, both quantitative and qualitative studies are needed. In the context of these general studies, specific attention needs to be paid to the interplay of social inequality and marginalization around substance use and problems. Priority should be given to studies of what happens when some aspect or component of social inequality or marginalization changes. These studies can be at the aggregate or the individual level; wherever possible, they should include both levels of change.

Along with planned experiments and interventions, these studies can include longitudinal studies in the individual life-course and 'natural experiments' when a relevant policy changes.

12

Globalization: Poverty, Inequality, and Democracy

INTRODUCTION

On April 26-28, the global Network of Democracy Research Institutes convened a conference on "Poverty, Inequality, and Democracy" in Bratislava, Slovakia. The meeting was consponsored by three member institutes of the NDRI-the Washingtonbased International Forum for Democratic Studies of the National Endowment for Democracy, Slovakia's Institute for Public Affairs and Stanford University's Centre for Democracy, Development, and the Rule of Law-and made possible by financial support from the United Nations Democracy Fund.

Four documents presented at the conference will be published in the October 2009 issue of the Journal of Democracy. The conference was opened by Grigorij Mesežnikov, president of IVO, who underscored the importance of studying how poverty and inequality impede democratization and how democracy, while a good in its own right, could also be instrumental in tackling social and economic ills, especially in the context of the challenges posed by the worldwide economic recession.

Next, Marc F. Plattner, director of the IFDS, discussed the increasing relevance of the relation between democracy and social policy. He noted that, in recent years, numerous scholars have called for more attention to be paid to these issues and to how they might be more effectively addressed by democrats, especially amidst the rise of populist movements in South America led by politicians with questionable democratic credentials. Plattner then explained that the conference stems from current efforts by the IFDS to examine how the so-called social agenda affects democratic development. These efforts have included a meeting in Washington in September 2007, a workshop on social policy at the World Movement for Democracy's Fifth Assembly, "Making Democracy Work: From Principles to Performance," held on April 6-9, 2008, in Kyiv, Ukraine, and the publication of a cluster of four objects on the topic in the October 2008 issue of the Journal of Democracy.

Finally, Kathryn Stoner-Weiss, deputy director for research and senior research scholar at CDDRL, highlighted the exigency of the questions the conference sought to answer. What follows is a brief report of the most relevant issues addressed by the document presenters, commentators, and participants.

THEORIZING POVERTY, INEQUALITY, AND DEMOCRACY

Opening the conference's first session, Professor Nancy Bermeo presented a document examining the nature of inequality and its relation to democracy. Focusing on the period between 1990 and 2005, Bermeo observed that, although the number of democracies rose dramatically and economic growth accelerated at a rapid pace, economic inequality remained constant or even increased in some cases.

Taking this disjunction as her starting point, Bermeo attempted to explain it and explore its implications. Bermeo dealt first with some conceptual matters pertaining to the definitions of inequality and poverty. She defined inequality as the condition of having different, and therefore unequal, command of resources valuable for well-being.

From an empirical point of view, one cannot define inequality without a modifier-political inequality, gender inequality, economic inequality, and so on. Democratization diminishes political inequality by creating an even field for all citizens, but it does not directly affect the private realm of family or the market. Poverty, on the other hand, refers to levels of income that are inadequate for well-being, or to deficits in capability that derive from an insufficiency of economic means.

Thus, economic inequality is a matter of the distribution of economic resources that arises when economic units are ranked just as to the wealth they earn or possess. Whereas inequality exists on a gradient, poverty is intrinsically dyadic, dividing the population between poor and non-poor. As two distinct phenomena, economic inequality and poverty are not necessarily correlative.

Having made this clarification, Bermeo asked if democracy diminishes inequality. Democracy presumptively leads to a demand for greater economic equality, and many scholars indeed think of democracy as a "game of redistribution." Yet as measured by Gini coefficients, income inequality in the majority of democracies has either remained constant or increased. Reversing the question, Bermeo asked if economic inequality affects the quality of democracy.

The harmful effects of inequality could hypothetically include a disproportionate influence of the wealthy, political detachment on the part of a large sector of the population, support for populism, support for personalist rule, corruption, and low levels of accountability. While cautioning about the reliability and comparability of some data, Bermeo reported a strong negative correlation between income inequality and measures of voice and accountability- evidence of the threat that inequality poses to the quality of democracy.

Third, Bermeo investigated whether democracies are at risk, and concluded that economic inequality by itself will not be a cause of democracy's collapse since the breakdown of democracy requires "coup coalitions"-critical masses of counter-elites who have the capacity to topple regimes. Coup coalitions are not easy or likely to form for a number of reasons.

For one, international actors have raised the cost of coups. Also, wealthy classes that once backed coups have come to believe that they have more power in an electoral democracy than in an authoritarian regime. In addition, democracy enjoys powerful appeal across regions, in many cases offering opportunities for radical change that are less risky than seizures of power. So, in spite of its deleterious effects, inequality does not pose an imminent risk for democracies.

COMPARING SOCIAL POLICIES

While Bermeo's document emphasized the relationship between inequality and democracy, the document by Professors Stephan Haggard and Robert Kaufman focused primarily on the different strategies that new democracies have employed in dealing with poverty and other social welfare issues. They noted that there are two principal kinds of strategies that states have pursued.

The first emphasizes universal policies of social assistance, while the second seeks to target assistance more narrowly to make sure that it benefits the poor. Comparing the experience of Central and Eastern Europe with that of Latin America, Haggard and Kaufman examined the effects of democratization on social policy. Democracy generates electoral incentives for politicians to compete by advocating redistribution and expanded welfare commitments.

It also guarantees freedom for previously excluded groups to organize. To ascertain the actual impact of democratization, however, one has to pay close attention to the authoritarian legacy in each of these regions. The effects of authoritarianism linger, conditioning the characteristics of present-day democracies. Critical realignments and political coalitions produced distinctive authoritarian models, which, in turn, created constituencies that influenced the course of social policy in new democracies.

In Latin America, for example, the reform coalitions that pushed and implemented the transition from oligarchic rule that took place from 1910 to about 1950 were comprised not only of labour unions, but also of dissident factions of the oligarchy. These cross-class reform coalitions excluded rural peasants and unorganized urban workers, perpetuating their political marginalization. While post-war importsubstitution industrialization strategies accommodated welfare entitlements for the organized urban working class, they largely failed to address the impoverishment of these politically excluded classes. In short, these political realignments and ISI strategies resulted in a highly skewed welfare system that benefited the middle class and upper echelons of the blue-collar working class.

In Central and Eastern Europe, where the authoritarian legacy is that of communism, critical alignments in the transition to communist rule repressed all other parties and tightly controlled labour. Statesocialist welfare systems were founded on a social contract that produced a fundamentally different social welfare trajectory.

Communist development in Central and Eastern Europe was characterized by central planning, including manpower planning and effective employment guarantees; nationalization that led to state provision of social insurance and services, particularly pensions and health insurance but also family allowances; and collectivization of agriculture that extended the system into the countryside and universalized guarantees. There were intra-regional variations, of course, but the convergence of Central and East European state-socialist welfare systems was much greater than that of welfare systems in Latin America. In his presentation, Haggard presented data on government spending in the last two decades of the twentieth-century to demonstrate the enduring effects of welfare legacies on contemporary social policy.

Reflecting the state-socialist legacy, social security spending from 1980 through 2000 in Central and Eastern Europe and Central Asia represented about 13 to 14 per cent of GDP. By comparison, in Latin America social security spending represented only between 6 and 9 per cent of GDP, while in East and Southeast Asia it represented merely about 1 per cent of GDP.

Health spending follows the same pattern as social security spending. Central and Eastern Europe and Central Asia spend about 4 per cent of GDP on health while Latin America spends a lower percentage, and East and Southeast

Asia even less. Education spending, however, follows a different pattern. East and Southeast Asian countries spend on the order of 4 to 4.5 per cent of GDP on education, whereas Central and Eastern Europe, Central Asia, and Latin America exhibit much lower rates.

Haggard and Kauffman demonstrated that the effects of democracy on social policy are clearly conditioned by the distribution and organization of interests. They highlighted the importance of historical legacies, drawing attention to the constraints that these place on countries in terms of the social policies they can pursue.

CENTRAL AND EASTERN EUROPE

In their document, Professors Béla Greskovits and Dorothee Bohle asked what remedies for poverty and inequality have been adopted by Central and East European states and to what degree they have been successful. Greskovits and Bohle explored the strategic differences between the model adopted by the Visegrad group plus Slovenia and the model followed by the Baltic group, despite the common features of their transition from communist rule.

The authors also examined how these postcommunist states integrated themselves into the global economy. Both groups of countries exited their previous economic system through a process of export-oriented development that was very successful in attracting foreign investment. Their economic policies, generally speaking, were biased in favour of international corporations and tended to neglect small and medium-sized domestic enterprises. "Jobless growth" was a function of the private sector's limited employment capacity, and depressed wages were insufficient for survival in some sectors.

The Visegrad-4 and Slovenia reindustrialized along the lines of what might be called "core-like" specializations, emphasizing such sophisticated products as cars, electronics, machinery, and chemicals. This reindustrialization created a dualism between the transnational corporations' workers, who live in the more developed regions, and workers in more traditional sectors of the economy. In contrast, the Baltic States, as well as Bulgaria and Romania, followed a more "semi-peripheral" path of reform involving de-industrialization, de-skilling, and the development of less advanced specializations. These semi-peripheral sectors tend to produce lower wages, a function of the low-cost, union-free sweatshops run by the highly mobile transnational corporations that proliferated following the fall of Soviet enterprise.

The costs of this precarious transnationalization were paid by the sweatshops' working poor. The two different models of welfare capitalism adopted by the Visegrád and the Baltic countries are reflected in differences in the relative size and volume of social benefits, public-sector employment, and education spending, as well as in the treatment of minority ethnic groups. Social spending in the Baltic countries averaged between 12 and 13 per cent of GDP, whereas the Visegrad-4 plus Slovenia spent much more, 19 to 23 per cent-though this amount is still below that of the EU-15 countries.

In terms of the cost of social benefits per person between 2004 and 2006, the Baltic States spent approximately €1,500. The Visegrád-4 countries spent a significantly greater amount, €2,661, while Slovenia, a more economically advanced country, spent €4,470. Spending per person in the EU-15 is approximately €6,700. As for public-sector employment, one can observe a much higher level in the Baltic-3 than the Visegrád-4.

Additionally, in the Baltic States, the at risk of poverty rate after social transfers is 20 per cent, while only 14 per cent of the population in the Visegrád-4 countries is at risk, and only 12 per cent in Slovenia-rates much better than the 16 per cent in the EU-15. Poverty and inequality in Central and Eastern Europe have a strong ethnic dimension. In Estonia and Latvia, many of the working poor are ethnic Russians.

Similarly, in the Visegrád-4 countries, a considerable segment of the long-term unemployed are ethnic Roma. The high number of unemployed minorities carries significant political implications since it is particularly difficult to build redistribution coalitions on the basis of sectors that are considered foreign by the majority of the population. The ethnic dimension of poverty further compounds its alienating effect.

The question of why the Baltic and Visegrád models are so different is intriguing given that both groups of states inherited similar industrial and welfare legacies and had similar transformative visions built on "returning to the West." The answer, just as to Greskovits and Bohle, is that popular consent for policy and social legitimacy was sought via different sorts of appeals.

In the case of the Visegrád countries, consent was sought on the basis of a welfarist model- assuring the population that its socioeconomic welfare would be taken care of. In the Baltic States, by contrast, the basis of legitimacy was more nationalist. The new social contracts in the Baltic States, which had been Soviet colonies, emphasized the recovery of national independence rather than the welfarist promises that were central in the Visegrád-4.

TURKEY

Later at the conference, Öykü Uluçay discussed the case of Turkey. Turkey has one of the highest levels of poverty among OECD countries, but by the standards of most developing countries its level of poverty is very low, affecting only 12 to 13 per cent of the population. A looser definition of poverty yields a rate of 31 per cent, but pensions and social transfers reduce it to 25 per cent.

This is a very modest result when compared to the performance of the EU-15, where pensions and transfers reduce the level of poverty by 15 percentage points. Turkey has a very complex welfare system grounded not only in state services, but also in social structures independent of the state.

Alongside the state system, Turkey has a traditional welfare regime-a safety net that is based more on societal than government-provided services, and includes the diversification of economic activities within extended families, urban-rural linkages, informal housing, and extended networks of kinship.

EAST AND SOUTH ASIA

Professor Jaeyeol Yee gave a presentation on East Asia, emphasizing the cases of Korea and Taiwan. With Gini indexes of .24 and .34, respectively, Taiwan and Korea have extremely low coefficients of inequality compared to countries such as Argentina (.51), Bolivia (.68), Brazil (.59), Botswana (.63), and Zambia (.53). Yet the amount of social spending in Korea and Taiwan is also low, an apparent contradiction that needs further exploration.

Things may be changing in East Asia, however, where the Gini index has been increasing since 1992. Yee averred that inequality is deepening in both Korea and Taiwan, especially in the former. Between 1991 and 2006, the ranks of the middle classes decreased by 13 per cent while the low-income and highincome classes increased by 7 and 5 per cent, respectively.

Moreover, in 1996, 41 per cent of Koreans perceived themselves as being middle class, whereas now that percentage is only 28 per cent. With respect to India, Partha Mokhopadhyay traced the evolution from the anti-poverty policies started by Indira Gandhi in the mid-1970s to the more universal policies of the present. Suhas Palshikar pointed out in his remarks that politics in India is becoming less focused on identity issues and more on public welfare.

LATIN AMERICA

Alberto Díaz-Cayeros presented a document that focused on the panoply of targeted programmes known as conditional cash transfers, which have been quite successful in reducing poverty in Latin America. In Brazil, for example, more than 11 million people benefit from the Bolsa Familia programme. In Colom Alberto Díaz-Cayeros presented a document that focused on the panoply of targeted programmes known as conditional cash transfers which have been quite successful in reducing poverty in Latin America.

In Brazil, for example, more than 11 million people benefit from the Bolsa Familia programme. In Colombia, about 5 per cent of the population benefit from similar targeted programmes . In Mexico, there are 5 million families-about 25 million people-who benefit from such programmes . In Peru, there are some 230,000 families-about 1 million people.

The prevailing way of addressing poverty in Latin America has been not to reform the overall welfare system, but to develop specific anti-poverty policies. Poverty in Latin America has dropped significantly over the past five years from about 42 per cent to about 36 per cent.

The effect of the current economic crisis remains to be seen. Significantly, centrist governments were the first to begin to apply these kinds of programmes . Rightist governments followed suit, while leftist governments adopted these policies much later.

AFRICA

Professor Larry Diamond gave a presentation on the case of Africa. Inspired by Peter Lewis's "Growth Without Prosperity in Africa," which appeared in the October 2008 issue of the Journal of Democracy, Diamond noted that African states have the highest percentages of poverty, with about 51 per cent of Africans living below the poverty line. Africa also has the greatest levels of economic inequality: The richest quintile of the population captures 65 per cent of the national income while the lowest quintile shares in only a very small percentage of the wealth.

As Diamond commented, if CCT programmes were to be applied in Africa, they would have to cover the overwhelming majority of the population. Diamond pointed out that African states are unique in terms of governance as well. In most of the cases the conference addressed, the presumption is that the state acts with a desire to advance the collective public good, but such an understanding does not exist in many African states where primordial structures hinder effective governance based on universalist concerns.

Instead, the norm too often is pursuit of particularistic concerns within hierarchical sociopolitical structures. Suggesting that effective policies must move the concerns of African states from the particular to the universal, Diamond criticized foreign aid schemes that pay insufficient attention to governance and accountability.

COMMON THREADS AND CONCERNS

The discussions at the conference manifested a number of common threads and concerns. One was the impact of historical legacies, in regard to which two distinct patterns can be discerned. In the first, as exemplified by the cases of East Asia and of Central and Eastern Europe, new democracies came into being with lower levels of poverty and lesser degrees of inequality. In the case of Central and Eastern Europe, these were the legacy of the former communist regimes.

In East Asia, they were a product of post- World War II reform, especially land redistribution. The second pattern, as manifest in the cases of Latin America and Africa, is characterized by high levels of poverty and inequality, the lingering legacies of colonialism and oligarchic rule. Another common thread uniting these different regional experiences is the structure of constraints that limited the choices available to governments.

These limitations in choice are also a function of countries' historical legacies. Countries with high levels of poverty, such as those in Latin America, tended to prioritize targeted policies, while other countries focused on reforming or strengthening the overall welfare system. Such policy decisions are determined by the constraints under which policymakers operate. A third common thread is the matrix of consequences resulting from market policies.

Although these policies helped achieve macroeconomic stability and opened up economies, they also had unintended consequences, often weakening already frail welfare systems. In Latin America, two paths opened as a result of government policies towards poverty. Countries reluctant to address poverty fell prey to populist authoritarian forces while governments that addressed these issues successfully have been able to build more stable democracies. In South and Southeast Asia, governments that have addressed the challenges of poverty have fared well. The popularity of

Thailand's ousted prime minister Thaksin Shinawatra can in part be attributed to his anti-poverty policies and introduction of a universal healthcare system. As Nancy Bermeo noted in her document, Thailand has exhibited an exceptional record of reducing inequality. In India, the recent electoral success of the Congress Party can also be partly attributed to its effective antipoverty policy. India is a success story not only in terms of democracy, but also in terms of reducing poverty from 50-to-55 per cent to current levels of about 20-to-25 per cent.

This success is a function of the implementation of a consistent, sustained, and effective anti-poverty policy that has been in place since the 1970s, as well as of the tremendous economic growth India has experienced in the past 10 to 15 years. Central and Eastern Europe has experienced a similar success story, though today the Visegrád countries seem to be handling the economic crisis better than the Baltic States. In Turkey, the continued success of the Justice and Development Party can in part be attributed to its social welfare policies.

CONCLUSIONS

High levels of poverty and inequality not only lower the quality of democracy, but may pave the way for the emergence of authoritarian populists and democratic backsliding. Therefore, addressing the social question, which warrants attention in its own right, is critical to the sustainability and quality of democracy. There are different ways to confront the challenge of poverty and inequality, depending on historical legacies, the structure of constraints, and the impact of previous economic policies.

There is no single recipe, yet the comparative analysis presented at the Bratislava conference, and the four conference documents that will appear in the October 2009 Journal of Democracy, shed considerable light upon the advantages and drawbacks of these different approaches.

13

Gender and Gender Inequality

UNDERSTANDING SEX AND GENDER

Although the terms sex and gender are sometimes used interchangeably and do in fact complement each other, they nonetheless refer to different aspects of what it means to be a woman or man in any society.

Sex refers to the anatomical and other biological differences between females and males that are determined at the moment of conception and develop in the womb and throughout childhood and adolescence. Females, of course, have two X chromosomes, while males have one X chromo-XXXXXXXXXXsome and one Y chromosome. From this basic genetic difference spring other biological differences. The first to appear are the different genitals that boys and girls develop in the womb and that the doctor and parents look for when a baby is born so that the momentous announcement, "It's a boy!" or "It's a girl!" can be made.

The genitalia are called primary sex characteristics, while the other differences that develop during puberty are called secondary sex characteristics and stem from hormonal differences between the two sexes. In this difficult period of adolescents' lives, boys generally acquire deeper voices, more body hair, and more muscles from their flowing testosterone. Girls develop breasts and wider hips and begin menstruating as nature prepares them for possible pregnancy and childbirth. For better or worse, these basic biological differences between the sexes affect many people's perceptions of what it means to be female or male, as we shall soon discuss.

GENDER AS A SOCIAL CONSTRUCTION

Female sex is a biological concept, then gender is a social concept. It refers to the social and cultural differences a society assigns to people based on their sex. A related concept, gender roles, refers to a society's expectations of people's behaviour and attitudes based on whether they are females or males. Understood in this way, gender is a social construction.

How we think and behave as females and males is not etched in stone by our biology but rather is a result of how society expects us to think and behave based on what sex we are. As we grow up, we learn these expectations as we develop our gender identity, or our beliefs about ourselves as females or males. These expectations are called femininity and masculinity. Femininity refers to the cultural expectations we have of girls and women, while masculinity refers to the expectations we have of boys and men.

As this nursery rhyme suggests, our traditional notions of femininity and masculinity indicate that we think females and males are fundamentally different from each other. In effect, we think of them as two sides of the same coin of being human. What we traditionally mean by femininity is captured in the adjectives, both positive and negative, we traditionally ascribe to women: gentle, sensitive, nurturing, delicate, graceful, cooperative, decorative, dependent, emotional, passive, and weak.

Thus, when we say that a girl or woman is very feminine, we have some combination of these traits, usually the positive ones, in mind: she is soft, dainty, pretty, even a bit flighty. What we traditionally mean by masculinity is captured in the adjectives, again both positive and negative, our society traditionally ascribes to men: strong, assertive, brave, active, independent, intelligent, competitive, insensitive, unemotional, and aggressive.

When we say that a boy or man is very masculine, we have some combination of these traits in mind: he is tough, strong, and assertive. These traits might sound like stereotypes of females and males in today's society, and to some extent they are, but differences between men and women in attitudes and behaviour do in fact exist. For example, women cry more often than men do. Men are more physically violent than women. Women take care of children more than men do. Women smile more often than men. Men curse more often than women.

When women talk with each other, they are more likely to talk about their personal lives than men are when they talk with each other. The two sexes even differ when they hold a cigarette. When a woman holds a cigarette, she usually has the palm of her cigarette-holding hand facing upward. When a man holds a cigarette, he usually has his palm facing downward.

THE DEVELOPMENT OF GENDER DIFFERENCES

What accounts for differences in female and male behaviour and attitudes? Do the biological differences between the sexes account for differences between these other differences? Or do these latter differences stem, as most sociologists think, from cultural expectations and from differences in the ways in which the sexes are socialized? These are critical questions, for they ask whether the differences between boys and girls and women and men stem more from biology or from society.

Biological explanations for human behaviour implicitly support the status quo. If we think behavioural and other differences between the sexes are due primarily to their respective biological makeups, we are saying that these differences are inevitable or nearly so and that any attempt to change them goes against biology and will likely fail.

As an example, consider the obvious biological fact that women bear and nurse children and men do not. Couple this with the common view that women are also more gentle and nurturing than men, and we end up with a "biological recipe" for women to be the primary caretakers of children. Many people think this means women are therefore much better suited than men to take care of children once they are born, and that the family might be harmed if mothers work outside the home or if fathers are the primary caretakers. That more than one-third of the public agrees that "it is much better for everyone involved if the man is the achiever outside the home and the woman takes care of the home and family." To the extent this belief exists, women may not want to work outside the home or, if they choose to do so, they face difficulties from employers, family, and friends.

Conversely, men may not even think about wanting to stay at home and may themselves face difficulties from employees, family, and friends if they want to do so. A belief in a strong biological basis for differences between women and men implies, then, that there is little we can or should do to change these differences. It implies that "anatomy is destiny," and destiny is, of course, by definition inevitable. Agreement or disagreement with statement that "it is much better for everyone involved if the man is the achiever outside the home and the woman takes care of the home and family."

This implication makes it essential to understand the extent to which gender differences do, in fact, stem from biological differences between the sexes or, instead, stem from cultural and social influences. If biology is paramount, then gender differences are perhaps inevitable and the status quo will remain. If culture and social influences matter much more than biology, then gender differences can change and the status quo may give way.

With this backdrop in mind, let's turn to the biological evidence for behavioural and other differences between the sexes and then examine the evidence for their social and cultural roots.

BIOLOGY AND GENDER

Several biological explanations for gender roles exist, and we discuss two of the most important ones here. One explanation is from the related fields of sociobiology and evolutionary psychology and argues an evolutionary basis for traditional gender roles.

Scholars advocating this view reason as follows. In prehistoric societies, few social roles existed. A major role centered on relieving hunger by hunting or gathering food.

The other major role centered on bearing and nursing children. Because only women could perform this role, they were also the primary caretakers for children for several years after birth. And because women were frequently pregnant, their roles as mothers confined them to the home for most of their adulthood. Meanwhile, men were better suited than women for hunting because they were stronger and quicker than women.

In prehistoric societies, then, biology was indeed destiny: for biological reasons, men in effect worked outside the home while women stayed at home with their children. Evolutionary reasons also explain why men are more violent than women. In prehistoric times, men who were more willing to commit violence against and even kill other men would "win out" in the competition for female mates. They thus were more likely than less violent men to produce offspring, who would then carry these males' genetic violent tendencies. By the same token, men who were prone to rape women were more likely to produce offspring, who would then carry these males' "rape genes."

This early process guaranteed that rape tendencies would be biologically transmitted and thus provides a biological basis for the amount of rape that occurs today. If the human race evolved along these lines, sociobiologists and evolutionary psychologists continue, natural selection favoured those societies where men were stronger, braver, and more aggressive and where women were more fertile and nurturing. Such traits over the millennia became fairly instinctual, meaning that men's and women's biological natures evolved differently.

Men became, by nature, more assertive, daring, and violent than women, and women are, by nature, more gentle, nurturing, and maternal than men. To the extent this is true, these scholars add, traditional gender roles for women and men make sense from an evolutionary standpoint, and attempts to change them go against the sexes' biological natures. This in turn implies that existing gender inequality must continue because it is rooted in biology. As the title of a book presenting the evolutionary psychology argument summarizes this implication, "biology at work: rethinking sexual equality". Critics challenge the evolutionary explanation on several grounds. First, much greater gender variation in behaviour and attitudes existed in prehistoric times than the evolutionary explanation assumes. Second, even if biological differences did influence gender roles in prehistoric times, these differences are largely irrelevant in today's world, in which, for example, physical strength is not necessary for survival.

Third, human environments throughout the millennia have simply been too diverse to permit the simple, straightforward biological development that the evolutionary explanation assumes. Fourth, evolutionary arguments implicitly justify existing gender inequality by implying the need to confine women and men to their traditional roles. Recent anthropological evidence also challenges the evolutionary argument that men's tendency to commit violence, including rape, was biologically transmitted. This evidence instead finds that violent men have trouble finding female mates who would want them and that the female mates they find and the children they produce are often killed by rivals to the men.

The recent evidence also finds those rapists' children are often abandoned and then die. As one anthropologist summarizes the rape evidence, "The likelihood that rape is an evolved adaptation extremely low. It just wouldn't have made sense for men in the to use rape as a reproductive strategy, so the argument that it's preprogrammed into us doesn't hold up". A second biological explanation for traditional gender roles centres on hormones and specifically on testosterone, the so-called male hormone.

One of the most important differences between boys and girls and men and women in the United States and many other societies is their level of aggression. Simply put, males are much more physically aggressive than females and in the United States commit about 85%-90% of all violent crimes. Why is this so? This gender difference is often attributed to males' higher levels of testosterone. To see whether testosterone does indeed raise aggression, investigators typically assess whether males with higher testosterone levels are more aggressive than those with lower testosterone levels. Several studies find that this is indeed the case. For example, a widely cited study of Vietnam-era male veterans found that those with higher levels of testosterone had engaged in more violent behaviour.

However, this correlation does not necessarily mean that their testosterone increased their violence: as has been found in various animal species, it is also possible that their violence increased their testosterone. Because studies of human males can't for ethical and practical reasons manipulate their testosterone levels, the exact meaning of the results from these testosterone-aggression studies must remain unclear, just as to a review sponsored by the National Academy of Sciences. Another line of research on the biological basis for sex differences in aggression involves children, including some as young as ages 1 or 2, in various situations.

They might be playing with each other, interacting with adults, or writing down solutions to hypothetical scenarios given to them by a researcher. In most of these studies, boys are more physically aggressive in thought or deed than girls, even at a very young age. Other studies are more experimental in nature. In one type of study, a toddler will be playing with a toy, only to have it removed by an adult. Boys typically tend to look angry and to try to grab the toy back, while girls tend to just sit there and whimper. Because these gender differences in aggression are found at very young ages, researchers often say they must have some biological basis.

However, critics of this line of research counter that even young children have already been socialized along gender lines, a point to which we return later. To the extent this is true, gender differences in children's aggression may simply reflect socialization and not biology. In sum, biological evidence for gender differences certainly exists, but its interpretation remains very controversial. It must be weighed against the evidence, to which we next turn, of cultural variations in the experience of gender and of socialization differences by gender. One thing is clear: to the extent we accept biological explanations for gender, we imply that existing gender differences and gender inequality must continue to exist.

This implication prompts many social scientists to be quite critical of the biological viewpoint. As Linda L. Lindsey notes, "Biological arguments are consistently drawn upon to justify gender inequality and the continued oppression of women." In contrast, cultural and social explanations of gender differences and gender inequality promise some hope for change. Let's examine the evidence for these explanations.

CULTURE AND GENDER

Some of the most compelling evidence against a strong biological determination of gender roles comes from anthropologists, whose work on preindustrial societies demonstrates some striking gender variation from one culture to another. This variation underscores the impact of culture on how females and males think and behave. Margaret Mead was one of the first anthropologists to study cultural differences in gender.

In New Guinea she found three tribes-the Arapesh, the Mundugumor, and the Tchambuli-whose gender roles differed dramatically. In the Arapesh both sexes were gentle and nurturing. Both women and men spent much time with their children in a loving way and exhibited what we would normally call maternal behaviour. In the Arapesh, then, different gender roles did not exist, and in fact, both sexes conformed to what Americans would normally call the female gender role.

The situation was the reverse among the Mundugumor. Here both men and women were fierce, competitive, and violent. Both sexes seemed to almost dislike children and often physically punished them. In the Mundugumor society, then, different gender roles also did not exist, as both sexes conformed to what we Americans would normally call the male gender role. In the Tchambuli, Mead finally found a tribe where different gender roles did exist. One sex was the dominant, efficient, assertive one and showed leadership in tribal affairs, while the other sex liked to dress up in frilly clothes, wear makeup, and even giggle a lot. Here, then, Mead found a society with gender roles similar to those found in the United States, but with a surprising twist. In the Tchambuli, women were the dominant, assertive sex that showed leadership in tribal affairs, while men were the ones wearing frilly clothes and makeup.

Mead's research caused a firestorm in scholarly circles, as it challenged the biological view on gender that was still very popular when she went to New Guinea. In recent years, Mead's findings have been challenged by other anthropologists. Among other things, they argue that she probably painted an overly simplistic picture of gender roles in her three societies. Other anthropologists defend Mead's work and note that much subsequent research has found that gender-linked attitudes and behaviour do differ widely from one culture to another. If so, they say, the impact of culture on what it means to be a female or male cannot be ignored.

Extensive evidence of this impact comes from anthropologist George Murdock, who created the Standard Cross-Cultural Sample of almost 200 preindustrial societies studied by anthropologists. Murdock found that some tasks in these societies, such as hunting and trapping, are almost always done by men, while other tasks, such as cooking and fetching water, are almost always done by women.

These patterns provide evidence for the evolutionary argument, as they probably stem from the biological differences between the sexes. Even so there were at least some societies in which women hunted and in which men cooked and fetched water.

More importantly, Murdock found much greater gender variation in several of the other tasks he studied, including planting crops, milking, and generating fires. Men primarily performed these tasks in some societies, women primarily performed them in other societies, and in still other societies both sexes performed them equally.

The gender responsibility for yet another task, weaving. Women are the primary weavers in about 61% of the societies that do weaving, men are the primary weavers in 32%, and both sexes do the weaving in 7% of the societies. Murdock's findings thesis how gender roles differ from one culture to another and imply they are not biologically determined.

Anthropologists since Mead and Murdock have continued to investigate cultural differences in gender. Some of their most interesting findings concern gender and sexuality. Although all societies distinguish "femaleness" and "maleness," additional gender categories exist in some societies.

The Native Americans known as the Mohave, for example, recognize four genders: a woman, a woman who acts like a man, a man, and a man who acts like a woman. In some societies, a third, intermediary gender category is recognized. Anthropologists call this category the berdache, who is usually a man who takes on a woman's role. This intermediary category combines aspects of both femininity and masculinity of the society in which it is found and is thus considered an androgynous gender.

Although some people in this category are born as intersexed individuals, meaning they have genitalia of both sexes, many are born biologically as one sex or the other but adopt an androgynous identity. An example of this intermediary gender category may be found in India, where the hirja role involves males who wear women's clothing and identify as women.

The hirja role is an important part of Hindu mythology, in which androgynous figures play key roles both as humans and as gods. Today people identified by themselves and others as hirjas continue to play an important role in Hindu practices and in Indian cultural life in general. Serena Nanda calls hirjas "human beings who are neither man nor woman" and says they are thought of as "special, sacred beings" even though they are sometimes ridiculed and abused.

Anthropologists have found another androgynous gender composed of women warriors in 33 Native American groups in North America. Walter L. Williams calls these women "amazons" and notes that they dress like men and sometimes even marry women. In some tribes girls exhibit such "masculine" characteristics from childhood, while in others they may be recruited into "amazonhood."

In the Kaska Indians, for example, a married couple with too many daughters would select one to "be like a man." When she was about 5 years of age, her parents would begin to dress her like a boy and have her do male tasks. Eventually she would grow up to become a hunter.

The androgynous genders found by anthropologists remind us that gender is a social construction and not just a biological fact. If culture does affect gender roles, socialization is the process through which culture has this effect. What we experience as girls and boys strongly influences how we develop as women and men in terms of behaviour and attitudes. To thesis this important dimension of gender, let's turn to the evidence on socialization.

SOCIALIZATION AND GENDER

The several agents of socialization, including the family, peers, schools, the mass media, and religion. Such socialization helps boys and girls develop their gender identity. Socialization into gender roles begins in infancy, as almost from the moment of birth parents begin to socialize their children as boys or girls without even knowing it.

Many studies document this process. Parents commonly describe their infant daughters as pretty, soft, and delicate and their infant sons as strong, active, and alert, even though neutral observers find no such gender differences among infants when they do not know the infants' sex. From infancy on, parents play with and otherwise interact with their daughters and sons differently.

They play more roughly with their sons-for example, by throwing them up in the air or by gently wrestling with them-and more quietly with their daughters. When their infant or toddler daughters cry, they warmly comfort them, but they tend to let their sons cry longer and to comfort them less. They give their girls dolls to play with and their boys "action figures" and toy guns. While these gender differences in socialization are probably smaller now than a generation ago, they certainly continue to exist. Go into a large toy store and you will see pink aisles of dolls and cooking sets and blue aisles of action figures, toy guns, and related items.

Peers

Peer influences also encourage gender socialization. As they reach school age, children begin to play different games based on their gender. Boys tend to play sports and other competitive team games governed by inflexible rules and relatively large numbers of roles, while girls tend to play smaller, cooperative games such as hopscotch and jumping rope with fewer and more flexible rules.

Although girls are much more involved in sports now than a generation ago, these gender differences in their play as youngsters persist and continue to reinforce gender roles. For example, they encourage competitiveness in boys and cooperation and trust among girls. Boys who are not competitive risk being called "sissy" or other words by their peers. The patterns we see in adult males and females thus have their roots in their play as young children.

Schools

School is yet another agent of gender socialization. First of all, school playgrounds provide a location for the gender-linked play activities just described to occur. Second, and perhaps more important, teachers at all levels treat their female and male students differently in subtle ways of which they are probably not aware. They tend to call on boys more often to answer questions in class and to praise them more when they give the right answer. They also give boys more feedback about their assignments and other school work. At all grade levels, many and other books still portray people in gender-stereotyped ways. It is true that the newer books do less of this than older ones, but the newer books still contain some stereotypes, and the older books are still used in many schools, especially those that cannot afford to buy newer volumes.

Mass Media

Gender socialization also occurs through the mass media. On children's television shows, the major characters are male. On Nickelodeon, for example, the very popular Sponge Bob Square Pants is a male, as are his pet snail, Gary; his best friend, Patrick Star; their neighbour, Squidward Tentacles; and SpongeBob's employer, Eugene Crabs. Of the major characters in Bikini Bottom, only Sandy Cheeks is a female.

For all its virtues, Sesame Street features Bert, Ernie, Cookie Monster, and other male characters. Most of the Muppets are males, and the main female character, Miss Piggy, depicted as vain and jealous, is hardly an admirable female role model. As for adults' prime-time television, more men than women continue to fill more major roles in weekly shows, despite notable women's roles in shows such as The Good Wife and Grey's Anatomy. Women are also often portrayed as unintelligent or frivolous individuals who are there more for their looks than for anything else. Television commercials reinforce this image. Cosmetic ads abound, suggesting not only that a major task for women is to look good but also that their sense of self-worth stems from looking good.

Other commercials show women becoming ecstatic over achieving a clean floor or sparkling laundry. Judging from the world of television commercials, then, women's chief goals in life are to look good and to have a clean house. At the same time, men's chief goals, judging from many commercials, are to drink beer and drive cars. Women's and men's magazines reinforce these gender images. Most of the magazines intended for teenage girls and adult women are filled with pictures of thin, beautiful models, advice on dieting, cosmetic ads, and substances on how to win. Conversely, the magazines intended for teenage boys and men are filled with ads and substances on cars and sports, advice on how to succeed in careers and other endeavors, and pictures of thin, beautiful women.

Religion

Another agent of socialization, religion, also contributes to traditional gender stereotypes. Many traditional interpretations of the Bible yield the message that women are subservient to men. This message begins in Genesis, where the first human is Adam, and Eve was made from one of his ribs. The major figures in the rest of the Bible are men, and women are for the most part depicted as wives, mothers, temptresses, and prostitutes; they are praised for their roles as wives and mothers and condemned for their other roles. More generally, women are constantly depicted as the property of men. The Ten Commandments includes a neighbour's wife with his house, ox, and other objects as things not to be coveted and many biblical passages say explicitly that women belong to men, such as this one from the New Testament:

- Wives be subject to your husbands, as to the Lord. For the husband is the head of the wife as Christ is the head of the Church. As the Church is subject to Christ, so let wives also be subject in everything to their husbands.

Several passages in the Old Testament justify the rape and murder of women and girls. The Koran, the sacred book of Islam, also contains passages asserting the subordinate role of women. This discussion suggests that religious people should believe in traditional gender views more than less religious people, and research confirms this relationship.

To thesis this shows the relationship in the General Social Survey between frequency of prayer and the view that "it is much better for everyone involved if the man is the achiever outside the home and the woman takes care of the home and family." People who pray more often are more likely to accept this traditional view of gender roles.

Percentage agreeing that "it is much better for everyone involved if the man is the achiever outside the home and the woman takes care of the home and family."

A FINAL WORD ON THE SOURCES OF GENDER

Scholars in many fields continue to debate the relative importance of biology and of culture and socialization for how we behave and think as girls and boys and as women and men. The biological differences between females and males lead many scholars and no doubt much of the public to assume that masculinity and femininity are to a large degree biologically determined or at least influenced. In contrast, anthropologists, sociologists, and other social scientists tend to view gender as a social construction. Even if biology does matter for gender, they say, the significance of culture and socialization should not be underestimated. To the extent that gender is indeed shaped by society and culture, it is possible to change gender and to help bring about a society where both men and women have more opportunity to achieve their full potential.

GENDER INEQUALITY

We have said that the women's movement changed American life in many ways but that gender inequality persists. Let's look at examples of such inequality, much of it taking the form of institutional discrimination, which can occur even if it is not intended to happen. We start with gender inequality in income and the workplace and then move on to a few other spheres of life.

INCOME AND WORKPLACE INEQUALITY

In the last few decades, women have entered the workplace in increasing numbers, partly, and for many women mostly, out of economic necessity and partly out of desire for the sense of self-worth and other fulfillment that comes with work. This is true not only in the United States but also in other nations, including Japan, where views of women are more traditional than those in the United States.

In February 2010, 58.9% of U.S. women age 16 or older were in the labour force, compared to only 43.3% in 1970; comparable figures for men were 71.0% in 2010 and 79.7% in 1970. Thus while women's labour force participation continues to lag behind men's, they have narrowed the gap. The figures just cited include women of retirement age. When we just look at younger women, labour force participation is even higher. For example, 76.1% of women aged 35-44 were in the labour force in 2008, compared to only 46.8% in 1970.

Despite the gains women have made, problems persist. Perhaps the major problem is a gender gap in income. Women have earned less money than men ever since records started being kept. In the United States in the early 1800s, full-time women workers in agriculture and manufacturing earned less than 38% of what men earned. By 1885 they were earning about 50% of what men earned in manufacturing jobs.

As the 1980s began, full-time women workers' median weekly earnings were about 65% of men's. Women have narrowed the gender gap in earnings since then: their weekly earnings now are 80.2% of men's among full-time workers. Still, this means that for every $10,000 men earn, women earn only about $8,002. To turn that around, for every $10,000 women earn, men earn $12,469. This gap amounts to hundreds of thousands of dollars over a lifetime of working. Although such practices and requirements are now illegal, they still continue. The sex segregation they help create contributes to the continuing gender gap between female and male workers. Occupations dominated by women tend to have lower wages and salaries. Because women are concentrated in low-paying jobs, their earnings are much lower than men's.

This gender gap exists for all levels of education and even increases with higher levels of education. On the average, college-educated women working full-time earn almost $17,700 less per year than their male counterparts. What accounts for the gender gap in earnings? A major reason is sex segregation in the workplace, which accounts for up to 45% of the gender gap. Although women have increased their labour force participation, the workplace remains segregated by gender. Almost half of all women work in a few low-paying clerical and service jobs, while men work in a much greater variety of jobs, including high-paying ones.

Part of the reason for this segregation is that socialization affects what jobs young men and women choose to pursue, and part of the reason is that women and men do not want to encounter difficulties they may experience if they took a job traditionally assigned to the other sex. A third reason is that sex-segregated jobs discriminate against applicants who are not the "right" sex for that job. Employers may either consciously refuse to hire someone who is the "wrong" sex for the job or have job requirements and workplace rules that unintentionally make it more difficult for women to qualify for certain jobs.

This fact raises an important question: why do women's jobs pay less than men's jobs? Is it because their jobs are not important and require few skills? The evidence indicates otherwise: women's work is devalued precisely because it is women's work, and women's jobs thus pay less than men's jobs because they are women's jobs. Studies of comparable worth support this argument.

Researchers rate various jobs in terms of their requirements and attributes that logically should affect the salaries they offer: the importance of the job, the degree of skill it requires, the level of responsibility it requires, the degree to which the employee must exercise independent judgment, and so forth. They then use these dimensions to determine what salary a job should offer. Some jobs might be "better" on some dimensions and "worse" on others but still end up with the same predicted salary if everything evens out. When researchers make their calculations, they find that certain women's jobs pay less than men's even though their comparable worth is equal to or even higher than the men's jobs. For example, a social worker may earn less money than a probation officer, even though calculations based on comparable worth would predict that a social worker should earn at least as much.

The comparable worth research demonstrates that women's jobs pay less than men's jobs of comparable worth and that the average working family would earn several thousand dollars more annually if pay scales were reevaluated based on comparable worth and women paid more for their work. Even when women and men work in the same jobs, women often earn less than men and men are more likely than women to hold leadership positions in these occupations. Census data provide ready evidence of the lower incomes women receive than men even in the same occupations. For example, female marketing and sales managers earn only 68% of what their male counterparts earn; female human resource managers earn only 68% of what their male counterparts earn; female claims adjusters earn only 83%; female accountants earn only 72%; female elementary and middle school teachers earn only 90%; and even female secretaries and clerical workers earn only 86%.

When variables like number of years on the job, number of hours worked per week, and size of firm are taken into account, these disparities diminish but do not disappear altogether, and it is very likely that sex discrimination by employers accounts for much of the remaining disparity. Litigation has suggested or revealed specific instances of sex discrimination in earnings and employment.

In July 2009, the Dell computer company, without admitting any wrongdoing, agreed to pay $9.1 million to settle a class action lawsuit, brought by former executives, that alleged sex discrimination in salaries and promotions. Earlier in the decade, a Florida jury found Outback Steakhouse liable for paying a woman site development assistant only half what it paid a man with the same title. After she trained him, Outback assigned him most of her duties, and when she complained, Outback transferred her to a clerical position. The jury awarded her $2.2 million in compensatory and punitive damages.

Some of the sex discrimination in employment reflects the existence of two related phenomena, the glass ceiling and the glass escalator. Women may be promoted in a job only to find they reach an invisible "glass ceiling" beyond which they cannot get promoted, or they may not get promoted in the first place.

In the largest U.S. corporations, women constitute only about 16% of the top executives, and women executives are paid much less than their male counterparts. Although these disparities stem partly from the fact that women joined the corporate ranks much more recently than men, they also reflect a glass ceiling in the corporate world that prevents qualified women from rising up above a certain level. Men, on the other hand, can often ride a "glass escalator" to the top, even in female occupations. An example is seen in elementary school teaching, where principals typically rise from the ranks of teachers. Although men constitute only about 20% of all public elementary school teachers, they account for about 44% of all elementary school principals. Whatever the reasons for the gender gap in income, the fact that women make so much less than men means that female-headed families are especially likely to be poor.

In 2008, about 31% of these families lived in poverty, compared to only 6.7% of married-couple families. The term feminization of poverty refers to the fact that female-headed households are especially likely to be poor. The gendering of poverty in this manner is one of the most significant manifestations of gender inequality in the United States.

Sexual Harassment

Another workplace problem is sexual harassment, which, as defined by federal guidelines and legal rulings and statutes, consists of unwelcome sexual advances, requests for sexual favours, or physical conduct of a sexual nature used as a condition of employment or promotion or that interferes with an individual's job performance and creates an intimidating or hostile environment.

Although men can be, and are, sexually harassed, women are more often the targets of sexual harassment, which is often considered a form of violence against women. This gender difference exists for at least two reasons, one cultural and one structural. The cultural reason centres on the depiction of women and the socialization of men. As our discussion of the mass media and gender socialization indicated, women are still depicted in our culture as sexual objects who exist for men's pleasure.

At the same time, our culture socializes men to be sexually assertive. These two cultural beliefs combine to make men believe that they have the right to make verbal and physical advances to women in the workplace. When these advances fall into the guidelines listed here, they become sexual harassment. The second reason that most targets of sexual harassment are women is more structural. Reflecting the gendered nature of the workplace and of the educational system, typically the men doing the harassment are in a position of power over the women they harass. A male boss harasses a female employee, or a male professor harasses a female student or employee. These men realise that subordinate women may find it difficult to resist their advances for fear of reprisals: a female employee may be fired or not promoted, and a female student may receive a bad grade.

How common is sexual harassment? This is difficult to determine, as the men who do the sexual harassment are not about to shout it from the rooftops, and the women who suffer it often keep quiet because of the repercussions just listed. But anonymous surveys of women employees in corporate and other settings commonly find that 40%-65% of the respondents report being sexually harassed. In a survey of 4,501 women physicians, 36.9% reported being sexually harassed either in medical school or in their practice as physicians. Sexual harassment cases continue to make headlines.

In one recent example, the University of Southern Mississippi paid $112,500 in September 2009 to settle a case brought by a women's tennis graduate assistant against the school's women's tennis coach; the coach then resigned for personal reasons. That same month, the CEO of a hospital in Washington State was reprimanded after a claim of sexual harassment was brought against him, and he was also fired for unspecified reasons.

WOMEN OF COLOUR: A TRIPLE BURDEN

Earlier we mentioned multicultural feminism, which stresses that women of colour face difficulties for three reasons: their gender, their race, and, often, their social class, which is frequently near the bottom of the socioeconomic ladder. They thus face a triple burden that manifests itself in many ways. For example, women of colour experience "extra" income inequality. Earlier we discussed the gender gap in earnings, with women earning 79.4% of what men earn, but women of colour face both a gender gap and a racial/ethnic gap. We see a racial/ethnic gap among both women and men, as African Americans and Latinos of either gender earn less than whites, and we also see a gender gap between men and women, as women earn less than men within any race or ethnicity.

These two gaps combine to produce an especially high gap between African American and Latina women and white men: African American women earn only 67.6% of what white men earn, and Latina women earn only 60% of what white men earn. These differences in income mean that African American and Latina women are poorer than white women. We noted earlier that about 31% of all female-headed families are poor.

This masks race/ethnic differences among such families: 21.5% of families headed by non-Latina white women are poor, compared to 40.5% of families headed by African American women and also 40.5% of families headed by Latina women. While white women are poorer than white men, African American and Latina women are clearly poorer than white women.

SEXUAL ORIENTATION AND INEQUALITY

A recent report by a task force of the American Psychological Association stated that "same-sex sexual and romantic attractions, feelings, and behaviours are normal and positive variations of human sexuality". A majority of Americans do not share this opinion. In the 2008 General Social Survey, 52% of respondents said that "sexual relations between two adults of the same sex" is "always wrong." Although, represents a substantial decline from the survey's 1973 finding of 74%, it is clear that many Americans remain sharply opposed to homosexuality.

Not surprisingly, then, sexual orientation continues to be the source of much controversy and no small amount of abuse and discrimination directed towards members of the gay, lesbian, bisexual, and transgendered community. These individuals experience various forms of abuse, mistreatment, and discrimination that their heterosexual counterparts do not experience. In this respect, their sexuality is the source of a good deal of inequality. For example, gay teenagers are very often the targets of taunting, bullying, physical assault, and other abuse in schools and elsewhere that sometimes drives them to suicide or at least to experience severe emotional distress.

In 38 states, individuals can be denied employment or fired from a job because of their sexual orientation, even though federal and state laws prohibit employment discrimination for reasons related to race and ethnicity, gender, age, religious belief, and national origin. And in 45 states as of April 2010, same-sex couples are legally prohibited from marrying.

In most of these states, this prohibition means that same-sex couples lack hundreds of rights, responsibilities, and benefits that spouses enjoy, including certain income tax and inheritance benefits, spousal insurance coverage, and the right to make medical decisions for a partner who can no longer communicate because of disease or traumatic injury.

HOUSEHOLD INEQUALITY

Someone has to do housework, and that someone is usually a woman. It takes many hours a week to clean the bathrooms, cook, shop in the grocery store, vacuum, and do everything else that needs to be done. The best evidence indicates that women married to or living with men spend two to three times as many hours per work on housework as men spend.

This disparity holds true even when women work outside the home, leading sociologist Arlie Hochschild to observe in a widely cited book that women engage in a "second shift" of unpaid work when they come home from their paying job. The good news is that gender differences in housework time are smaller than a generation ago. The bad news is that a large gender difference remains. As one study summarized the evidence on this issue, "women invest significantly more hours in household labour than do men despite the narrowing of gender differences in recent years". In the realm of household work, then, gender inequality persists.

VIOLENCE AGAINST WOMEN

Violence against women is a technical term used to collectively refer to violent acts that are primarily or exclusively committed against women. Similar to a hate crime, this type of violence targets a specific group with the victim's gender as a primary motive.

The United Nations General Assembly defines "violence against women" as "any act of gender-based violence that results in, or is likely to result in, physical, sexual or mental harm or suffering to women, including threats of such acts, coercion or arbitrary deprivation of liberty, whether occurring in public or in private life."

The 1993 Declaration on the Elimination of Violence Against Women noted that this violence could be perpetrated by assailants of either gender, family members and even the "State" itself. Worldwide governments and organizations actively work to combat violence against women through a variety of programmes. A UN resolution designated November 25 as International Day for the Elimination of Violence against Women. Some historians believe that the history of violence against women is tied to the history of women being viewed as property and a gender role assigned to be subservient to men and also other women.

The UN Declaration on the Elimination of Violence against Women states that "violence against women is a manifestation of historically unequal power relations between men and women, which have led to domination over and discrimination against women by men and to the prevention of the full advancement of women, and that violence against women is one of the crucial social mechanisms by which women are forced into a subordinate position compared with men."

In the 1870s courts in the United States stopped recognizing the common-law principle that a husband had the right to "physically chastise an errant wife". In the UK the traditional right of a husband to inflict moderate corporal

marriages which suggests that "over time a husband's battering may abate somewhat, but perhaps because he has successfully intimidated his wife. The risk of violence remains strong in a marriage in which it has been a feature in the past. Thus, treatment is essential here; the clinician cannot just wait and watch." The most urgent clinical priority is the protection of the wife because she is the one most frequently at risk, and clinicians must be aware that supporting assertiveness by a battered wife may lead to more beatings or even death.

ACTIVISM

Many activists believe that working towards the elimination of domestic violence means working to eliminate a societal hierarchy enforced through sexism. INCITE! Women of Colour Against Violence cited racism within the anti-violence movement and suggest that violence against women will not end until the anti-violence movement redirects its goal from "ending violence against women "to "ending violence against women of colour." The same conclusion can be drawn for other systems of oppression.

RAPE

Susan Griffin began a classic thesis on rape in 1971 with this startling statement:

- I have never been free of the fear of rape. From a very early age I, like most women, have thought of rape as a part of my natural environment-something to be feared and prayed against like fire or lightning. I never asked why men raped; I simply thought it one of the many mysteries of human nature.

What do we know about rape? Why do men rape? Our knowledge about the extent and nature of rape and reasons for it comes from three sources: the FBI Uniform Crime Reports and the National Crime Victimization Survey and surveys of and interviews with women and men conducted by academic researchers. From these sources we have a fairly good if not perfect idea of how much rape occurs, the context in which it occurs, and the reasons for it. What do we know?

THE BENEFITS AND COSTS OF BEING MALE

Most of the discussion so far has been about women, and with good reason: in a sexist society such as our own, women are the subordinate, unequal sex. But "gender" means more than "female," and a few comments about men are in order.

BENEFITS

We talked about "white privilege," the advantages that whites automatically have in a racist society whether or not they realise they have these advantages. Many scholars also talk about male privilege, or the advantages that males automatically have in a patriarchal society whether or not they realise they have these advantages.

A few examples thesis male privilege. Men can usually walk anywhere they want or go into any bar they want without having to worry about being raped or sexually harassed. Susan Griffin was able to write "I have never been free of the fear of rape" because she was a woman: it is no exaggeration to say that few men could write the same thing and mean it. Although some men are sexually harassed, most men can work at any job they want without having to worry about sexual harassment.

Men can walk down the street without having strangers make crude remarks about their looks, dress, and sexual behaviour. Men can apply for most jobs without worrying about being rejected or, if hired, not being promoted because of their gender. We could go on with many other examples, but the fact remains that in a patriarchal society, men automatically have advantages just because they are men, even if race, social class, and sexual orientation affect the degree to which they are able to enjoy these advantages.

COSTS

Yet it is also true that men pay a price for living in a patriarchy. Without trying to claim that men have it as bad as women, scholars are increasingly pointing to the problems men face in a society that promotes male domination and traditional standards of masculinity such as assertiveness, competitiveness, and toughness. Socialization into masculinity is thought to underlie many of the emotional problems men experience, which stem from a combination of their emotional inexpressiveness and reluctance to admit to, and seek help for, various personal problems. Sometimes these emotional problems build up and explode, as mass shootings by males at schools and elsewhere indicate, or express themselves in other ways.

Compared to girls, for example, boys are much more likely to be diagnosed with emotional disorders, learning disabilities, and attention deficit disorder, and they are also more likely to commit suicide and to drop out of high school. Men experience other problems that put themselves at a disadvantage compared to women. They commit much more violence than women do and, apart from rape, also suffer a much higher rate of violent victimization. They die earlier than women and are injured more often. Because men are less involved than women in child-rearing, they also miss out on the joy of parenting that women are much more likely to experience.

Growing recognition of the problems males experience because of their socialization into masculinity has led to increased concern over what is happening to American boys. Citing the strong linkage between masculinity and violence, some writers urge parents to raise their sons differently in order to help our society reduce its violent behaviour. In all of these respects, boys and men-and our nation as a whole-are paying a very real price for being male in a patriarchal society.

Bibliography

Alexander, John M.: *Inequality, Poverty and Affirmative Action: Contemporary Trends in India,* Finland: United Nations University, Helsinki, 2003.

Berry, R. A.: *Agrarian Structure and Productivity in Developing Countries,* Helsinki: Johns Hopkins University Press, 2001.

Chambers, R.: *Voices of the Poor: Crying out for Change,* New York: Oxford University Press, 2000.

Chambers, Robert: *Whose Reality Counts? Putting the First Last,* London: Intermediate Technology Publicatiions, 2000.

Cramer, H.: *Mathematical Methods for Statistics,* Princeton: Princeton University Press, 2005.

Daly, Herman: *Steady-State Economics,* Washington: Island Press, 2009.

Deininger, K.: *Explaining Agricultural and Agrarian Policies in Developing Countries,* New Haven: Yale University Press, 2006.

Dreze, Jean: *India: Economic Development and Social Opportunity,* Delhi: Oxford University Press, 2002.

Hogg, Robert: *Probability and Statistical Inference,* New Jersey: Prentice Hall, 2004.

Kendall, Maurice: *The Advanced Theory of Statistics,* London: Griffin, 2002.

Krugman, Paul: *Development, Geography and Economic Theory,* Cambridge, Helsinki: Massachusetts Institute of Technology Press, 2005.

Kuznets, Simon: *Modern Economic Growth: Rate, Structure and Spread,* New Haven: Yale University Press, 2006.

Milton, J.: *Local Organization for Rural Development: Analysis of Asian Experience*, New York: Cornell University, 2006.

Narayan, D.: *Voices of the Poor: Can Anyone Hear Us?,* New York: Oxford University Press, 2003.

Narayan, D.: *Voices of the Poor: Crying Out for Change*, New York: Oxford University Press, 2000.

Niaz, M.: *Social Divisions in School Participation and Attainment in India*, India: IDB Working Paper, 2009.

Ormerod, P.: *Butterfly Economics: A New General Theory of Social and Economic Behavior*, New York: Oxford University Press, 1998.

Petesch, P.: *Voices of the Poor*, New York: Oxford University Press, 2000.

Rademacher, A.: *Social, Economic and Educational Status of the Muslim Community of India*, New York: Oxford University Press, 2003.

Roemer, John: *Equality of Opportunities*, Cambridge: Harvard University Press, 2008.

Ronald, J.: *Land to the Tiller: The Political Economy of Agrarian Reform in South Asia*, New Haven: Yale University Press, 2005.

Sen, Amartya: *Development as Freedom*, U.K: Oxford University Press, 2001.

Shrestha, R.: *The Use and Misuse of Social Science in Nepal*, Kathmandu: Tribhuvan University, 2001.

Singer, Hans: *The Notion of Human Investment*, London: Intermediate Technology Publications, 2002.

Stone, L.: *The Use and Misuse of Social Science in Nepal*, Kathmandu: Tribhuvan University, 1989.

Index